On creativity

"The artist is originally a man who turns from reality . . . and who then in phantasy-life allows full play to his erotic and ambitious wishes. But he finds a way of return from this world of phantasy back to reality; with his special gifts he moulds his phantasies into a new kind of reality, and men concede them a justification as valuable reflections of actual life."

On narcissism

"It seems very evident that one person's narcissism has a great attraction for those others who have renounced part of their own narcissism and are seeking after object-love; the charm of a child lies to a great extent in his narcissism, his self-sufficiency and in-accessibility, just as does the charm of certain animals which seem not to concern themselves about us, such as cats and the large beasts of prey."

On loving

"Perhaps we shall come to a better understanding of the manifold opposites of loving if we reflect that our mental life as a whole is governed by *three polarities,* namely, the following antitheses; Subject (ego)—Object (external world), Pleasure—Pain, Active—Passive."

On masochism in men

"The masochist wants to be treated like a little, helpless, dependent child, but especially like a naughty child. . . . If one has the opportunity of studying cases in which the masochistic phantasies have undergone especially rich elaboration, one easily discovers that in them the subject is placed in a situation characteristic of womanhood, *i.e.* they mean that he is being castrated, is playing the passive part in coitus, or is giving birth."

Volumes in
The Collected Papers of Sigmund Freud

Each volume has an Introduction by the Editor, Philip Rieff.

General Psychological Theory

PAPERS ON METAPSYCHOLOGY

SIGMUND FREUD

WITH AN INTRODUCTION BY THE EDITOR
PHILIP RIEFF

A TOUCHSTONE BOOK
Published by Simon & Schuster

TOUCHSTONE
Rockefeller Center
1230 Avenue of the Americas
New York, NY 10020

First Touchstone Edition 1997

TOUCHSTONE and colophon are registered
trademarks of Simon & Schuster Inc.

Manufactured in the United States of America

9 10 8

Library of Congress-in-Publication Data is available.

ISBN-13:   978-0-684-84292-9
ISBN-10:   0-684-84292-0

Contents

Introduction

This volume contains much of the best Freud wrote on psychological theory. Among other texts to which the reader might refer for more on this subject: Chapter 7 of *The Interpretations of Dreams;* the unfinished early "Project for a Scientific Psychology" (1895); two letters to Fliess, Numbers 39 and 52, in the standard edition of the Fliess letters, entitled *The Origins of Psychoanalysis;* Lectures 22 and 26 of the *Introductory Lectures;* the whole of two short books, *Beyond the Pleasure Principle* and *The Ego and the Id;* Lectures 31 and 32 of the *New Introductory Lectures;* and finally, the entire *An Outline of Psychoanalysis.*

"Metapsychology" and "general psychological theory" may be understood as interchangeable terms. Yet the term "metapsychology" is somewhat misleading; Freud never went beyond psychology, as the qualifying "meta" would ordinarily imply. On the contrary, his metapsychology is useful precisely because it permits him to psychologize about every object of his scientific attention. A metapsychological level of analysis provided Freud, and the discipline of psychoanalysis as such, with a set of stable conceptual cues that could elicit a wide variety of responses from the empirical data. It is in this sense that Freud's metapsychological papers constitute the most general of psychological theories, so general, indeed, that psychoanalysis can even imply, to its devoted adherents, a cosmology. Freud's metapsychological papers show the classic purpose of all theorizing: to construct a canon of concepts that will give the analyst steady points of reference from which to map journeys leading, in this case, into the jungle of the emotions.

Freud rarely wrote academically neat and easily catalogued essays. In consequence, some duplication of material becomes both necessary and useful. Among Freud's greatest efforts in metapsychology, the third part of his analysis of Dr. Schreber needs special mention. I include it in a volume of Freud's theoretical papers despite the fact that it is an integral part of one of his major case histories; it is even more significantly a major contribution to his metapsychology.

In the second, larger part of this introduction, I shall try to supply the general reader with some interpretative categories that may prove helpful in grasping Freud's meta-psychology—in particular, that aspect of his theory of the instincts fundamental to psychoanalysis as a doctrine of man in society. I take this option because Freud considered his own the master science of society upon which, at last, the entire range of social sciences could find a secure foundation.[1]

Analogical Method

The method by which Freud implicated all the sciences under his own was not new; pre-Renaissance science, as well as theology and politics, not to speak of poetry, was dependent on exactly this method. Yet "we must look around for analogies,"[2] Freud commands, not simply as rhetorical expedients to make comprehension easier but because analogy was the method of natural, untrained knowing and when transformed by a new content became the mode of scientific, trained knowledge. The new content of trained analogizing was, as Nietzsche said, found in the aggressive motives of mankind, and with this new content and old form Freud constructed a science which appeared to him larger, at once more difficult to acquire and more personal than any other intellectual discipline. This fusion of the most profound content with the most easily transferable method did indeed put Freud's science above the conventional divisions of rational knowledge and set his movement gathering in the remotest fields: grammar, history, the plastic arts, mythology, politics, theology, children's games, dress, poetry, mathematics, jurisprudence, everything and all.

Serious criticism of Freud is most often criticism of his analogical method. It is the routine caveat raised by social scientists. Yet of all methods, analogy, if difficult to defend, is also most difficult to criticize fairly. To the literalist, Freud's analogies must seem equivocal, and the quick changes in context leave out something the reader is used to finding: the common sense. What is obvious is set aside by Freud's method as evidence of its own falsehood, and the common reader, bewildered, gropes about for what is absent and puzzles his head for a kind of literalism Freud rejects. Thus, the entire

[1] See Ernest Jones, *Life and Work,* III (New York, 1957), p. 339.

[2] *Moses and Monotheism* (New York, 1949), p. 109.

Freudian use of "quantities" is allegorical; quantities are not measured, but only compared, as quantities of libido become quantities of aggressive urges.[3] Fundamentally diverse methods cannot be translated into one another; it is pointless to object to a non-literal method because it fails to provide literal truths, and it is no proper criticism of Freud to point out that he is not doing what his method does not allow him to do. In the method of analogy, the distinctions between fixed and fluid terms, between proof and dialectic, are without meaning. Freud's literal inconsistencies disappear when they are correctly distributed over the entire range of his contextual interpretations, and the unity of his method and his data emerges, in full view, as a circle well known in the history of argument.

MICROCOSM AND MACROCOSM

Freud's analogical method begins with the self as the first of his stock of images, and from this all others derive. His greatness is in his thorough self-study, for while he studied he found he was something more than himself, a microcosm, a veritable little world, the experience of which led him inevitably to draw the analogy of the big. Imagination, not God or Capitalism, has uttered the curse of bigness. Freud did not resist the ambition of his mind and, especially in later writings, permitted it every opportunity for large comparisons. Within the individual, Freud discovered the entire macrocosm of creation. Indeed, "the test of science is fully circumscribed if we confine it to showing how the world must appear to us in consequence of the particular character of our organization." Mind was prior to reality, a useful discovery for a master-science that is also a psychology. Understanding was possible because "our mental apparatus . . . itself is a constituent part of that world which we are to investigate."[4] The self was no alien from the natural world; we were conscious of being not only subjects but objects of nature among other natural objects.

Freud threw an old bridge across the chasm between the

[3] Such transformations of quantities take as an assumption the convertibility of instinctual energy, which is the key to the psychoanalytic metapsychology.

[4] *The Future of an Illusion* (London, 1943), p. 97.

thinking subject and the objective world, one that looked to many like Schopenhauer's assumption of the analogy of all being. Schopenhauer had found the essence of the world analogous to the essence of the psyche. The tendency of heavy bodies to fall and for crystals to form, the teleology of the magnetic needle, the obscurest processes of proto- plasmic irritability, the desire of the cactus for sand and the treetop for light, the flight of birds and the plundering of beasts, the development of embryos, the interminable murders that comprise human history, sleep and dreams, motives and conscious acts, the universe entire, is the play of will. Plainly, Freud found Schopenhauer's Will, renamed, everywhere, but first of all in an inventory of the unconscious. All life was derivative, in complex permutations of fusion and defusion, of instincts analogous to those found in the mind. By the method of analogy, Freud dignified the natural capacity of the "mental apparatus" to know objects according to what it finds in itself. The question is only what is there originally to be found. The rationalists had found Intellect, and argued, by analogy, that all beings think in some degree. Freud found intellect only a hope, not a description, and the essential and fundamental thing Instinct. Thought was a derived or sec- ondary phenomenon, like neuroses an inevitable accident of frustrated Instinct.

So, far from the mind knowing itself as an object, Freud assumed it natural for mind to consider objects and the objective world not as "it is" but as "I am." All Freudian child psychologies ask this epistemological question. The child's natural imagination first sees objects as part of its own being. "Originally the ego includes everything, later it detaches from itself the external world." The "oceanic feel- ing" his friend Romain Rolland described as the validation of mystic identity, Freud thought "only a shrunken vestige" of the natural imagination.[5] The process of an absorption of objects into the subject continued to exist in later life, not only latently as a regression to the primitive form of psychic life (narcissism), but also in all the affective relations to objects, after the reality principle has forced the natural imagination to relinquish them. "Object" is a favorite term

[5] *Civilization and Its Discontents* (London, 1939), p. 13.

of the Freudian method and we shall examine other uses of it later; its epistemological one is clear here. Freud moved from mind to the world, from subject to object.

To those who objected that his was "not natural science, it is the philosophy of Schopenhauer," he replied that, after all, "everything had been said already." He would not object to the association. "Ladies and gentlemen, why should not a bold thinker have divined things that a sober and painstaking investigation of details subsequently confirms?" Freudianism was, in any case, "not even true Schopenhauer." Freud did not "assert that death is the only aim of life; we do not overlook the presence of life by the side of death."[6] He recognized two fundamental instincts; Schopenhauer recognized only one. Freud considered Empedocles his truest predecessor, not only because he appeared to be the first complete dualist, but because "Empedocles ascribed to the whole universe the same animistic principle as is manifested in each individual organism." Freud accepted Empedocles' "cosmic phantasy" of love and hate as his own, however much he considered his own overlaid and confined by the temporary fashion of biological models.[7]

Even the word "cosmic" seemed to Freud appropriate to his theory. Cosmic events left their impressions upon the human, and these impressions were the instincts, defined as tendencies "innate in living organic matter impelling it towards the reinstatement of an earlier condition."[8] The compulsion to return to the earliest satisfaction, if only by the detour of a lifetime, seemed to Freud intelligible as the "death instinct." But the short road from death to death is diverted by life; the activities of "pleasure" or "love." The pleasures, too, were instincts, inserting themselves between the original inorganic state and its prompt reinstatement after matter has once come alive. Life was the absence of a perfect equilibrium of the instincts, and death a seeking after that perfection. The instincts, therefore, were the compensations generated by

---

[6] *New Introductory Lectures on Psychoanalysis* (London, 1949), p. 139. Cf. *Beyond the Pleasure Principle* (London, 1922), p. 63.

[7] Yet it is well known that Freud aspired to maintain his biological models. The rhetoric of drives appeared to avoid obvious moralizing.

[8] *Beyond the Pleasure Principle*, p. 44.

change. They are the exemplary modes in Freud's equilibrium theory, for they are expressed only where some past state has given way to another, whenever living matter is obliged to alter itself.

Catastrophe Theory

Freud held a catastrophe theory of the genesis of instincts (which later provided Otto Rank with the theoretical model of his schism). In the beginning, the forces compelling change came from without in the shape of astronomical and geological events. Freud was most impressed by two of the many catastrophes available to his ingenuity: 1) the dessication which threw life out of a watery existence onto land and 2) the glacial period, which must have inhibited sexual instincts and directed them into cultural channels. Both categories repeated themselves psychologically in the dichronous onset of sexual development which is separated by what Freud called the "latency period" (approximately ages five to twelve), itself the microcosm of transition.[9] Other prehistoric catastrophes, however subtle or large, could be read analogically, too. The form of all relations—personal and physical—in the Freudian method is between giver and receiver, and for the world at large this could mean only the relation of the sun which alone is life-giving to the earth. Instinctive behavior recorded processes in the universe and changes in the relationships of the heavenly bodies out of the remotest past.

In the last resort it must have been the evolution of our earth, and its relation to the sun, that has left its imprint on the development of the organism. The conservative organic instincts have absorbed every one of these enforced alterations in the course of life and have stored them for repetition; they thus present the delusive appearance of forces striving after change and progress, while they are merely endeavouring to reach an old goal (death) by ways both old and new.[10]

In *Beyond the Pleasure Principle* Freud made of the influence of the stars upon human life something more than

[9] *The Ego and the Id* (London, 1947), p. 46.
[10] *Beyond the Pleasure Principle*, pp. 46–47.

astrological fancy, and Sandor Ferenczi's "Thalassa" (1921), though Freud disapproved, is worthy of this very special Freud. Ferenczi's cenogenesis, the theory that mankind retains an unconscious memory of its phylogenetic history, returns to an even wider application of the principle that ontogeny recapitulates phylogeny (which Freud assumed), calling on Haeckel and the *naturphilosophen*, as well as on Freud himself. The disciple offered five, not two, catastrophes in all: 1) the origin of organic life; 2) the origin of individual unicellular organisms; 3) the beginning of sexual propagation and the development of marine life; 4) the recession of the ocean and adaptation to terrestrial existence, and the development of animal species with organs of copulation; 5) the Ice Ages and the coming of Man. "Thalassa" presents some ingenious elaborations of Freud's catastrophe theory; their basis remains Freud's *todestrieb*, the tendency of all organisms to strive toward a state of absence of irritability and finally "the deathlike repose of the inorganic world."[11]

Dualistic Theory

As Freud expected, his "dualistic theory" of Eros and Thanatos "met with little general acceptance and has not really established itself even among psychoanalysts." It is still the least acceptable part of the master's legacy. The meliorist spirit rules within the movement particularly in the United

[11] See Sandor Ferenczi, Chapter Six of "Thalassa: A Theory of Genitality," *Psychoanalytic Quarterly*, Vol. III, no. 1 (January, 1934), pp. 1-29. Regression is the basic concept in Ferenczi's theory. He sees regression in the act of sexual intercourse: a striving toward the moist interior of the mother's body and ultimately toward the aquatic mode of existence abandoned in primeval times. Not only is coitus a symbolic action in which the individual re-experiences the pleasure of intra-uterine existence, the anxiety of birth, and the subsequent pleasure in surmounting this danger successfully, but also he repeats symbolically the danger of death which his animal ancestors overcame in the geological cataclysm of the drying up of the sea. Noting the recurrent symbol of penis as *fish* and woman as *water*, Ferenczi concluded that birth is nothing but "a recapitulation on the part of the individual of the great catastrophe which at the time of the recession of the ocean forced many animals . . . to adapt themselves to a land existence, above all to renounce gill-breathing and provide themselves with organs for the respiration of air."

States, and the notion that individuals are aggressive no matter what the social system is most repugnant to the meliorist temper. But it has suited the new wind of acquiescence in things as they are, blowing like a death wish now over the world.

Freud's first formulation of the death instinct was timid, even apologetic, a rare shading of his clear style. If he thought a tactic of modesty would bring some favor, it brought little; nearly at the end of his life, in 1937, Freud could be heard insisting quite dogmatically that "internal conflicts" are "certainly . . . the correct equivalent of the external conflicts" of the universe. Life is the irritation of an uneasy stalemate. "Only by the concurrent or opposing action of the two primal instincts—Eros and the death-instinct—never by one or the other alone, can the motley variety of vital phenomena be explained."[12] World War I and Freud's studies of traumatic war neuroses upset the earlier hegemony of the pleasure-principle in his psychological method. Even though he had maintained a double-instinct theory before 1920 (sex and hunger, then sex and ego instincts), the sexual had obviously taken precedence in all Freud's explanations. Now Freud discovered that though "it is simply the pleasure-principle which draws up the programme of life's purpose," this program is "in conflict with the whole world, with the macrocosm as much as with the microcosm."[13] The dream could not be a wish-fulfillment alone, the wish was not for pleasure alone, the joke left something necessary to it necessarily unsaid. ". . . we shall have to abandon the belief that mental processes are governed exclusively by a striving after pleasure,"[14] or by any other exclusive striving.

Despite Freud's attempt after 1920 to construct a genuine parity between the two instincts, a fundamental disparity remained. The difference between life and death is that death has no character; life has three. The Freudian characterology is entirely of the development of the libido into three stages: the oral, the anal, and the genital. It is an important sign of

[12] *Therapy and Technique,* "Analysis Terminable and Interminable," p. 261, Collier Books edition BS 189V.
[13] *Civilization and Its Discontents,* p. 27.
[14] *Therapy and Technique, op. cit.,* p. 261.

Freud's failure to equalize the life and death instincts that in a doctrine free with name-givings, there is no name for the energy of the death instinct equivalent to "libido" ("aggression" is not an energy), and no characterology for aggression, the microcosmic expression of the death instinct to parallel the libidinal.[15]

With this single, grave disjunction, the Freudian psychology is a consistent structure of resemblances between levels, between visible and primal worlds. The highest science, Freud reassured his followers, detailed the intuition of the greatest poetry. The instincts dividing and uniting personality are dereistic, agents of "heavenly" forces, as the "instinct of aggression is the derivative and main representative of the death instinct . . . found alongside Eros, sharing his rule over the earth." It is in the end of no value to think only of aggression and of libido. Freud insists the perceptible facts of instinctual forces cannot be understood except with reference to their cosmological predicates. Psychology was scandalized to be drawn so far above itself, and many of Freud's disciples have been concerned to pull him down from the clouds, suggesting he meant only "entropy" or this or that other familiar thing in his old and speculative age. There is a kind of horror among the orthodox that Freud had swerved too close to the Scylla of Jung, in repudiating the neo-Freudian (Adler and the sociologues) Charybdis. But this hierarchy reaching down from the heavens to the psyche is no fuddling of Freud's old age. His moral interest simply had enlarged beyond the human accident to the nonaccidental, and he delivered pride yet another blow: man's emotions were not his own; they were derivatives of the cold emotions of the universe. Thus the "name libido can . . . be used to denote the manifestation of the power of Eros." Both Eros and libido tend to preserve "the organic substance . . . binding it into ever larger units."[16] Freud used the one statically, the other in a dynamic and

[15] The Freudians excuse this lapse by remarking that since Freud discovered death thirty years after libido, "research" has yet to catch up. But the utopia of research will never end, and a characterology of aggression distinct from the libidinal will never be found. The structure of the theory itself admits of no academic excuses.

[16] *Civilization and Its Discontents*, pp. 97, 101–103, 114, 144.

fluid process. Eros is universal; libido is particular, wracked with "vicissitudes," reversals, impurities. Eros is the life force to the universe, as libido is to the personality; Eros is immutable, libido, happily, mutable. Freud may speak of "eternal Eros," never of "eternal libido."

There is no danger here of confusion with Jung, who expanded libido to include Eros, losing a discrimination that lessened the power of his theory. Jung diluted the terror of death to an imprudent habit of the libido to go to extremes and so induce from nature or purchase from science a more or less painful equilibration. Underneath his erudite veneer of Romanticism, he is much more mechanical than Freud. Indeed, the entire Jungian doctrine is Romanticism mechanized, not unlike Wilhelm Reich's repudiation of the death instinct as simply a cessation of the function of vital mechanisms.

For Freud, instincts were prior to their exhibitions in individual actions. They were also prior to their exhibitions in socal action. By his use of the image of microcosm-macrocosm, Freud reconstructed the stock parallels between nature and the individual, and finally a continuum between these two and society. Each is implicit in the other and all are arranged in a hierarchy, as in an evolutionary doctrine. Freud's eternal polarities, wedded and irreconcilable, have an infinite variety of derivatives: quarrels among cats and cellular disintegration are as much derived from Thanatos as the aggressions of humans, and within human life aggression may become conscience or cruelty or, mixed in the most delicate combinations and put out to work in familiar ways. The two instincts were never unmixed; neither is their relation. Freud's insight made all relations a little more dangerous and everyone a little more wary of their complexities. The doctrine urged men and women to be simpler, or else their complexes would overwhelm them.

The psyche was mediatory between nature and society, containing both orders representatively in its own structure. It played the same role between nature and society that ego plays between id and super-ego. The "personality" as a phenomenon more social than the "psyche" is the compromise nature and society work out together. The continuum of nature, individual, and society made Freudianism a social science, simple and complete. Individuals will manifest the condition of the society in which they live, as both will manifest the condition of nature. If persons are corrupt, society must be corrupt. If they are aggressive, there is aggression in society as there is Thanatos in the universe. Personality, rightly understood, is the measure and the clue, society writ large, made up of the bits and pieces of the great world jostling each other in the small.

Society as Neurosis

Having warned his readers against the dangers of analogy ("it behooves us to be very careful"),[17] Freud proceeded to the confident elaboration of the most dangerous, "the only really satisfactory analogy": that between individual and society. "Individual Psychology is from the very first the same as Social Psychology," Freud announced.[18] In the case of any social phenomenon, Freud had "no difficulty in finding a full analogy to it in the mental life of an individual." History became mass psychology. The analogy between individual and mass, being indispensable, "is rather in the nature of an axiom."[19] Jung, too, accepted the method of analogy as axiomatic; "the analogical method," a major Jungian writes, "is indispensable in every psychological investigation. There could, in fact, be no extension of our scientific borders without it, only it must be tempered by a vigilant sense of reality. . . . In philosophy, history and psychology, the analogical method has now been reinstated as the method par excellence."[20] Although Jung's sense of reality has not been as vigilant as Freud's, there is some danger that in an examination of Freud's analogies the inevitable similarity to Jung will appear too great. Their differences are important, but their similarities in the subject of this introduction are greater than either camp will admit.

ROLE OF RELIGION

The most obvious analogy Freud discovered was between

[17] *Op. cit.*, p. 141.
[18] *Group Psychology and the Analysis of the Ego* (London, 1949), p. 2.
[19] *Moses and Monotheism*, p. 117.
[20] H. G. Baynes, *Mythology of the Soul* (London, 1949), p. 110.

individual sickness and institutional religion. Since *Totem and Taboo* (1912), he had never doubted that religious phenomena are to be understood only on the model of the neurotic symptoms of the individual.[21] Obsessional neurosis is private religion, and religion is mass obsessional neurosis. Subjective psychological experience was analogous to objective social experience, as individual history was to race history.[22] Neurotics were simply the pious of an earlier culture, no longer pious enough. Penances were obsessional acts, within an institutional guarantee. The identity of the "origin of neurotic ceremonial" and "the psychological processes of religious life" depended entirely upon the inferences analogy emboldened Freud to draw about the latter from its functional resemblances to the former.[23] He needed no other evidence, no study of religious ceremonials or social events in themselves.

There is great ease in the Freudian method. The husk of events is removed and only kernels of meaning remain. Actions become transparent and at last one can look inside at what is really interesting, the agents; and inside the agents, there are the emotions making everything move. Freud provided gossip with a theory and made history nothing more than the quintessence of gossip. His method would halt the perverse quoting of state papers, as if they were significant data, and return social research to its original concern with the oddities of personality and the regularities of events, as if this movement or that did not differ from those of the "heavenly forces." Historians, who aspire to something more impersonal and respect more obvious facts like the impotence of a revolution as well as the impotence of a revolutionary, accuse Freud of encouraging the barbarism of the historyless. The historians, though they are too hostile, may be correct. Freud's analogies permit uncontrolled shifts in the presentation of evidence and arbitrary devaluations of the larger contexts within which given psychological processes operate. The results survive him in a remarkable narrowing of his-

[21] *Moses and Monotheism*, p. 89.
[22] *Op. cit.*, p. 126.
[23] Cf. "Obsessive Acts and Religious Practices," pp. 17, 24, *Character and Culture*, Collier Books edition BS 193V.

torical interest among those he influenced. Contemporaneity, the failure of memory, is the characteristic mark of modern barbarism.

But the new barbarism induces an ease greater than the mere condensation of history into psychology. By a strange chemistry it dissolves worlds of moral difference into the absurd sameness of psychological roles. Hitler and Christ are both father-images, and fathers must be moral. One does not choose one's father. Psychology makes it all quite accidental which morality one acquires, discerning a natural morality that precedes Bibles and swords and makes of them only the narrowest family prejudice. Psychoanalysis can too easily arraign substantive issues of justice, morality, and freedom as evocations of psychic functions. Freud's social theory is dependent on the reduction of susbtantive to functional, public to private. The psychological was primary and causative, while the historical event was the secondary, or resultant.

The analogy between the individual and the group, Freud insisted, unmasked neuroses as an individual bewilderment of "the great social productions of art, religion, and philosophy." This is not quite to say that healthy minds have no art, worship nothing, and never bother about universals. On the other hand, healthy minds, in order to become so, may produce all three or, at least, participate in their use. Where the "productions" are not social enough or when wear and tear have rendered them no longer usable, as in the case of Christianity, they fall away and leave man with the terrible choice of neurosis or health. A free person will choose to cultivate his garden, uncomplicated by art and unsolaced by religion. One unfree will choose the substitute art; if he succeeds, he too will be saved, although imperfectly. But if he fails, if his substitution is too imperfect, he falls into illness. ". . . Hysteria is a caricature of a work of art, . . . an obsessional neurosis is a caricature of a religion and . . . a paranoiac delusion is a caricature of a philosophical system. Culture is a social, not an individual formation."[24] Individual neuroses are asocial forms; they mistake accomplishment by private means for what arose in society by collective effort.

[24] *Totem and Taboo,* standard edition, vol. XIII (London, 1955), p. 73.

Freud's analogies reveal the sharpness of his polemic. Philosophers are not simply ingenious moralists; there are gods who are not fathers, or before that, mothers; a nun counting beads is not an obsessional counting buttons. They are not; but Freud's analogies imply guilt by association. He explained the connection between the private motive and the public action genetically; but genesis does not tell right from wrong, good from bad. Indeed, saintliness may be a development of the oral character, but certain emotional states, certain developments of character are, if not inherently then by inspection of consequences, known to be good; a satisfactory explanation can not discount them as pathological. The good need not be pathological because it is rare or because it is no progression beyond a certain stage of development.

If neuroses are caricatures, then aesthetic, religious, and intellectual achievements are not to be discounted as psychological precipitates. Art is normal; only disease is abnormal. Freud, indeed, tolerates the possibility. He saw art, after all, as the normalizing of sickness and judged we were all sick. Only the failure of art to do its work pushes us beyond the illness cruel nature has imposed. Thus, the Freudian theory of culture is more problematic than can be understood by converting the psychological level into the "base" and the cultural level into the "superstructure." It is at least necessary to enter a caveat against interpreting Freud simply as devaluing culture. Sublimations are not just substitutes for the genuine sexual article, when sexuality is so ubiquitous as to include them. Culture is something quite different from neurosis. Freud was not unaware of the reductionist element in his analogical modes. Essential distortions of meaning arise when "the same process is applied to a different kind of object."[25] The distortions of applying the same process to such different objects as culture and personality served Freud's polemical intention as well as his scientific one. At times, the polemic and the science are hardly distinguishable, and this helps account for a science that has been, from its beginnings, a factor in the moral revolution of our time.

University of Pennsylvania   PHILIP RIEFF
1962

[25] *Civilization and Its Discontents*, p. 133.

I

Formulations Regarding the Two Principles in Mental Functioning[1] (1911)

WE HAVE LONG observed that every neurosis has the result, and therefore probably the purpose, of forcing the patient out of real life, of alienating him from actuality. Nor could a fact such as this escape the observation of Pierre Janet; he spoke of a loss of "*la fonction du réel*" as being a special characteristic of the neurotic, but without discovering the connection of this disturbance with the fundamental conditions of neurosis.[2] By introducing the concept of repression into the genesis of the neuroses we have been able to gain some insight into this connection. The neurotic turns away from reality because he finds it unbearable—either the whole or parts of it. The most extreme type of this alienation from reality is shown in certain cases of hallucinatory psychosis which aim at denying the existence of the particular event that occasioned the outbreak of insanity (Griesinger). But actually every neurotic does the same with some fragment of reality.[3] And now we are confronted with the task of investigating the development of the relation of the neurotic and of mankind in general to reality, and of so bringing the psychological significance of the real outer world into the structure of our theory.

In the psychology which is founded on psychoanalysis we have accustomed ourselves to take as our starting-point the unconscious mental processes, with the peculiarities of which we have become acquainted through analysis. These we consider to be the older, primary processes, the residues of a

[1] First published in *Jahrbuch*, Bd. iii., 1911; reprinted in *Sammlung*, Dritte Folge. [Translated by M. N. Searl.]

[2] Pierre Janet, *Les Névroses*, 1909.

[3] A remarkably clear presentiment of this causation has recently been pointed out by Otto Rank in Schopenhauer's *The World as Will and Idea* (*Zentralblatt*, 1910).

phase of development in which they were the only kind of mental processes. The sovereign tendency obeyed by these primary processes is easy of recognition; it is called the pleasure-pain (*Lust-Unlust*) principle, or more shortly the pleasure-principle. These processes strive towards gaining pleasure; from any operation which might arouse unpleasantness ("pain") mental activity draws back (repression). Our nocturnal dreams, our waking tendency to shut out painful impressions, are remnants of the supremacy of this principle and proofs of its power.

In presupposing that the state of mental equilibrium was originally disturbed by the peremptory demands of inner needs, I am returning to lines of thought which I have developed in another place.[4] In the situation I am considering, whatever was thought of (desired) was simply imagined in an hallucinatory form, as still happens to-day with our dream-thoughts every night.[5] This attempt at satisfaction by means of hallucination was abandoned only in consequence of the absence of the expected gratification, because of the disappointment experienced. Instead, the mental apparatus had to decide to form a conception of the real circumstances in the outer world and to exert itself to alter them. A new principle of mental functioning was thus introduced; what was conceived of was no longer that which was pleasant, but that which was real, even if it should be unpleasant.[6] This institution of the *reality-principle* proved a momentous step.

[4] The General Section of *Die Traumdeutung*.

[5] The state of sleep can recover the likeness of mental life as it was before the recognition of reality, because a prerequisite of sleep is a deliberate rejection of reality (the wish to sleep).

[6] I will attempt to amplify the above schematic presentation with some further details. It will rightly be objected that an organization which is a slave to the pleasure-principle and neglects the reality of the outer world could not maintain itself alive for the shortest time, so that it could not have come into being at all. The use of a fiction of this kind is, however, vindicated by the consideration that the infant, if one only includes the maternal care, does almost realize such a state of mental life. Probably it hallucinates the fulfilment of its inner needs; it betrays its "pain" due to increase of stimulation and delay of satisfaction by the motor discharge of crying and struggling and then experiences

1. In the first place the new demands made a succession of adaptations necessary in the mental apparatus, which, on account of insufficient or uncertain knowledge, we can only detail very cursorily.

The increased significance of external reality heightened the significance also of the sense-organs directed towards that outer world, and of the *consciousness* attached to them; the latter now learned to comprehend the qualities of sense in addition to the qualities of pleasure and "pain" which hitherto had alone been of interest to it. A special function was instituted which had periodically to search the outer world, in order that its data might be already familiar if an urgent inner need should arise; this function was *attention*. Its activity meets the sense-impressions halfway, instead of awaiting their appearance. At the same time there was probably introduced a system of *notation*, whose task was to deposit the results of this periodical activity of consciousness—a part of that which we call *memory*.

In place of repression, which excluded from cathexis as productive of "pain" some of the emerging ideas, there developed an impartial *passing of judgement*, which had to decide whether a particular idea was true or false, that is, was in agreement with reality or not; decision was determined by comparison with the memory-traces of reality.

A new function was now entrusted to motor discharge,

---

the hallucinated satisfaction. Later, as a child, it learns to employ intentionally these modes of discharge as means of expression. Since the care of the infant is the prototype of the later care of the child, the supremacy of the pleasure-principle can end in actuality only with complete mental detachment from the parents. A beautiful example of a state of mental life shut off from the stimuli of the outer world, and able to satisfy even its nutritional requirements autistically (to use Bleuler's word), is given by the bird inside the egg together with its food supply; for it, maternal care is limited to the provision of warmth. I shall not look upon it as a correction, but as an amplification of the scheme in question, if anyone demands by what devices the system living according to the pleasure-principle can withdraw itself from the stimuli of reality. These contrivances are only the correlate of "repression," which treats inner "painful" stimuli as if they were outer, *i.e.* reckons them as belonging to the outer world.

which under the supremacy of the pleasure-principle had served to unburden the mental apparatus of accretions of stimuli, and in carrying out this task had sent innervations into the interior of the body (mien, expressions of affect); it was now employed in the appropriate alteration of reality. It was converted into *action*.

Restraint of motor discharge (of action) had now become necessary, and was provided by means of the process of *thought*, which was developed from ideation. Thought was endowed with qualities which made it possible for the mental apparatus to support increased tension during a delay in the process of discharge. It is essentially an experimental way of acting, accompanied by displacement of smaller quantities of cathexis together with less expenditure (discharge) of them. For this purpose conversion of free cathexis into "bound" cathexes was imperative, and this was brought about by means of raising the level of the whole cathectic process. It is probable that thinking was originally unconscious, in so far as it rose above mere ideation and turned to the relations between the object-impressions, and that it became endowed with further qualities which were perceptible to consciousness only through its connection with the memory-traces of words.

2. There is a general tendency of our mental apparatus which we can trace back to the economic principle of saving in expenditure; it seems to find expression in the tenacity with which we hold on to the sources of pleasure at our disposal, and in the difficulty with which we renounce them. With the introduction of the reality-principle one mode of thought-activity was split off; it was kept free from reality-testing and remained subordinated to the pleasure-principle alone.[7] This is the act of *phantasy-making*, which begins already in the games of children, and later, continued as *day-dreaming*, abandons its dependence on real objects.

3. The supersession of the pleasure-principle by the reality-principle with all the mental consequences of this, which is

[7] Just as a nation whose wealth rests on the exploitation of its land yet reserves certain territory to be preserved in its original state and protected from cultural alterations, *e.g.* Yellowstone Park.

here schematically condensed in a single sentence, is not in reality accomplished all at once; nor does it take place simultaneously along the whole line. For while this development is going on in the ego-instincts, the sexual instincts become detached from them in very significant ways. The sexual instincts at first behave auto-erotically; they find their satisfaction in the child's own body and therefore do not come into the situation of frustration which enforces the installation of the reality-principle. Then when later on they begin to find an object, this development undergoes a long interruption in the latency period, which postpones sexual development until puberty. These two factors—auto-erotism and latency period —bring about the result that the mental development of the sexual instincts is delayed and remains far longer under the supremacy of the pleasure-principle, from which in many people it is never able to withdraw itself at all.

In consequence of these conditions there arises a closer connection, on the one hand, between the sexual instincts and phantasy and, on the other hand, between the ego-instincts and the activities of consciousness. Both in healthy and in neurotic people this connection strikes us as very intimate, although the considerations of genetic psychology put forward above lead us to recognize it as *secondary*. The perpetuated activity of auto-erotism makes possible a long retention of the easier momentary and phantastic satisfaction in regard to the sexual object, in place of real satisfaction in regard to it, the latter requiring effort and delay. In the realm of phantasy, repression remains all-powerful; it brings about the inhibition of ideas *in statu nascendi* before they can be consciously noticed, should cathexis of them be likely to occasion the release of "pain." This is the weak place of our mental organization, which can be utilized to bring back under the supremacy of the pleasure-principle thought-processes which had already become rational. An essential part of the mental predisposition to neurosis thus lies in the delayed training of the sexual instincts in the observance of reality and, further, in the conditions which make this delay possible.

4. Just as the pleasure-ego can do nothing but *wish*, work towards gaining pleasure and avoiding "pain," so the reality-ego need do nothing but strive for what is *useful* and guard

itself against damage.[8] Actually, the substitution of the reality-principle for the pleasure-principle denotes no dethronement of the pleasure-principle, but only a safeguarding of it. A momentary pleasure, uncertain in its results, is given up, but only in order to gain in the new way an assured pleasure coming later. But the end psychic impression made by this substitution has been so powerful that it is mirrored in a special religious myth. The doctrine of reward in a future life for the—voluntary or enforced—renunciation of earthly lusts is nothing but a mythical projection of this revolution in the mind. In logical pursuit of this prototype, *religions* have been able to effect absolute renunciation of pleasure in this life by means of the promise of compensation in a future life; they have not, however, achieved a conquest of the pleasure-principle in this way. It is *science* which comes nearest to succeeding in this conquest; science, however, also offers intellectual pleasure during its work and promises practical gain at the end.

5. *Education* can without further hesitation be described as an incitement to the conquest of the pleasure-principle, and to its replacement by the reality-principle; it offers its aid, that is, to that process of development which concerns the ego; to this end it makes use of rewards of love from those in charge, and thus it fails if the spoilt child thinks it will possess this love whatever happens and can in no circumstances lose it.

6. *Art* brings about a reconciliation of the two principles in a peculiar way. The artist is originally a man who turns from reality because he cannot come to terms with the demand for the renunciation of instinctual satisfaction as it is first made, and who then in phantasy-life allows full play to his erotic and ambitious wishes. But he finds a way of return from this world of phantasy back to reality; with his special gifts he moulds his phantasies into a new kind of reality, and men concede them a justification as valuable reflections of actual life. Thus by a certain path he actually becomes the

[8] The superiority of the reality-ego over the pleasure-ego is aptly expressed by Bernard Shaw in these words: "To be able to choose the line of greatest advantage instead of yielding in the direction of least resistance." (*Man and Superman: A Comedy and a Philosophy*.)

hero, king, creator, favourite he desired to be, without pursuing the circuitous path of creating real alterations in the outer world. But this he can only attain because other men feel the same dissatisfaction as he with the renunciation demanded by reality, and because this dissatisfaction, resulting from the displacement of the pleasure-principle by the reality-principle, is itself a part of reality.[9]

7. While the ego goes through its transformation from a *pleasure-ego* into a *reality-ego*, the sexual instincts undergo the changes that lead them from their original auto-erotism through various intermediate phases to object-love in the service of procreation. If it is correct that every step of these two processes of development may become the seat of a predisposition to later neurotic illness, it seems to follow that the decision as regards the form of the subsequent illness (election of neurosis) will depend on the particular phase of ego-development and libido-development in which the inhibition of development has occurred. The chronological characteristics of the two developments, as yet unstudied, their possible variations in speed with respect to each other, thus receive unexpected significance.

8. There is a most surprising characteristic of unconscious (repressed) processes to which every investigator accustoms himself only by exercising great self-control; it results from their entire disregard of the reality-test; thought-reality is placed on an equality with external actuality, wishes with fulfilment and occurrence, just as happens without more ado under the supremacy of the old pleasure-principle. Hence also the difficulty of distinguishing unconscious phantasies from memories which have become unconscious. One must, however, never allow oneself to be misled into applying to the repressed creations of the mind the standards of reality; this might result in undervaluing the importance of phantasies in symptom-formation on the ground that they are not actualities; or in deriving a neurotic sense of guilt from another source because there is no proof of actual committal of any crime. One is bound to employ the currency that prevails in the country one is exploring; in our case it is the neurotic

[9] Cf. the similar position taken by Otto Rank in *Der Künstler*, 1907.

currency. For example, one may try to solve such a dream as the following. A man who had at one time looked after his father through a long and painful illness up to his death, informed me that in the months following his father's decease he had repeatedly dreamt as follows: *his father was again alive and he was talking to him as of old. But as he did so he felt it exceedingly painful that his father was nevertheless dead, only not aware of the fact.* No other way leads to the understanding of this seemingly senseless dream than the addition of "as the dreamer wished," or "as a result of his wish," after the words "that his father was nevertheless dead"; and the further addition of "that he wished it" to the last words. The dream thought then runs: it was a painful memory for him that he must have desired his father's death (as a release) while he still lived, and how terrible it would have been had his father had any suspicion of it. It is thus a matter of the familiar case of self-reproaches after the loss of a loved person, and in this case the reproach goes back to the infantile significance of the death-wish against the father.

The deficiencies of this short paper, which is rather introductory than expository, are perhaps only to a slight extent excused if I acknowledge them to be unavoidable. In the meagre sentences on the mental consequences of adaptation to the reality-principle I was obliged to intimate opinions which I should have preferred to withhold, the vindication of which will certainly require no small exertion. But I hope that benevolent readers will not fail to observe how even in this work the sway of the reality-principle is beginning.

II

On the Mechanism of Paranoia (1911)

WE HAVE HITHERTO been dealing with the father complex, which was the dominant element in Schreber's case[1] and with the wish-phantasy round which the illness centred. But in all of this there is nothing characteristic of the form of disease known as paranoia, nothing that might not be found (and that has not in fact been found) in other kinds of neuroses. The distinctive character of paranoia (or of dementia paranoides) must be sought for elsewhere, namely, in the particular form assumed by the symptoms; and we shall expect to find that this is determined, not by the nature of the complexes themselves, but by the mechanism by which the symptoms are formed or by which repression is brought about. We should be inclined to say that what was characteristically paranoiac about the illness was the fact that the patient, as a means of warding off a homosexual wish-phantasy, reacted precisely with delusions of persecution of this kind.

These considerations therefore lend an added weight to the circumstance that we are in point of fact driven by experience to attribute to the homosexual wish-phantasy an intimate (perhaps an invariable) relation to this particular form of disease. Distrusting my own experience on the subject, I have during the last few years joined with my friends C. G. Jung of Zurich and S. Ferenczi of Budapest in investigating upon this single point a number of cases of paranoid disorder which have come under observation. The patients whose histories provided the material for this inquiry included both men and women, and varied in race, occupation, and social standing. Yet we were astonished to find that in all of these cases a defence against a homosexual wish was clearly recognizable at the very centre of the conflict which underlay the disease, and that it was in an attempt to master an unconsciously reinforced current of homosexuality that they had all of them

[1] [All page references in this essay relate, unless the contrary is stated, to Schreber's "Denkwürdigkeiten."—P.R.]

come to grief.[2] This was certainly not what we had expected. Paranoia is a disorder in which a sexual aetiology is by no means obvious; on the contrary, the strikingly prominent features in the causation of paranoia, especially among males, are social humiliations and slights. But if we go into the matter only a little more deeply, we shall be able to see that the really operative factor in these social injuries lies in the part played in them by the homosexual components of affective life. So long as the individual is functioning normally and it is consequently impossible to see into the depths of his mental life, there is justification for doubting whether his emotional relations to his neighbours in society have anything to do with sexuality, either actually or genetically. But the development of delusions never fails to unmask these relations and to trace back the social feelings to their roots in a purely sensual erotic wish. So long as he was healthy, even Dr. Schreber, whose delusions culminated in a wish-phantasy of an unmistakably homosexual nature, had, by all accounts, shown no signs of homosexuality in the ordinary sense of the word.

I shall now endeavour (and I think the attempt is neither unnecessary nor unjustifiable) to show that the knowledge of psychological processes which, thanks to psychoanalysis, we now possess already enables us to understand the part played by a homosexual wish in the development of paranoia. Recent investigations[3] have directed our attention to a stage in the development of the libido which it passes through on the way from auto-erotism to object-love.[4] This stage has been given the name of narcissism.[5] Its nature is as follows. There comes

[2] Further confirmation is afforded by A. Maeder's analysis of a paranoid patient J. B. ("Psychologische Untersuchungen an Dementia praecox-Kranken," 1910). The present paper, I regret to say, was completed before I had an opportunity of reading Maeder's work.

[3] I. Sadger, "Ein Fall von multipler Perversion mit hysterischen Absenzen," 1910. Freud, *Eine Kindheitserinnerung des Leonardo da Vinci,* 1910.

[4] Freud, *Drei Abhandlungen zur Sexualtheorie,* Second Edition, 1910.

[5] [In the original this sentence reads: "This stage has been described as *"Narzissismus"*; I prefer to give it the name of *"Narzissmus,"* which may not be so correct, but is shorter and less cacophonous."—*Trans.*]

a time in the development of the individual at which he unifies his sexual instincts (which have hitherto been engaged in auto-erotic activities) in order to obtain a love-object; and he begins by taking himself, his own body, as his love-object, and only subsequently proceeds from this to the choice of some person other than himself as his object. This half-way phase between auto-erotism and object-love may perhaps be indispensable to the normal course of life; but it appears that many people linger unusually long in this condition, and that many of its features are carried over by them into the later stages of their development. The point of central interest in the self which is thus chosen as a love-object may already be the genitals. The line of development then leads on to the choice of an outer object with similar genitals—that is, to homosexual object-choice—and thence to heterosexuality. Persons who are manifest homosexuals in later life have, it may be presumed, never emancipated themselves from the binding condition that the object of their choice must possess genitals like their own; and in this connection the infantile sexual theories which attribute the same kind of genitals to both sexes exert a considerable influence.

After the stage of heterosexual object-choice has been reached, the homosexual tendencies are not, as might be supposed, done away with or brought to a stop; they are merely deflected from their sexual aim and applied to fresh uses. They now combine with portions of the ego-instincts and, as "anaclitic" components,[6] help to constitute the social instincts, thus contributing an erotic factor to friendship and comradeship, to *esprit de corps* and to the love of mankind in general. How large a contribution is in fact derived from erotic sources (though with the sexual aim inhibited) could scarcely be guessed from the normal social relations of mankind. But it is not irrelevant to note that it is precisely manifest homosexuals, and among them again precisely those that struggle against an indulgence in sensual acts, who distinguish themselves by taking a particularly active share in the general interests of humanity—interests which have themselves sprung fr⟩ a sublimation of erotic instincts.

[6] [That is, as libidinal components "leaning up against" or supp⟩ting themselves upon the ego-instincts.—*Trans.*]

In my *Drei Abhandlungen zur Sexualtheorie* I have expressed the opinion that each stage in the development of psycho-sexuality affords a possibility for the occurrence of a "fixation" and thus for the laying down of a disposition to illness in later life. Persons who have not freed themselves completely from the stage of narcissism, who, that is to say, have at that point a fixation which may operate as a disposing factor for a later illness, are exposed to the danger that some unusually intense wave of libido, finding no other outlet, may lead to a sexualization of their social instincts and so undo the work of sublimation which they had achieved in the course of their development. This result may be produced by anything that causes the libido to flow backwards (*i.e.* that causes a "regression"): whether, on the one hand, for instance, the libido becomes collaterally reinforced owing to some disappointment over a woman, or is directly dammed up owing to a mishap in social relations with other men—both of these would be instances of "frustration"; or whether, on the other hand, there is a general intensification of the libido, so that it becomes too powerful to find an outlet along the channels which are already open to it, and consequently bursts through its banks at the weakest spot. Since our analyses show that paranoiacs *endeavour to protect themselves against any such sexualization of their social instinctual cathexes,* we are driven to suppose that the weak spot in their development is to be looked for somewhere between the stages of auto-erotism, narcissism and homosexuality, and that their disposition to illness (which may perhaps be susceptible of more precise definition) must be located in that region. A similar disposition would have to be assigned to patients suffering from Kraepelin's dementia praecox or (as Bleuler has named it) *schizophrenia;* and we shall hope later on to find clues which will enable us to trace back the differences between the two disorders (as regards both the form they take and the course they run) to corresponding differences in the patients' dispositional fixations.

We consider, then, that what lies at the core of the conflict in cases of paranoia among males is a homosexual wish-phantasy of *loving a man.* But we have not in the least forgotten that the confirmation of such an important hypothesis can only follow upon the investigation of a large number of instances of every variety of paranoiac disorder. We must therefore be prepared, if need be, to limit our assertion to a single type of paranoia. Nevertheless, it is a remarkable fact that the familiar principal forms of paranoia can all be represented as contradictions of the single proposition: "*I* (a man) *love him* (a man)," and indeed that they exhaust all the possible ways in which such contradictions could be formulated.

The proposition "I (a man) love him" is contradicted by:

(*a*) Delusions of persecution; for it loudly asserts:

"I do not *love* him—I *hate* him."

This contradiction, which could be expressed in no other way in the unconscious,[7] cannot, however, become conscious to a paranoiac in this form. The mechanism of symptom-formation in paranoia requires that internal perceptions, or feelings, shall be replaced by external perceptions. Consequently the proposition "I hate him" becomes transformed by *projection* into another one: "*He hates* (persecutes) *me*, which will justify me in hating him." And thus the unconscious feeling, which is in fact the motive force, makes its appearance as though it were the consequence of an external perception:

"I do not *love* him—I *hate* him, because HE PERSECUTES ME."

Observation leaves room for no doubt that the persecutor is some one who was once loved.

(*b*) Another element is chosen for contradiction in *erotomania*, which remains totally unintelligible on any other view:

"I do not love *him*—I love *her*."

And in obedience to the same need for projection, the proposition is transformed into: "I notice that *she* loves me."

"I do not love *him*—I love *her*, because SHE LOVES ME." Many cases of erotomania might give an impression that they could be satisfactorily explained as being exaggerated or distorted heterosexual fixations, if our attention were not attracted by the circumstance that these infatuations invariably begin, not with any internal perception of loving, but with an external perception of being loved. But in this form of

---

[7] Or in the "root-language," as Schreber would say.

paranoia the intermediate proposition "I love *her*" can also become conscious, because the contradiction between it and the original proposition is not such a diametrical one as that between love and hate: it is, after all, possible to love both *her* and *him*. It can thus come about that the proposition which has been substituted by projection ("*she loves me*") may make way again for the "root-language" proposition "I love *her*."

(*c*) The third way in which the original proposition can be contradicted leads us to delusions of jealousy, which we can study in the characteristic forms in which they appear in each sex.

(*a*) Let us first consider alcoholic delusions of jealousy. The part played by alcohol in this disorder is thoroughly intelligible. We know that drink removes inhibitions and undoes the work of sublimation. It is not infrequently disappointment over a woman that drives a man to drink—which means, as a rule, that he resorts to the public-house and to the company of men, who afford him the emotional satisfaction which he has failed to get from his wife at home. If now these men become the objects of a strong libidinal cathexis in his unconscious, he will ward it off with the third kind of contradiction:

"It is not *I* who love the man—*she* loves him," and he suspects the woman in relation to all the men whom he himself is tempted to love.

Distortion by means of projection is necessarily absent in this instance, since, with the change of the subject who loves, the whole process is anyhow thrown outside the ego. The fact that the woman loves the men is a matter of external perception to him; whereas the facts that he himself does not love but hates, or that he himself loves not this but that person, are matters of internal perception.

(*β*) Delusions of jealousy in women are exactly analogous. "It is not *I* who love the women—but *he* loves them." The jealous woman suspects her husband in relation to all the women by whom she is herself attracted owing to her homosexuality and the dispositional effect of her excessive narcissism. The influence of the time of life at which her fixation occurred is clearly shown by the selection of the love-objects which she imputes to her husband; they are often old and quite inappropriate for a real love relation—revivals of the nurses and servants and girl friends of her childhood, or actually of sisters who were her rivals.

Now it might be supposed that a proposition consisting of three terms, such as *"I love him,"* could only be contradicted in three different ways. The delusion of jealousy contradicts the subject, delusions of persecution contradict the verb, and erotomania contradicts the object. But in fact a fourth kind of contradiction is possible, namely, one which rejects the proposition as a whole:

"I do not love at all—I do not love any one." And since, after all, one's libido must go somewhere, this proposition seems to be the psychological equivalent of the proposition: "I love only myself." So that this kind of contradiction would give us megalomania, which we may regard as a *sexual over-estimation of the ego* and may thus set beside the over-estimation of the love-object with which we are already familiar.[8]

It is of some importance in connection with other parts of the theory of paranoia to notice that we can detect an element of megalomania in most other forms of paranoiac disorder. We are justified in assuming that megalomania is essentially of an infantile nature and that, as development proceeds, it is sacrificed to social considerations. Similarly, an individual's megalomania is never so vehemently suppressed as when he is in the grip of an overpowering love:

> "Denn wo die Lieb' erwachet, stirbt
> das Ich, der finstere Despot."[9]

After this discussion of the unexpectedly important part played by homosexual wish-phantasies in paranoia, let us

[8] *Drei Abhandlungen zur Sexualtheorie* (1905), Sixth Edition, 1925, p. 23. The same view and the same formulation will be found in the papers by Abraham and Maeder to which I have already referred.

[9] Jelaleddin Rumi, translated by Rückert.
["For when the flames of Love arise,
Then Self, the gloomy tyrant, dies."]

return to the two factors in which, from the nature of things, we originally expected to find the distinguishing marks of paranoia, namely, the mechanism *by which the symptoms are formed* and the mechanism *by which repression is brought about.*

We certainly have no right to begin by assuming that these two mechanisms are identical, and that symptom-formation follows the same path as repression, each proceeding along it, perhaps, in an opposite direction. Nor does there seem to be any great probability that such an identity exists. Nevertheless, we shall refrain from expressing any opinion on the subject until we have completed our investigation.

The most striking characteristic of symptom-formation in paranoia is the process which deserves the name of *projection*. An internal perception is suppressed, and, instead, its content, after undergoing a certain degree of distortion, enters consciousness in the form of an external perception. In delusions of persecution the distortion consists in a transformation of affect; what should have been felt internally as love is perceived externally as hate. We should feel tempted to regard this remarkable process as the most important element in paranoia and as being absolutely pathognomonic for it, if we were not opportunely reminded of two things. For, in the first place, projection does not play the same part in all forms of paranoia; and, in the second place, it makes its appearance not only in paranoia but under other psychological conditions as well, and in fact it has a regular share assigned to it in our attitude towards the external world. For when we refer the causes of certain sensations to the external world, instead of looking for them (as we do in the case of the others) inside ourselves, this normal proceeding also deserves to be called projection. Having thus been made aware that more general psychological problems are involved in the question of the nature of projection, let us make up our minds to postpone the investigation of it (and with it that of the mechanism of paranoiac symptom-formation in general) until some other occasion; and let us now turn to consider what ideas we can collect on the subject of the mechanism of repression in paranoia. I should like to say at once, however, that this temporary renunciation will turn out to be well justified; for we shall find that the manner in which the process of repression occurs is far more intimately connected with the developmental history of the libido and with the disposition to which it gives rise than is the manner in which the symptoms are formed.

In psychoanalysis we have been accustomed to look upon pathological phenomena as being derived in a general way from repression. If we examine what is spoken of as "repression" more closely, we shall find reason to split the process up into three phases which are easily distinguishable from one another conceptually.

(1) The first phase consists in *fixation*, which is the precursor and necessary condition of every "repression." Fixation can be described in this way. One instinct or instinctual component fails to accompany the rest along the anticipated normal path of development, and, in consequence of this inhibition in its development, it is left behind at a more infantile stage. The libidinal current in question then behaves in regard to later psychological structures as though it belonged to the system of the unconscious, as though it were repressed. We have already pointed out that these instinctual fixations constitute the basis for the disposition to subsequent illness, and we may now add that they constitute above all the basis for the determination of the outcome of the third phase of repression.

(2) The second phase of repression is that of repression proper—the phase to which most attention has hitherto been given. It emanates from the more highly developed systems of the ego—systems which are capable of being conscious—and may in fact be described as a process of "after-expulsion." It gives an impression of being an essentially active process, while fixation appears rather to be a passive lagging behind. What undergo repression may either be the psychical derivatives of the original lagging instincts, when these have become reinforced and so come into conflict with the ego (or egosyntonic instincts), or they may be psychical trends which have for other reasons aroused strong aversion. But this aversion would not in itself lead to repression, unless some connection had been established between the unwelcome trends about to be repressed and those which have been

repressed already. Where this is so, the repulsion exercised by the conscious system and the attraction exercised by the unconscious one tend in the same sense, namely, towards bringing about repression. The two possibilities which are here treated separately may in practice, perhaps, be less sharply differentiated, and the distinction between them may merely depend upon the greater or lesser degree in which the primarily repressed instincts contribute to the result.

(3) The third phase, and the most important as regards pathological phenomena, is that of miscarriage of repression, of *irruption*, of *return of the repressed*. This irruption takes its start from the point of fixation, and it involves a regression of the libidinal development to that point.

We have already alluded to the multiplicity of the possible points of fixation; there are, in fact, as many as there are stages in the development of the libido. We must be prepared to find a similar multiplicity of the mechanisms of repression proper and of the mechanisms of irruption (or of symptom-formation), and we may already begin to suspect that it will not be possible to trace back all of these multiplicities to the developmental history of the libido alone.

It is easy to see that this discussion is beginning to trench upon the problem of "choice of neurosis," which, however, cannot be taken in hand until preliminary work of another kind has been accomplished. Let us bear in mind for the present that we have already dealt with fixation, and that we have postponed the subject of symptom-formation; and let us restrict ourselves to the question of whether the analysis of Schreber's case throws any light upon the mechanism employed in paranoia for the purpose of repression proper.

At the climax of his illness, under the influence of visions which were "partly of a terrifying character, but partly, too, of an indescribable grandeur" (p. 73), Schreber became convinced of the imminence of a great catastrophe, of the end of the world. Voices told him that the work of the past 14,000 years had now come to nothing, and that the earth's allotted span was only 212 years more (p. 71); and during the last part of his stay in Prof. Flechsig's sanatorium he believed that that period had already elapsed. He himself was "the only real man still surviving," and the few human shapes that he still saw—the physician, the attendants, the other patients—he explained as being "men miracled up, cursory contraptions." Occasionally the converse current of feeling also made itself apparent; a newspaper was put into his hands in which there was a report of his own death (p. 81), he himself existed in a second, inferior shape, and in this second shape he one day quietly passed away (p. 73). But the form of his delusion in which his ego was retained and the world sacrificed proved itself by far the more powerful. He had various theories of the cause of the catastrophe. At one time he had in mind a process of glaciation owing to the withdrawal of the sun; at another it was to be destruction by an earthquake, in the occurrence of which he, in his capacity of "seer," was to act a leading part, just as another seer was alleged to have done in the earthquake of Lisbon in 1755 (p. 91). Or again, Flechsig was the culprit, since he had sown fear and terror among men, had wrecked the foundations of religion, and spread abroad neurotic states and general immorality, so that devastating pestilences had descended upon mankind (p. 91). In any case the end of the world was the consequence of the conflict which had broken out between him and Flechsig, or, according to the aetiology adopted in the second phase of his delusion, of the indissoluble bond which had been formed between him and God; it was, in fact, the inevitable result of his illness. Years afterwards, when Dr. Schreber had returned to human society, he could find no trace in the books, the musical scores, or the other articles of daily use, which fell into his hands once more, of anything to bear out his theory that there had been a gap of vast duration in the history of mankind; he was therefore forced to admit that his view was untenable: ". . . I can no longer avoid recognizing that, *externally considered,* everything is as it used to be. *Whether, nevertheless, there may not have been a profound internal change* is a question to which I shall recur later" (p. 85). He could not bring himself to doubt that during his illness the world had come to an end and that, in spite of everything, the one that he now saw before him was a different one.

Ideas of this kind about a world-catastrophe are not infrequently reported as occurring during the agitated stage in other cases of paranoia.[10] If we take our stand upon the theory of libidinal cathexis, and if we follow the hint given by Schreber's view of other people as being "cursory contraptions," we shall not find it difficult to explain these catastrophes.[11] The patient has withdrawn from the persons in his environment and from the external world generally the libidinal cathexis which he has hitherto directed on to them. Thus all things have become indifferent and irrelevant to him, and have to be explained by means of a secondary rationalization as being "miracled up, cursory contraptions." The end of the world is the projection of this internal catastrophe; for his subjective world has come to an end since he has withdrawn his love from it.[12]

After Faust has uttered the curses which free him from the world, the Chorus of Spirits sings:

> "Weh! Weh!
> Du hast sie zerstört,
> die schöne Welt,
> mit mächtiger Faust!
> sie stürzt, sie zerfällt!
> Ein Halbgott hat sie zerschlagen!
>
> .   .   .   .   .
>
> Mächtiger
> der Erdensöhne,
> Prächtiger

[10] An "end of the world" based upon other motives is to be found at the climax of a lovers' ecstasy (cf. Wagner's *Tristan und Isolde*); in this case it is not the ego but the single love-object which absorbs all the cathexes directed upon the external world.

[11] Cf. Abraham, "Die psychosexuellen Differenzen der Hysterie und der Dementia praecox," 1908, and Jung, *Über die Psychologie der Dementia Praecox*, 1907. Abraham's short paper contains almost all the essential views put forward in the present study of the case of Schreber.

[12] He has perhaps withdrawn from it not only his libidinal cathexis, but his interest in general—that is the cathexes that proceed from his ego as well. This question is discussed below.

> baue sie wieder,
> in deinem Busen baue sie auf!"[13]

And the paranoiac builds it up again, not more splendid, it is true, but at least so that he can once more live in it. He builds it up by the work of his delusions. *The delusion-formation, which we take to be a pathological product, is in reality an attempt at recovery, a process of reconstruction.* Such a reconstruction after the catastrophe is more or less successful, but never wholly so; in Schreber's words, there has been a "profound internal change" in the world. But the man has recaptured a relation, and often a very intense one, to the people and things in the world, although the relation may be a hostile one now, where formerly it was sympathetic and affectionate. We may conclude, then, that the process of repression proper consists in a detachment of the libido from people—and things—that were previously loved. It happens silently; we receive no intelligence of it, but can only infer it from subsequent events. What forces itself so noisily upon our attention is the process of recovery, which undoes the work of repression and brings back the libido again on to the people it had abandoned. In paranoia this process is carried out by the method of projection. It was incorrect of us to say that the perception which was suppressed internally was projected outwards; the truth is rather, as we now see, that what was abolished internally returns from without. The thorough examination of the process of projection which we have post-

---

[13] [Literally:

> "Woe! Woe!
> Thou hast destroyed it,
> The beautiful world,
> With mighty fist!
> It tumbles, it falls in pieces!
> A demigod has shattered it!
>
> . . . . .
> Mighty
> Among the sons of earth,
> More splendid
> Build it again,
> Build it up in thy bosom!"
>
> GOETHE, *Faust*, Part 1.]

poned to another occasion will clear up our remaining doubts on this subject.

In the meantime, however, it is a source of some satisfaction to find that our newly acquired knowledge involves us in a number of further discussions.

(1) Our first reflection will tell us that this detachment of the libido cannot occur in paranoia only; nor, on the other hand, where it does occur elsewhere, can it have such disastrous consequences. It is quite possible that a detachment of the libido is the essential and regular mechanism of every repression. We can have no positive knowledge on that point until the other disorders that are based upon repression have been similarly examined. But it is certain that in normal mental life (and not only in periods of mourning) we are constantly detaching our libido in this way from people or from other objects without falling ill. When Faust freed himself from the world by uttering his curses, the result was not a paranoia or any other neurosis but simply a particular frame of mind. The detachment of the libido, therefore, cannot in itself be the pathogenic factor in paranoia; there must be some special characteristic which distinguishes a paranoiac detachment of the libido from other kinds. And it is not difficult to suggest what that characteristic may be. What use is made of the libido after it has been set free by the process of detachment? A normal person will at once begin looking about for a substitute for the lost attachment; and until that substitute has been found the liberated libido will be kept in suspension within his mind, and will there give rise to tensions and colour all his moods. In hysteria the liberated libido becomes transformed into somatic innervations or into anxiety. But in paranoia the clinical evidence goes to show that the libido, after it has been withdrawn from the object, is put to a special use. It will be remembered that the majority of cases of paranoia exhibit traces of megalomania, and that megalomania can by itself constitute a paranoia. From this it may be concluded that in paranoia the liberated libido becomes fixed on to the ego, and is used for the aggrandizement of the ego. A return is thus made to the stage of narcissism (familiar to us in the development of the libido), in which a person's only sexual object is his own ego. On the basis of this

clinical evidence we can suppose that paranoiacs are endowed
with a *fixation at the stage of narcissism,* and we can assert
that the amount of *regression* characteristic of paranoia is
indicated by the length of *the step back from sublimated
homosexuality to narcissism.*

(2) An equally obvious objection can be based upon
Schreber's case history, as well as upon many others. For it
can be urged that the delusions of persecution (which were
directed against Flechsig) unquestionably made their appearance at an earlier date than the phantasy of the end of the
world; so that what is supposed to have been a return of
the repressed actually preceded the repression itself—which
is patent nonsense. In order to meet this objection we must
leave the high ground of generalization and descend to the
detailed consideration of actual circumstances—which are
undoubtedly very much more complicated. We must admit
the possibility that a detachment of the libido such as we are
discussing might just as easily be a partial one, a drawing
back from some single complex, as a general one. A partial
detachment should be by far the commoner of the two, and
should precede a general one, since to begin with it is only
for a partial detachment that the influences of life provide a
motive. The process may stop at the stage of a partial detachment or it may spread to a general one, which will loudly pro-
claim its presence by means of the symptoms of megalomania.
Thus, in spite of the objection raised above, the detachment
of the libido from the figure of Flechsig may have been the
primary process in the case of Schreber; it was immediately
followed by the appearance of the delusion, which brought
back the libido on to Flechsig again (though with a negative
sign to mark the fact that repression had taken place) and
thus annulled the work of repression. And now the battle of
repression broke out anew, but this time with more powerful
weapons. In proportion as the object of contention became
the most important thing in the external world, trying on the
one hand to draw the whole of the libido on to itself, and on
the other hand mobilizing all the resistances against itself, so
the struggle raging around this single object became more
and more comparable to a general engagement; till at length
a victory for the forces of repression could find expression in

a conviction that the world had come to an end and that the self alone survived. If we review the ingenious constructions which were raised by Schreber's delusion in the domain of religion—the hierarchy of God, the qualified souls, the forecourts of Heaven, the lower and the upper God—we can gauge in retrospect the wealth of sublimations which were brought down in ruin by the catastrophe of the general detachment of his libido.

(3) A third consideration which arises from the views that have been developed in these pages is as follows. Are we to suppose that a general detachment of the libido from the external world would be an effective enough agent to account for the idea of the "end of the world"? Or would not the egoistic cathexes which still remained in existence have been sufficient to maintain *rapport* with the external world? To meet this difficulty we should either have to assume that what we call libidinal cathexis (that is, interest emanating from erotic sources) coincides with interest in general, or we should have to consider the possibility that a very widespread disturbance in the distribution of the libido may bring about a corresponding disturbance in the egoistic cathexes. But these are problems with which we are still quite unaccustomed to deal, and before which we stand helpless. It would be otherwise if we could start out from some well-grounded theory of instincts; but in fact we have nothing of the kind at our disposal. We regard instinct as being a term situated on the frontier-line between the somatic and the mental, and consider it as denoting the mental representative of organic forces. Further, we accept the popular distinction between egoistic instincts and a sexual instinct; for such a distinction seems to agree with the biological conception that the individual has a double orientation, aiming on the one hand at self-preservation and on the other at the preservation of the species. But beyond this are only hypotheses, which we have taken up—and are quite ready to drop again—in order to help us to find our bearings in the chaos of the obscurer processes of the mind. What we expect from psychoanalytic investigations of pathological mental processes is precisely that they shall drive us to some conclusions on questions involving the theory of instincts. These investigations, however, are in their

infancy and are only being carried out by isolated workers, so that the hopes we place in them must still remain unfulfilled. We can no more dismiss the possibility that disturbances of the libido may react upon the egoistic cathexes than we can overlook the converse possibility—namely, that a secondary or induced disturbance of the libidinal processes may result from abnormal changes in the ego. Indeed, it is probable that processes of this kind constitute the distinctive characteristic of psychoses. How much of all this may apply to paranoia it is impossible at present to say. There is one consideration, however, on which I should like to lay stress. It cannot be asserted that a paranoiac, even at the height of the repressive process, withdraws his interest from the external world so completely as must be considered to occur in certain other kinds of hallucinatory psychosis (such as Meynert's amentia). The paranoiac perceives the external world and takes into account any alterations that may happen in it, and the effect it makes upon him stimulates him to invent explanatory theories (such as Schreber's description of men as "cursory contraptions"). It therefore appears to me far more probable that the paranoiac's altered relation to the world is to be explained entirely or in the main by the loss of his libidinal interest.

(4) It is impossible to avoid asking (in view of the close connection between the two disorders) how far this conception of paranoia will affect our conception of dementia praecox. I am of opinion that Kraepelin was entirely justified in taking the step of separating off a large part of what had hitherto been called paranoia and merging it, together with catatonia and certain other varieties of disease, into a new clinical unit—though "dementia praecox" was a particularly unhappy name to choose for it. The designation chosen by Bleuler for the same group of varieties—"schizophrenia"—is also open to the objection that the name appears appropriate only so long as we forget its literal meaning. For otherwise it prejudices the issue, since the name connotes a theoretically postulated characteristic of the disease—a characteristic, moreover, which does not belong exclusively to it, and which, in the light of other considerations, cannot be regarded as the essential one. However, it is not on the whole of very great

importance what names we give to clinical pictures. What seems to me more essential is that paranoia should be maintained as an independent clinical type, however frequently the picture it presents may be complicated by the presence of schizophrenic features. For, from the standpoint of the libido theory, while it would resemble dementia praecox in so far as the repression proper would in both disorders have the same principal feature—detachment of the libido, together with its regression on to the ego—it would be distinguished from dementia praecox by having its dispositional point of fixation differently located and by having a different mechanism for the return of the repressed (that is, for the formation of symptoms). It would seem to me the most convenient plan to give dementia praecox the name of *paraphrenia*. This term has no special connotation, and it would serve to indicate a relationship with paranoia (a name which may be regarded as fixed) and would further recall hebephrenia, an entity which is now merged in dementia praecox. It is true that the name has already been proposed for other purposes; but this need not concern us, since the alternative applications have not passed into general use.

Abraham has very convincingly shown[14] that the turning away of the libido from the external world is a particularly clearly-marked feature in dementia praecox. It is from this feature that we infer the fact that the repression is effected by means of detachment of the libido. Here we may regard the phase of agitated hallucinations as a struggle between repression and an attempt at recovery (an endeavour to bring the libido back again on to its objects). Jung, with extraordinary analytic acumen, has perceived that the "flight of ideas" and motor stereotypes occurring in this disorder are the relics of former object-cathexes, clung to with convulsive energy. This attempt at recovery (which observers mistake for the disease itself) does not, as in paranoia, make use of projection, but employs a hallucinatory (hysterical) mechanism. This is one of the great distinctions between dementia praecox and paranoia; and light can be thrown upon its genesis from another quarter. The second distinction is shown

---

[14] In the paper already quoted.

by the issue of the disease in those cases where the process has become sufficiently general. The prognosis is on the whole more unfavourable than in paranoia; the victory lies with the forces of repression and not, as in the former, with those of reconstruction. Regression travels back not merely to the stage of narcissism (manifesting itself in the shape of megalomania) but to a complete abandonment of object-love and to a restoration of infantile auto-erotism. The dispositional point of fixation must therefore be situated further back than in paranoia, and must lie somewhere at the beginning of the course of development from auto-erotism to object-love. Moreover, it is not at all likely that homosexual impulses, which are so frequently (perhaps invariably) to be found in paranoia, play an equally important part in the aetiology of that far more comprehensive disorder, dementia praecox.

Our hypotheses as to the dispositional fixations in paranoia and paraphrenia make it easy to see that a case may begin with paranoiac symptoms and may yet develop into a dementia praecox, and that paranoid and schizophrenic phenomena may be combined in any proportion. And we can understand how a clinical picture such as Schreber's can come about, and merit the name of a paranoid dementia, from the fact that in its production of a wish-phantasy and of hallucinations it shows paraphrenic traits, while in its exciting cause, in its use of the mechanism of projection, and in its final issue it exhibits a paranoid character. For it is possible for several fixations to be left behind in the course of development, and each of these in succession may allow an irruption of the ousted libido—beginning, presumably, with the later acquired fixations, and then, as the illness develops, affecting the original ones that lie nearer the starting-point. We should be glad to know to what conditions the relatively favourable issue of the present case is due; for we cannot willingly attribute the whole responsibility for the outcome to anything so casual as the "improvement due to change of residence,"[15] which set in after the patient's removal from Prof. Flechsig's sanatorium. But our insufficient acquaintance with the intimate circumstances of the history of the case makes it impossible to give

[15] Cf. Riklin, "Über Versetzungsbesserungen," 1905.

an answer to this interesting question. It may be suspected, however, that what enabled Schreber to reconcile himself to his homosexual phantasy, and so made it possible for his illness to terminate in something approximating to a recovery, may have been the fact that his father-complex was in the main positively toned and that in real life the later years of his relationship with an excellent father had probably been unclouded.

Since I neither fear the criticism of others nor shrink from criticizing myself, I have no motive for avoiding the mention of a similarity which may possibly damage our libido theory in the estimation of many of my readers. Schreber's "rays of God," which are made up of a condensation of the sun's rays, of nerve-fibres, and of spermatozoa, are in reality nothing else than a concrete representation and external projection of libidinal cathexes; and they thus lend his delusions a striking similarity with our theory. His belief that the world must come to an end because his ego was attracting all the rays to itself, his anxious concern at a later period, during the process of reconstruction, lest God should sever his ray-connection with him,—these and many other details of Schreber's delusional formation sound almost like endopsychic perceptions of the processes whose existence I have assumed in these pages as the basis of our explanation of paranoia. I can nevertheless call a friend and fellow-specialist to witness that I had developed my theory of paranoia before I became acquainted with the contents of Schreber's book. It remains for the future to decide whether there is more delusion in my theory than I should like to admit, or whether there is more truth in Schreber's delusion than other people are as yet prepared to believe.

Lastly, I cannot conclude the present work, which is once again only a fragment of a larger whole, without fore-shadowing the two chief theses towards the establishment of which the libido theory of the neuroses and psychoses is advancing, namely, that the neuroses arise in the main from a conflict between the ego and the sexual instinct, and that the forms which the neuroses assume bear the imprint of the course of development followed by the libido—and by the ego.

III

A Note on the Unconscious in Psychoanalysis[1] (1912)

I WISH TO EXPOUND in a few words and as plainly as possible what the term "unconscious" has come to mean in psychoanalysis and in psychoanalysis alone.

A conception—or any other mental element—which is now *present* to my consciousness may become *absent* the next moment, and may become *present again*, after an interval, unchanged, and, as we say, from memory, not as a result of a fresh perception by our senses. It is this fact which we are accustomed to account for by the supposition that during the interval the conception has been present in our mind, although *latent* in consciousness. In what shape it may have existed while present in the mind and latent in consciousness we have no means of guessing.

At this very point we may be prepared to meet with the philosophical objection that the latent conception did not exist as an object of psychology, but as a physical disposition for the recurrence of the same psychical phenomenon, *i.e.* of the said conception. But we may reply that this is a theory far overstepping the domain of psychology proper; that it simply begs the question by asserting "conscious" to be an identical term with "mental," and that it is clearly at fault in denying psychology the right to account for its most common facts, such as memory, by its own means.

Now let us call "conscious" the conception which is present to our consciousness and of which we are aware, and let this be the only meaning of the term "conscious." As for latent conceptions, if we have any reason to suppose that they exist in the mind—as we had in the case of memory—let them be denoted by the term "unconscious."

Thus an unconscious conception is one of which we are not

[1] Written (in English) at the request of the Society for Psychical Research and first published in a Special Medical Supplement of their *Proceedings,* Part lxvi., Vol. xxvi., 1912.

aware, but the existence of which we are nevertheless ready to admit on account of other proofs or signs.

This might be considered an uninteresting piece of descriptive or classificatory work if no experience appealed to our judgement other than the facts of memory, or the cases of association by unconscious links. The well-known experiment, however, of "post-hypnotic suggestion" teaches us to insist upon the importance of the distinction between *conscious* and *unconscious* and seems to increase its value.

In this experiment, as performed by Bernheim, a person is put into a hypnotic state and is subsequently aroused. While he was in the hypnotic state, under the influence of the physician, he was ordered to execute a certain action at a certain fixed moment after his awakening, say half an hour later. He awakes, and seems fully conscious and in his ordinary condition; he has no recollection of his hypnotic state, and yet at the pre-arranged moment there rushes into his mind the impulse to do such and such a thing, and he does it consciously, though not knowing why. It seems impossible to give any other description of the phenomenon than to say that the order had been present in the mind of the person in a condition of latency, or had been present unconsciously, until the given moment came, and then had become conscious. But not the whole of it emerged into consciousness: only the conception of the act to be executed. All the other ideas associated with this conception—the order, the influence of the physician, the recollection of the hypnotic state—remained unconscious even then.

But we have more to learn from such an experiment. We are led from the purely descriptive to a *dynamic* view of the phenomenon. The idea of the action ordered in hypnosis not only became an object of consciousness at a certain moment, but the more striking aspect of the fact is that this idea grew *active*: it was translated into action as soon as consciousness became aware of its presence. The real stimulus to the action being the order of the physician, it is hard not to concede that the idea of the physician's order became active too. Yet this last idea did not reveal itself to consciousness, as did its outcome, the idea of the action; it remained unconscious, and so it was *active and unconscious* at the same time.

A post-hypnotic suggestion is a laboratory production, an artificial fact. But if we adopt the theory of hysterical phenomena first put forward by Pierre Janet and elaborated by Breuer and myself, we shall not be at a loss for plenty of natural facts showing the psychological character of the post-hypnotic suggestion even more clearly and distinctly.

The mind of the hysterical patient is full of active yet unconscious ideas; all her symptoms proceed from such ideas. It is in fact the most striking character of the hysterical mind to be ruled by them. If the hysterical woman vomits, she may do so from the idea of being pregnant. She has, however, no knowledge of this idea, although it can easily be detected in her mind, and made conscious to her, by one of the technical procedures of psychoanalysis. If she is executing the jerks and movements constituting her "fit," she does not even consciously represent to herself the intended actions, and she may perceive those actions with the detached feelings of an onlooker. Nevertheless analysis will show that she was acting her part in the dramatic reproduction of some incident in her life, the memory of which was unconsciously active during the attack. The same preponderance of active unconscious ideas is revealed by analysis as the essential fact in the psychology of all other forms of neurosis.

We learn therefore by the analysis of neurotic phenomena that a latent or unconscious idea is not necessarily a weak one, and that the presence of such an idea in the mind admits of indirect proofs of the most cogent kind, which are equivalent to the direct proof furnished by consciousness. We feel justified in making our classification agree with this addition to our knowledge by introducing a fundamental distinction between different kinds of latent or unconscious ideas. We were accustomed to think that every latent idea was so because it was weak and that it grew conscious as soon as it became strong. We have now gained the conviction that there are some latent ideas which do not penetrate into consciousness, however strong they may have become. Therefore we may call the latent ideas of the first type *preconscious*, while we reserve the term *unconscious* (proper) for the latter type which we came to study in the neuroses. The term *unconscious*, which was used in the purely descriptive sense before, now comes to imply something more. It designates not only latent ideas in general, but especially ideas with a certain dynamic character, ideas keeping apart from consciousness in spite of their intensity and activity.

Before continuing my exposition I will refer to two objections which are likely to be raised at this point. The first of these may be stated thus: instead of subscribing to the hypothesis of unconscious ideas of which we know nothing, we had better assume that consciousness can be split up, so that certain ideas or other psychical acts may constitute a consciousness apart, which has become detached and estranged from the bulk of conscious psychical activity. Well-known pathological cases like that of Dr. Azam seem to go far to show that the splitting up of consciousness is no fanciful imagination.

I venture to urge against this theory that it is a gratuitous assumption, based on the abuse of the word "conscious." We have no right to extend the meaning of this word so far as to make it include a consciousness of which its owner himself is not aware. If philosophers find difficulty in accepting the existence of unconscious ideas, the existence of an unconscious consciousness seems to me even more objectionable. The cases described as splitting of consciousness, like Dr. Azam's, might better be denoted as shifting of consciousness, —that function—or whatever it be—oscillating between two different psychical complexes which become conscious and unconscious in alternation.

The other objection that may probably be raised would be that we apply to normal psychology conclusions which are drawn chiefly from the study of pathological conditions. We are enabled to answer it by another fact, the knowledge of which we owe to psychoanalysis. Certain deficiencies of function of most frequent occurrence among healthy people, e.g. lapsus linguae, errors in memory and speech, forgetting of names, etc., may easily be shown to depend on the action of strong unconscious ideas in the same way as neurotic symptoms. We shall meet with another still more convincing argument at a later stage of this discussion.

By the differentiation of preconscious and unconscious

ideas, we are led on to leave the field of classification and to form an opinion about functional and dynamical relations in the action of the mind. We have found a *preconscious activity* passing into consciousness with no difficulty, and an *unconscious activity* which remains so and seems to be cut off from consciousness.

Now we do not know whether these two modes of psychical activity are identical or essentially divergent from their beginning, but we may ask why they should become different in the course of mental action. To this last question psychoanalysis gives a clear and unhesitating answer. It is by no means impossible for the product of unconscious activity to pierce into consciousness, but a certain amount of exertion is needed for this task. When we try to do it in ourselves, we become aware of a distinct feeling of *repulsion* which must be overcome, and when we produce it in a patient we get the most unquestionable signs of what we call his *resistance* to it. So we learn that the unconscious idea is excluded from consciousness by living forces which oppose themselves to its reception, while they do not object to other ideas, the preconscious ones. Psychoanalysis leaves no room for doubt that the repulsion from unconscious ideas is only provoked by the tendencies embodied in their contents. The next and most probable theory which can be formulated at this stage of our knowledge is the following. Unconsciousness is a regular and inevitable phase in the processes constituting our mental activity; every mental act begins as an unconscious one, and it may either remain so or go on developing into consciousness, according as it meets with resistance or not. The distinction between preconscious and unconscious activity is not a primary one, but comes to be established after repulsion has sprung up. Only then the difference between preconscious ideas, which can appear in consciousness and reappear at any moment, and unconscious ideas which cannot do so gains a theoretical as well as a practical value. A rough but not inadequate analogy to this supposed relation of conscious to unconscious activity might be drawn from the field of ordinary photography. The first stage of the photograph is the "negative"; every photographic picture has to pass through the "negative process," and some of these negatives which have held good in examination are admitted to the "positive process" ending in the picture.

But the distinction between preconscious and unconscious activity, and the recognition of the barrier which keeps them asunder, is not the last or the most important result of the psychoanalytic investigation of mental life. There is one mental product to be met with in the most normal persons, which yet presents a very striking analogy to the wildest productions of insanity, and was no more intelligible to philosophers than insanity itself. I refer to dreams. Psychoanalysis is founded upon the analysis of dreams; the interpretation of dreams is the most complete piece of work the young science has done up to the present. One of the most common types of dream-formation may be described as follows: a train of thoughts has been aroused by the working of the mind in the daytime, and retained some of its activity, escaping from the general inhibition of interests which introduces sleep and constitutes the mental preparation for sleeping. During the night this train of thoughts succeeds in finding connections with one of the unconscious tendencies present ever since his childhood in the mind of the dreamer, but ordinarily *repressed* and excluded from his conscious life. By the borrowed force of this unconscious help, the thoughts, the residue of the day's mental work, now become active again, and emerge into consciousness in the shape of the dream. Now three things have happened:

(1) The thoughts have undergone a change, a disguise and a distortion, which represents the part of the unconscious helpmate.

(2) The thoughts have occupied consciousness at a time when they ought not.

(3) Some part of the unconscious, which could not otherwise have done so, has emerged into consciousness.

We have learnt the art of finding out the "residual thoughts," the *latent thoughts of the dream*, and, by comparing them with the *manifest dream*, we are able to form a judgement on the changes they underwent and the manner in which these were brought about.

The latent thoughts of the dream differ in no respect from the products of our regular conscious activity; they deserve the name of preconscious thoughts, and may indeed have been conscious at some moment of waking life. But by entering into connection with the unconscious tendencies during the night they have become assimilated to the latter, degraded as it were to the condition of unconscious thoughts, and subjected to the laws by which unconscious activity is governed. And here is the opportunity to learn what we could not have guessed from speculation, or from another source of empirical information—that the laws of unconscious activity differ widely from those of the conscious. We gather in detail what the peculiarities of the *Unconscious* are, and we may hope to learn still more about them by a profounder investigation of the processes of dream-formation.

This inquiry is not yet half finished, and an exposition of the results obtained hitherto is scarcely possible without entering into the most intricate problems of dream-analysis. But I would not break off this discussion without indicating the change and progress in our comprehension of the Unconscious which are due to our psychoanalytic study of dreams.

Unconsciousness seemed to us at first only an enigmatical characteristic of a definite mental act. Now it means more for us. It is a sign that this act partakes of the nature of a certain mental category known to us by other and more important features, and that it belongs to a system of mental activity which is deserving of our fullest attention. The index-value of the unconscious has far outgrown its importance as a property. The system revealed by the sign that the single acts forming parts of it are unconscious we designate by the name "The Unconscious," for want of a better and less ambiguous term. In German, I propose to denote this system by the letters *Ubw,* an abbreviation of the German word "Unbewusst."[2] And this is the third and most significant sense which the term "unconscious" has acquired in psychoanalysis.

[2] [In English translations this is rendered Ucs; "consciousness" by Cs; "preconsciousness" by Pcs; "perception-consciousness" by Pcpt-Cs.]

On Narcissism: An Introduction[1] (1914)

1

The word narcissism is taken from clinical terminology and was chosen by P. Näcke[2] in 1899 to denote the attitude of a person who treats his own body in the same way as otherwise the body of a sexual object is treated; that is to say, he experiences sexual pleasure in gazing at, caressing and fondling his body, till complete gratification ensues upon these activities. Developed to this degree, narcissism has the significance of a perversion, which has absorbed the whole sexual life of the subject; consequently, in dealing with it we may expect to meet with phenomena similar to those for which we look in the study of all perversions.

Now those engaged in psychoanalytic observation were struck by the fact that isolated features of the narcissistic attitude are found in many people who are characterized by other aberrations—for instance, as Sadger states, in homosexuals—and at last it seemed that a disposition of the libido which must be described as narcissistic might have to be reckoned with in a much wider field, and that it might claim a place in the regular sexual development of human beings.[3] Difficulties in psychoanalytic work upon neurotics led to the same supposition, for it seemed as though this kind of narcissistic attitude in them was one of the factors limiting their susceptibility to influence. Narcissism in this sense would not be a perversion, but the libidinal complement to the egoism of the instinct of self-preservation, a measure of which may justifiably be attributed to every living creature.

A pressing motive for occupying ourselves with the conception of a primary and normal narcissism arose when the attempt was made to bring our knowledge of dementia praecox (Kraepelin), or schizophrenia (Bleuler), into line with the hypothesis upon which the libido-theory is based. Such patients, whom I propose to term paraphrenics, display

---

[1] First published in *Jahrbuch*, Bd. vi., 1914; reprinted in *Sammlung*, Vierte Folge. [Translated by Cecil M. Baines.]

[2] [In a later paper Professor Freud has corrected this slip and added the name of Havelock Ellis.]

[3] Otto Rank, "Ein Beitrag zum Narzissmus."

two fundamental characteristics: they suffer from mega-lomania and they have withdrawn their interest from the external world (people and things). In consequence of this latter change in them, they are inaccessible to the influence of psychoanalysis and cannot be cured by our endeavours. But this turning away of the paraphrenic from the outer world needs to be more precisely characterized. A patient suffering from hysteria or obsessional neurosis has also, as far as the influence of his illness goes, abandoned his relation to reality. But analysis shows that he has by no means broken off his erotic relations to persons and things. He still retains them in phantasy; *i.e.* he has, on the one hand, substituted for actual objects imaginary objects founded on memories, or has blended the two; while, on the other hand, he has ceased to direct his motor activities to the attainment of his aims in connection with real objects. It is only to this condition of the libido that we may legitimately apply the term *introversion* of the libido which is used by Jung indiscriminately. It is other-wise with the paraphrenic. He seems really to have withdrawn his libido from persons and things in the outer world, without replacing them by others in his phantasy. When this does happen, the process seems to be a secondary one, part of an effort towards recovery, designed to lead the libido back towards an object.[4]

The question arises: What is the fate of the libido when withdrawn from external objects in schizophrenia? The mega-lomania characteristic of these conditions affords a clue here. It has doubtless come into being at the expense of the object-libido. The libido withdrawn from the outer world has been directed on to the ego, giving rise to a state which we may call narcissism. But the megalomania itself is no new phe-nomenon; on the contrary, it is, as we know, an exaggeration and plainer manifestation of a condition which had already existed previously. This leads us to the conclusion that the narcissism which arises when libidinal cathexes are called in away from external objects must be conceived of as a second-

[4] Compare with these propositions my discussion of the "end of the world" in the analysis of Senatspräsident Schreber, *supra*, p. 38. Also Abraham, "Die psychosexuellen Differenzen der Hys-terie und der Dementia Praecox."

ary form, superimposed upon a primary one that is obscured by manifold influences.

Let me expressly state that I am not attempting here to explain or penetrate further into the problem of schizophrenia, but am merely putting together what has been said elsewhere, in order that I may justify this introduction of the concept of narcissism.

This development of the libido-theory—in my opinion, a legitimate development—receives reinforcement from a third quarter, namely, from the observations we make and the conceptions we form of the mental life of primitive peoples and of children. In the former we find characteristics which, if they occurred singly, might be put down to megalomania: an over-estimation of the power of wishes and mental processes, the "omnipotence of thoughts," a belief in the magical virtue of words, and a method of dealing with the outer world—the art of "magic"—which appears to be a logical application of these grandiose premises.[5] In the child of our own day, whose development is much more obscure to us, we expect a perfectly analogous attitude towards the external world.[6] Thus we form a conception of an original libidinal cathexis of the ego, part of which cathexis is later yielded up to objects, but which fundamentally persists and is related to the object-cathexes much as the body of a protoplasmic animalcule is related to the pseudopodia which it puts out. In our researches, taking, as they did, neurotic symptoms for their starting-point, this part of the disposition of the libido necessarily remained hidden from us at the outset. We were struck only by the emanations from this libido—the object-cathexes, which can be put forth and drawn back again. We perceive also, broadly speaking, a certain reciprocity between ego-libido and object-libido. The more that is absorbed by the one, the more impoverished does the other become. The highest form of development of which object-libido is capable is seen in the state of being in love, when the subject seems to yield up his whole personality in favour of object-cathexis;

[5] Cf. the corresponding sections on this subject in my *Totem und Tabu*, 1913.

[6] Cf. Ferenczi, "Stages in the Development of the Sense of Reality."

while we have the opposite condition in the paranoiac's phantasy (or self-perception) of the "end of the world."[7] Finally, with reference to the differentiation of the energies operating in the mind, we infer that at first in the narcissistic state they exist side by side and that our analysis is not a fine enough instrument to distinguish them; only where there is object-cathexis is it possible to discriminate a sexual energy—the libido—from an energy pertaining to the ego-instincts.

Before going any further I must touch on two questions which lead us to the heart of the difficulties of our subject. In the first place: what is the relation of the narcissism of which we are now speaking to auto-erotism, which we have described as an early state of the libido? And secondly: if we concede to the ego a primary cathexis of libido, why is there any necessity for further distinguishing a sexual libido from a non-sexual energy pertaining to the ego-instincts? Would not the assumption of a uniform mental energy save us all the difficulties of differentiating the energy of the ego-instincts from ego-libido, and ego-libido from object-libido? On the first point I would comment as follows: it is impossible to suppose that a unity comparable to the ego can exist in the individual from the very start; the ego has to develop. But the auto-erotic instincts are primordial; so there must be something added to auto-erotism—some new operation in the mind—in order that narcissism may come into being.

To be required to give a definite answer to the second question must occasion perceptible uneasiness in every psychoanalyst. One dislikes the thought of abandoning observation for barren theoretical discussions, but all the same we must not shirk an attempt at explanation. Conceptions such as that of an ego-libido, an energy pertaining to the ego-instincts, and so on, are certainly neither very easy to grasp nor is their content sufficiently rich; a speculative theory of these relations of which we are speaking would in the first place require as its basis a sharply defined concept. But I am of opinion that that is just the difference between a speculative theory and a science founded upon constructions arrived at empirically.

[7] There are two mechanisms in this "end of the world" idea: in one case, the whole libidinal cathexis is drained off to the loved object, while, in the other, it all flows back to the ego.

The latter will not begrudge to speculation its privilege of a smooth, logically unassailable structure, but will itself be gladly content with nebulous, scarcely imaginable conceptions, which it hopes to apprehend more clearly in the course of its development, or which it is even prepared to replace by others. For these ideas are not the basis of the science upon which everything rests: that, on the contrary, is observation alone. They are not the foundation-stone, but the coping of the whole structure, and they can be replaced and discarded without damaging it. The same thing is happening in our day in the science of physics, the fundamental notions of which as regards matter, centres of force, attraction, etc., are scarcely less debatable than the corresponding ideas in psychoanalysis.

The value of the concepts "ego-libido" and "object-libido" is that they are derived from the study of the essential characteristics of neurotic and psychotic processes. The differentiation of the libido into that which is proper to the ego and that which attaches itself to objects is a necessary extension of an original hypothesis which discriminated between ego-instincts and sexual instincts. At any rate, analysis of the pure transference neuroses (hysteria and the obsessional neurosis) compelled me so to discriminate, and I only know that all attempts to account for these phenomena by other means have been completely unsuccessful.

In the complete absence of any theory of the instincts which would help us to find our bearings, we may be permitted, or rather, it is incumbent upon us, in the first place to work out any hypothesis to its logical conclusion, until it either fails or becomes confirmed. There are various points in favour of the hypothesis of a primordial differentiation between sexual instincts and other instincts, ego-instincts, besides the usefulness of such an assumption in the analysis of the transference neuroses. I admit that this latter consideration alone would not be decisive, for it might be a question of an indifferent energy operating in the mind which was converted into libido only by the act of object-cathexis. But, in the first place, this differentiation of concepts corresponds to the distinction between hunger and love, so widely current. And, in the second place, there are biological considerations in its favour. The individual does actually carry on a double exist-

ence: one designed to serve his own purposes and another as
a link in a chain, in which he serves against, or at any rate
without, any volition of his own. The individual himself regards sexuality as one of his own ends; while from another
point of view he is only an appendage to his germ-plasm, to
which he lends his energies, taking in return his toll of
pleasure—the mortal vehicle of a (possibly) immortal substance—like the inheritor of an entailed property who is only
the temporary holder of an estate which survives him. The
differentiation of the sexual instincts from the ego-instincts
would simply reflect this double function of the individual.
Thirdly, we must recollect that all our provisional ideas in
psychology will some day be based on an organic substructure.
This makes it probable that special substances and special
chemical processes control the operation of sexuality and provide for the continuation of the individual life in that of the
species. We take this probability into account when we substitute special forces in the mind for special chemical substances.

Just because I try in general to keep apart from psychology
everything that is not strictly within its scope, even biological
thought, I wish at this point expressly to admit that the
hypothesis of separate ego-instincts and sexual instincts (that
is to say, the libido-theory) rests scarcely at all upon a psychological basis, but is essentially supported upon the facts of
biology. So I shall also be consistent enough to drop this
hypothesis if psychoanalytic work itself should suggest as
more valuable another hypothesis about the instincts. So far,
this has not happened. It may then be that—when we penetrate deepest and furthest—sexual energy, the libido, will be
found to be only the product of a differentiation in the energy
at work generally in the mind. But such a statement is of no
importance. It has reference to matters so remote from the
problems of our observation and so empty of available knowledge, that to dispute it is as idle as to affirm it; it is possible
that this primordial identity has as little to do with our analyti-
cal interests as the primordial kinship of all human races has
to do with the proof of kinship with a testator required by the
Probate Court. All these speculations lead nowhere; since we
cannot wait for another science to present us with a theory of
the instincts ready-made, it is far more to the purpose that

we should try to see what light may be thrown upon this basic problem of biology by a synthesis of psychological phenomena. Let us be fully aware of the possibility of error; but do not let us be deterred from carrying to its logical conclusion the hypothesis we first adopted of an antithesis between ego-instincts and sexual instincts (an hypothesis to which we were impelled by analysis of the transference neuroses), and so from seeing whether it turns out to be consistent and fruitful, and whether it may be applied to other affections also, *e.g.* to schizophrenia.

Of course, it would be a very different matter if it were proved that the libido-theory had already come to grief in the attempt to explain the last-named disease. That this is so has been maintained by C. G. Jung,[8] and so I have been obliged to enter upon this last disquisition, which I would gladly have been spared. I should have preferred, without any discussion of the premises, to follow out the course embarked upon in the analysis of the Schreber case. But Jung's assertion is, to say the least of it, premature. The grounds he gives for it are scanty. At the outset, he quotes me as saying that I myself have been obliged, owing to the difficulties of the Schreber analysis, to extend the conception of the libido, *i.e.* to give up its sexual content and to identify libido with psychic "interest" in general. Ferenczi, in an exhaustive criticism of Jung's work, has already said all that is necessary in correction of this erroneous interpretation.[9] I can only corroborate this critic and repeat that I have never thus retracted the libido-theory. Another argument of Jung's, namely, that we must not assume that the loss of the normal function of appreciating reality can be brought about only by the withdrawal of the libido, is no argument but a dictum. It begs the question, it anticipates the decision and waives discussion; for whether and how this is possible is just what has to be investigated. In his next large work,[10] Jung just misses the solution which I had long since indicated: "At the same time there is this to be taken into consideration, a point to which Freud refers in his work on the Schreber case, that the introversion of the *libido*

[8] "Wandlungen und Symbole der Libido."

[9] *Zeitschrift*, Bd. I., 1913.

[10] "Versuch einer Darstellung der psychoanalytischen Theorie."

sexualis leads to a cathexis of the 'ego,' and that possibly it is this that produces the effect of a loss of reality. It is indeed a tempting possibility to explain the psychology of the loss of reality in this fashion." But Jung discusses this possibility very little further. A few pages later he dismisses it with the remark that from this conditioning factor "would result, not dementia praecox, but the psychology of an ascetic anchorite." How little this inept comparison can help us to a conclusion may be learnt from the reflection that an anchorite who "tries to erase every trace of sexual interest" (but only in the popular sense of the word "sexual") does not even necessarily display any pathogenic disposition of the libido. He may have turned away his interest from human beings entirely, and yet may have sublimated it to a heightened interest in the divine, in nature, or in the animal kingdom, without his libido having undergone introversion to his phantasies or retrogression to his ego. This comparison would seem to rule out in advance the possibility of differentiating between interest emanating from erotic or that from other sources. Further, when we remember that the researches of the Swiss school, however meritorious, have elucidated only two features in the picture of dementia praecox—the existence of complexes common to healthy and neurotic persons alike, and the similarity of the phantasy-formations of that disease to popular myths—but have not been able to throw any further light on the pathogenic mechanism, we may repudiate Jung's assertion that the libido-theory has broken down in the attempt to understand dementia praecox, and is therefore rendered invalid for the other neuroses also.

2

It seems to me that certain peculiar difficulties lie in the way of a direct study of narcissism. Our chief means of access to an understanding of this condition will probably remain the analysis of paraphrenics. As the transference neuroses have enabled us to trace the libidinal instinctual impulses, so dementia praecox and paranoia will give us insight into the psychology of the ego. Once more, in order to arrive at what is normal and apparently so simple, we shall have to study the pathological with its distortions and exaggerations. At the same time, there are other sources from which we may derive a knowledge of narcissism, which I will now mention in their order—namely, the study of organic disease, of hypochondria, and of love between the sexes.

In estimating the influence of organic disease upon the distribution of the libido, I follow a suggestion of S. Ferenczi's, which he made to me in conversation. It is universally known, and seems to us a matter of course, that a person suffering organic pain and discomfort relinquishes his interest in the things of the outside world, in so far as they do not concern his suffering. Closer observation teaches us that at the same time he withdraws libidinal interest from his love-objects: so long as he suffers, he ceases to love. The banality of this fact is no reason why we should be deterred from translating it into terms of the libido-theory. We should then say: the sick man withdraws his libidinal cathexes back upon his own ego, and sends them forth again when he recovers. "Concentrated is his soul," says W. Busch, of the poet suffering from toothache, "in his jaw-tooth's aching hole." Here libido and ego-interest share the same fate and have once more become indistinguishable from each other. The familiar egoism of the sick person covers them both. We find it so natural because we are certain that in the same situation we should behave in just the same way. The way in which the readiness to love, however great, is banished by bodily ailments, and suddenly replaced by complete indifference, is a theme which has been sufficiently exploited by comic writers.

The condition of sleep, like illness, implies a narcissistic withdrawal of the libido away from its attachments back to the subject's own person, or, more precisely, to the single desire for sleep. The egoism of dreams fits in very well in this connection. In both states we have, if nothing else, examples of changes in the distribution of the libido which are consequent upon a change in the ego.

Hypochondria, like organic disease, manifests itself in distressing and painful bodily sensations and also concurs with organic disease in its effect upon the distribution of the libido. The hypochondriac withdraws both interest and libido—the latter specially markedly—from the objects of the outer world and concentrates both upon the organ which engages his attention. A difference between hypochondria and organic disease now becomes evident: in the latter, the distressing sensations are based upon demonstrable organic changes; in the former, this is not so. But it would be entirely in keeping with our general conception of the processes of neurosis if we decided to say that hypochondria must be right; organic changes cannot be absent in it either. Now in what could such changes consist?

Here we may fall back upon our experience, which shows that bodily sensations of a painful nature, comparable to those of hypochondria, are not lacking in the other neuroses. I have said once before that I am inclined to class hypochondria with neurasthenia and anxiety-neurosis as a third "actual neurosis." Probably it would not be going too far to put it in this way: that in the other neuroses too there is regularly present some small admixture of hypochondria. Perhaps we have the best example of this in the anxiety-neurosis and in the hysteria superimposed upon it. Now the familiar prototype of an organ sensitive to pain, in some way changed and yet not diseased in the ordinary sense, is that of the genital organ in a state of excitation. It becomes congested with blood, swollen, moist, and is the seat of manifold sensations. If we apply to that activity of a given bodily area which consists in conveying sexually exciting stimuli to the mind the term *erotogenicity,* and if we reflect that the conclusions of our theory of sexuality have long accustomed us to the notion that certain other areas of the body—the *erotogenic* zones—may act as substitutes for the genitals and behave analogously to them, we then have only one step further to venture here. We can make up our minds to regard erotogenicity as a property common to all organs and are then justified in speaking of an increase or decrease in the degree of it in any given part of the body. It is possible that for every such change in the erotogenicity of the organs there is a parallel change in the libidinal cathexis in the ego. In such factors may lie the explanation of what is at the bottom of hypochondria and what it is that can have upon the distribution of the libido the same effect as actual organic disease.

We see that, if we follow out this line of thought, we encounter the problem not only of hypochondria, but of the other "actual neuroses"—neurasthenia and anxiety-neurosis. Let us therefore stop at this point. It is not within the scope of a purely psychological inquiry to penetrate so far behind the frontiers of physiological research. Let us only mention that from this point of view we may surmise that the relation of hypochondria to paraphrenia is similar to that of the other actual neuroses to hysteria and to the obsessional neurosis: which is as much as to say that it is dependent on the ego-libido as the others are on the object-libido, and that hypo-chondriacal anxiety, emanating from the ego-libido, is the counterpart to neurotic anxiety. Further: since we are already familiar with the idea that the mechanism of disease and symptom-formation in the transference neuroses, the passage from introversion to regression, is to be connected with a damming-up of the object-libido,[11] we may come to closer quarters with the conception of a damming-up of the ego-libido also and may bring this conception into relation with the phenomena of hypochondria and paraphrenia.

Of course curiosity will here suggest the question why such a damming-up of libido in the ego should be experienced as "painful." There I shall content myself with the answer that "pain" is in general the expression of increased tension, and thus a *quantity* of the material event is, here as elsewhere, transformed into the *quality* of "pain" in the mind; nevertheless, it may be not the absolute amount of the physical process which is decisive for the development of pain, but rather a certain function of this absolute amount. At this point we may even venture to touch on the question: whence does that necessity arise that urges our mental life to pass on beyond the limits of narcissism and to attach the libido to objects? The answer which would follow from our line of thought would once more be that we are so impelled when the cathexis of the ego with libido exceeds a certain degree. A strong egoism is a protection against disease, but in the last resort we must begin to love in order that we may not fall ill, and must fall ill if, in consequence of frustration, we cannot love. Somewhat after this fashion does Heine conceive of the psychogenesis of the Creation:

[11] Cf. "Types of Neurotic Nosogenesis," *Sexuality and the Psychology of Love*, Collier Books edition BS 192V.

Krankheit ist wohl der letzte Grund
Des ganzen Schöpferdrangs gewesen;
Erschaffend konnte ich genesen,
Erschaffend wurde ich gesund.[12]

We have recognized our mental apparatus above all as a device for mastering excitations which would otherwise be felt as unpleasant or would have pathogenic effects. The "working-over" of stimuli in the mind accomplishes wonders for the internal discharge of excitations which are incapable of direct discharge outwards, or for which such a discharge is, for the moment, undesirable. Now it is in the first instance a matter of indifference whether the objects of this internal process of "working-over" are real or imaginary. The difference does not appear till later, when the turning of the libido towards unreal objects (introversion) has led to a damming-up. The megalomania of paraphrenics permits a similar internal working-over of the libido which has returned to the ego to be made; perhaps it is only when this process fails that the damming-up of the libido in the ego becomes pathogenic and starts the process of recovery which impresses us as being the disease itself.

I shall try here to penetrate a little further into the mechanism of paraphrenia and to put together those conceptions which to-day seem to me worthy of consideration. The difference between paraphrenic affections and the transference neuroses appears to me to lie in the circumstance that, in the former, the libido that is liberated by frustration does not remain attached to objects in phantasy, but returns to the ego; the megalomania then represents the mastery of this volume of libido, and thus corresponds with the introversion on to the phantasy-creations that is found in the transference neuroses; the hypochondria of paraphrenia, which is homologous to the anxiety of the transference neuroses, arises from a failure of this effort in the mental apparatus. We know that the anxiety of the neuroses can be relieved by further mental

[12] Disease at bottom brought about
    Creative urgence—for, creating,
    I soon could feel the pain abating,
    Creating, I could work it out.

"working-over," *e.g.* by conversion, reaction-formation or defence-formation (phobia). The corresponding process in paraphrenics is the effort towards recovery, to which the striking phenomena of the disease are due. Since frequently, if not usually, an only partial detachment of the libido from objects accompanies paraphrenia, we can distinguish in the clinical picture three groups of phenomena: (1) those representing such remains as there may be of a normal state or of neurosis (phenomena of a residual nature); (2) those representing the morbid process (the detachment of the libido from its objects and, further, megalomania, hypochondria, affective disturbance and every kind of regression); (3) those representing an attempt at recovery. In (3) the libido is once more attached to objects, after the manner of an hysteria (in dementia praecox or paraphrenia proper), or of an obsessional neurosis (in paranoia). This fresh libidinal cathexis takes place from another level and under other conditions than the primary one. The difference between the transference neuroses arising in this way and the corresponding formations where the ego is normal would afford us the deepest insight into the structure of our mental apparatus.

A third way in which we may study narcissism is by observing the behaviour of human beings in love, with its manifold differentiation in man and woman. In much the same way as the object-libido at first concealed from us the ego-libido, so in considering the object-choice of the child (and the adolescent) we first noticed that the sources from which he takes his sexual objects are his experiences of gratification. The first auto-erotic sexual gratifications are experienced in connection with vital functions in the service of self-preservation. The sexual instincts are at the outset supported upon the ego-instincts; only later do they become independent of these, and even then we have an indication of that original dependence in the fact that those persons who have to do with the feeding, care, and protection of the child become his earliest sexual objects: that is to say, in the first instance the mother or her substitute. Side by side with this type and source of object-choice, which may be called the *anaclitic* type,[13] a second type, the existence of which we had not suspected, has been revealed by psychoanalytic investigation. We have found, especially in persons whose libidinal development has suffered some disturbance, as in perverts and homosexuals, that in the choice of their love-object they have taken as their model not the mother but their own selves. They are plainly seeking themselves as a love-object and their type of object-choice may be termed *narcissistic*. This observation provides us with our strongest motive for regarding the hypothesis of narcissism as a necessary one.

Now this does not mean that human beings are to be divided into two sharply differentiated groups, according as their object-choice conforms to the anaclitic or to the narcissistic type; we rather assume that both kinds of object-choice are open to each individual, though he may show a preference for one or the other. We say that the human being has originally two sexual objects: himself and the woman who tends him, and thereby we postulate a primary narcissism in everyone, which may in the long run manifest itself as dominating his object-choice.

Further, the comparison of man and woman shows that there are fundamental differences between the two in respect of the type of object-choice, although these differences are of course not universal. Complete object-love of the anaclitic type is, properly speaking, characteristic of the man. It displays the marked sexual over-estimation which is doubtless derived from the original narcissism of the child, now transferred to the sexual object. This sexual over-estimation is the origin of the peculiar state of being in love, a state suggestive of a neurotic compulsion, which is thus traceable to an impoverishment of the ego in respect of libido in favour of the love-object. A different course is followed in the type most frequently met with in women, which is probably the purest and truest feminine type. With the development of puberty the maturing of the female sexual organs, which up till then

[13] [*Anlehnungstypus*. Literally, "leaning-up-against" type. In the first phase of their development the sexual instincts find their satisfaction through propping themselves upon or "leaning up against" the self-preservative instincts.]

have been in a condition of latency, seems to bring about an intensification of the original narcissism, and this is unfavourable to the development of a true object-love with its accompanying sexual over-estimation; there arises in the woman a certain self-sufficiency (especially when there is a ripening into beauty) which compensates her for the social restrictions upon her object-choice. Strictly speaking, such women love only themselves with an intensity comparable to that of the man's love for them. Nor does their need lie in the direction of loving, but of being loved; and that man finds favour with them who fulfils this condition. The importance of this type of woman for the erotic life of mankind must be recognized as very great. Such women have the greatest fascination for men, not only for aesthetic reasons, since as a rule they are the most beautiful, but also because of certain interesting psychological constellations. It seems very evident that one person's narcissism has a great attraction for those others who have renounced part of their own narcissism and are seeking after object-love; the charm of a child lies to a great extent in his narcissism, his self-sufficiency and inaccessibility, just as does the charm of certain animals which seem not to concern themselves about us, such as cats and the large beasts of prey. In literature, indeed, even the great criminal and the humorist compel our interest by the narcissistic self-importance with which they manage to keep at arm's length everything which would diminish the importance of their ego. It is as if we envied them their power of retaining a blissful state of mind—an unassailable libido-position which we ourselves have since abandoned. The great charm of the narcissistic woman has, however, its reverse side; a large part of the dissatisfaction of the lover, of his doubts of the woman's love, of his complaints of her enigmatic nature, have their root in this incongruity between the types of object-choice.

Perhaps it is not superfluous to give an assurance that, in this description of the feminine form of erotic life, no tendency to depreciate woman has any part. Apart from the fact that tendentiousness is alien to me, I also know that these different lines of development correspond to the differentiation of functions in a highly complicated biological connection; further, I am ready to admit that there are countless women

who love according to the masculine type and who develop
the over-estimation of the sexual object so characteristic of
that type.

Even for women whose attitude towards the man remains
cool and narcissistic there is a way which leads to complete
object-love. In the child to whom they give birth, a part of
their own body comes to them as an object other than themselves, upon which they can lavish out of their narcissism
complete object-love. Other women again do not need to wait
for a child in order to take the step in development from
(secondary) narcissism to object-love. Before puberty they
have had feelings of a likeness to men and have developed to
some extent on masculine lines; after this tendency has been
cut short when feminine maturity is reached, they still retain
the capacity of longing for a masculine ideal which is really
a survival of the boyish nature that they themselves once
owned.

We may conclude these suggestions with a short survey of
the paths leading to object-choice.

A person may love:

(1) According to the narcissistic type:

    (a) What he is himself (actually himself).

    (b) What he once was.

    (c) What he would like to be.

    (d) Someone who was once part of himself.

(2) According to the anaclitic type:

    (a) The woman who tends.

    (b) The man who protects;

and those substitutes which succeed them one after another.
The justification for inserting case (c) of the first type has yet
to be demonstrated later on in our discussion.

The significance of narcissistic object-choice for homosexuality in men must be appraised in another connection.

The primary narcissism of the child assumed by us, which
forms one of the hypotheses in our theories of the libido, is
less easy to grasp by direct observation than to confirm by
deduction from another consideration. If we look at the attitude of fond parents towards their children, we cannot but
perceive it as a revival and reproduction of their own, long
since abandoned narcissism. Their feeling, as is well known, is

characterized by over-estimation, that sure indication of a narcissistic feature in object-choice which we have already appreciated. Thus they are impelled to ascribe to the child all manner of perfections which sober observation would not confirm, to gloss over and forget all his shortcomings—a tendency with which, indeed, the denial of childish sexuality is connected. Moreover, they are inclined to suspend in the child's favour the operation of all those cultural acquirements which their own narcissism has been forced to respect, and to renew in his person the claims for privileges which were long ago given up by themselves. The child shall have things better than his parents; he shall not be subject to the necessities which they have recognized as dominating life. Illness, death, renunciation of enjoyment, restrictions on his own will, are not to touch him; the laws of nature, like those of society, are to be abrogated in his favour; he is really to be the centre and heart of creation, "His Majesty the Baby," as once we fancied ourselves to be. He is to fulfil those dreams and wishes of his parents which they never carried out, to become a great man and a hero in his father's stead, or to marry a prince as a tardy compensation to the mother. At the weakest point of all in the narcissistic position, the immortality of the ego which is so relentlessly assailed by reality, security is achieved by fleeing to the child. Parental love, which is so touching and at bottom so childish, is nothing but parental narcissism born again and, transformed though it be into object-love, it reveals its former character infallibly.

3

The disturbances to which the original narcissism of the child is exposed, the reactions with which he seeks to protect himself from them, the paths into which he is thereby forced —these are themes which I shall leave on one side, as an important field for work which still awaits exploration; the most important of these matters, however, can be isolated from the rest and, as the "castration complex" (in the boy, anxiety concerning the penis; in the girl, envy of the penis), be treated in connection with the effect of early sexual intimidation. Elsewhere, psychoanalytic research leads us to vicissitudes undergone by the libidinal instincts in which they are isolated from, and in opposition to, the ego-instincts; but where the castration complex is in question, our researches permit us to infer the existence of an epoch and a mental state in which the two groups of instincts are acting in harmony with each other, inseparably blent, as narcissistic interests. It is from this state of things that A. Adler has derived his conception of the "masculine protest," which he has exalted almost to the position of the sole motive power concerned in the formation of neurosis and also of character, and which he conceives of as having its origin, not in a narcissistic, and therefore still libidinal, trend, but in a social valuation. Psychoanalytic research has, from the very beginning, recognized the existence and significance of the "masculine protest," but has always regarded it, in opposition to Adler, as narcissistic in nature and derived from the castration complex. It appertains to the formation of character, into the genesis of which it enters along with many other factors, and it is completely inadequate to explain the problems of the neuroses, in which Adler will take account of nothing but the manner in which they serve the interests of the ego. I find it quite impossible to base the genesis of neurosis upon so narrow a foundation as the castration complex, however pre-eminent a part this may play in men amongst the resistances to the cure of a neurosis. Lastly, I know also of cases of neurosis in which the "masculine protest," or in our sense the castration complex, plays no pathogenic part, or does not appear at all.

Observation of normal adults shows that their former megalomania has been subdued and that the mental characteristics from which we inferred their infantile narcissism have vanished. What has become of their ego-libido? Are we to assume that the whole of it has passed over into object-cathexes? Such a possibility is plainly contrary to the whole trend of our argument; but in the psychology of repression we may find a clue to another answer to the question.

We have learnt that libidinal impulses are fated to undergo pathogenic repression if they come into conflict with the subject's cultural and ethical ideas. By this we do not ever mean: if the individual in question has a merely intellectual knowledge of the existence of these ideas; we always mean: if he recognizes them as constituting a standard for himself and acknowledges the claims they make on him. Repression, as we have said, proceeds from the ego; we might say with greater precision: from the self-respect of the ego. The very impressions, experiences, impulses and desires that one man indulges or at least consciously elaborates in his mind will be rejected with the utmost indignation by another, or stifled at once even before they enter consciousness. The difference between the two, however—and here we have the conditioning factor in repression—can easily be expressed in terms of the libido-theory. We may say that the one man has set up an *ideal* in himself by which he measures his actual ego, while the other is without this formation of an ideal. From the point of view of the ego this formation of an ideal would be the condition of repression.

To this ideal ego is now directed the self-love which the real ego enjoyed in childhood. The narcissism seems to be now displaced on to this new ideal ego, which, like the infantile ego, deems itself the possessor of all perfections. As always where the libido is concerned, here again man has shown himself incapable of giving up a gratification he has once enjoyed. He is not willing to forgo his narcissistic perfection in his childhood; and if, as he develops, he is disturbed by the admonitions of others and his own critical judgement is awakened, he seeks to recover the early perfection, thus wrested from him, in the new form of an ego-ideal. That which he projects ahead of him as his ideal is merely his substitute for the lost narcissism of his childhood—the time when he was his own ideal.

This suggests that we should examine the relation between this forming of ideals and sublimation. Sublimation is a process that concerns the object-libido and consists in the instinct's directing itself towards an aim other than, and remote from, that of sexual gratification; in this process the accent falls upon the deflection from the sexual aim. Idealization is a process that concerns the *object*; by it that object, without any alteration in its nature, is aggrandized and exalted in the mind. Idealization is possible in the sphere of the ego-libido as well as in that of the object-libido. For example, the sexual over-estimation of an object is an idealization of it. In so far as sublimation is a process that concerns the instinct and idealization one that concerns the object, the two concepts are to be distinguished one from the other.

The formation of the ego-ideal is often confounded with sublimation, to the detriment of clear comprehension. A man who has exchanged his narcissism for the worship of a high ego-ideal has not necessarily on that account succeeded in sublimating his libidinal instincts. It is true that the ego-ideal requires such sublimation, but it cannot enforce it; sublimation remains a special process which may be prompted by the ideal but the execution of which is entirely independent of any such incitement. It is just in neurotics that we find the highest degrees of tension between the development of their ego-ideal and the measure of their sublimation of primitive libidinal instincts, and in general it is far harder to convince the idealist of the inexpediency of the hiding-place found by his libido than the plain man whose demands in this respect are only moderate. Further, the formation of an ego-ideal and sublimation are quite differently related to the causation of neurosis. As we have learnt, the formation of the ideal increases the demands of the ego and is the most powerful factor favouring repression; sublimation is a way out, a way by which the claims of the ego can be met without involving repression.

It would not surprise us if we were to find a special institution in the mind which performs the task of seeing that narcissistic gratification is secured from the ego-ideal and that, with this end in view, it constantly watches the real ego and measures it by that ideal. If such an institution does exist, it cannot possibly be something which we have not yet discovered; we only need to recognize it, and we may say that what we call our *conscience* has the required characteristics. Recognition of this institution enables us to understand the so-called "delusions of observation" or, more correctly, of *being watched*, which are such striking symptoms in the paranoid diseases and may perhaps also occur as an isolated form of illness, or intercalated in a transference neurosis. Patients of this sort complain that all their thoughts are known and their actions watched and overlooked; they are informed of the functioning of this mental institution by voices which characteristically speak to them in the third person ("Now she is thinking of that again" . . . "now he is going out"). This complaint is justified—it describes the truth; a power of this kind, watching, discovering and criticizing all our intentions, does really exist; indeed, it exists with every one of us in normal life. The delusion of being watched presents it in a regressive form, thereby revealing the genesis of this function and the reason why the patient is in revolt against it.

For that which prompted the person to form an ego-ideal, over which his conscience keeps guard, was the influence of parental criticism (conveyed to him by the medium of the voice), reinforced, as time went on, by those who trained and taught the child and by all the other persons of his environment—an indefinite host, too numerous to reckon (fellow-men, public opinion).

Large quantities of libido which is essentially homosexual are in this way drawn into the formation of the narcissistic ego-ideal and find outlet and gratification in maintaining it. The institution of conscience was at bottom an embodiment, first of parental criticism, and subsequently of that of society; a similar process takes place when a tendency towards repression develops out of a command or prohibition imposed in the first instance from without. The voices, as well as the indefinite number of speakers, are brought into the foreground again by the disease, and so the evolution of conscience is regressively reproduced. But the revolt against this *censorial institution* springs from the person's desire (in accordance with the fundamental character of his illness) to liberate himself from all these influences, beginning with that of his parents, and from his withdrawal of homosexual libido from those influences. His conscience then encounters him in a regressive form as a hostile influence from without.

The lament of the paranoiac shows also that at bottom the self-criticism of conscience is identical with, and based upon, self-observation. That activity of the mind which took over the function of conscience has also enlisted itself in the service of introspection, which furnishes philosophy with the material for its intellectual operations. This must have something to do with the characteristic tendency of paranoiacs to form speculative systems.[14]

It will certainly be of importance to us if we can see in other fields evidence of the activity of this critically watching faculty, which becomes heightened into conscience and philosophic introspection. I would refer here to what Herbert Silberer has called the "functional phenomenon," one of the few indisputably valuable additions to the theory of dreams. Silberer, as is well known, has shown that in the states between sleeping and waking we can directly observe the translation of thoughts into visual images, but that in these circumstances we frequently have a presentation, not of a thought-content, but of the actual state of the mind (readiness, fatigue, etc.) of the person who is struggling with sleep. Similarly, Silberer has shown that often the end of a dream or some section of the dream-content signifies merely the dreamer's own perception of his sleeping and waking. He has thus demonstrated that self-observation—in the sense of the paranoiac's delusion of being watched—plays a part in dream-formation. This part is not invariable; probably I overlooked it because it does not appear in my own dreams to any great extent; in persons who are gifted philosophically and therefore accustomed to introspection it may become very clear.

We may here recall our discovery that dream-formation takes place under the sway of a censorship which compels distortion of the dream-thoughts. We did not picture this censorship as a special force, an entity, but we chose the term to designate a particular aspect of the repressive tendencies which control the ego: namely, their attitude towards the dream-thoughts. Penetrating further into the structure of the ego, we may recognize the *dream-censor* again in the ego-ideal and in the dynamic utterances of conscience. If this censor is to some extent on the alert even during sleep, we can understand that the necessary condition of its activity—

[14] I should like to add, merely by way of suggestion, that the process of development and strengthening of this watching institution might contain within it the genesis later on of (subjective) memory and of the time-factor, the latter of which has no application to unconscious processes.

self-observation and self-criticism—should contribute to the dream-content some such thoughts as these: "Now he is too sleepy to think . . . now he is waking up."[15]

At this point we may enter upon a discussion of the self-regarding attitude in normal persons and in neurotics.

First of all, the feeling of self-regard appears to us a measure of the ego; what various components go to make up that measure is irrelevant. Everything we possess or achieve, every remnant of the primitive feeling of omnipotence that experience has corroborated, helps to exalt the self-regard.

Applying our distinction between sexual and ego-instincts, we must recognize that the self-regard has a very intimate connection with the narcissistic libido. Here we are supported by two fundamental facts: that in paraphrenics the self-regard is exalted, while in the transference neuroses it is abased, and that where the erotic life is concerned not being loved lowers the self-regarding feelings, while being loved raises them. We have stated that to be loved is the aim and the satisfaction in a narcissistic object-choice.

Further, it is easy to observe that libidinal object-cathexis does not raise the self-regard. The effect of the dependence upon the loved object is to lower that feeling: the lover is humble. He who loves has, so to speak, forfeited a part of his narcissism, which can only be replaced by his being loved. In all these respects the self-regarding feelings seem to remain in a relation to the narcissistic element in the erotic life.

The realization of impotence, of one's own inability to love in consequence of mental or physical disorder, has an exceedingly lowering effect upon the self-regard. Here, as I judge, we shall find one of the sources of the feelings of inferiority of which patients suffering from the transference neuroses so readily complain to us. The main source of these feelings is, however, the impoverishment of the ego, due to the withdrawal from it of extraordinarily large libidinal cathexes—due, that is to say, to the injury sustained by the ego through the sexual trends which are no longer subject to control.

---

[15] I cannot here determine whether the differentiation of the censorial function from the rest of the ego is capable of forming the basis of the philosophic distinction between consciousness and self-consciousness.

A. Adler is right in maintaining that a person's realization of organic inferiorities in himself acts as a spur upon an active mental life, and produces by way of over-compensation a higher degree of ability. But it would be altogether an exaggeration if, following this lead of Adler's, we tried to prove that every fine achievement was conditioned by an original organic inferiority. Not all artists are handicapped with bad eyesight, nor did all orators originally stammer. And there are plenty of instances of excellent achievements springing from superior organic endowment. In the aetiology of neurosis organic inferiority and imperfect development play an insignificant part, much the same as that played by actual perceptual material in the formation of dreams. The neurosis makes use of such inferiorities as a pretext, just as it does of all other suitable factors. So surely as we credit the assertion of one neurotic patient that it was inevitable that she should fall ill, since she is ugly, deformed or lacking in charm and so no one could love her, the very next neurotic will convince us of our error; for she remains the victim of her neurosis and her aversion to sexuality, although she seems to be desirable, and indeed more desired than the average woman. The majority of hysterical women are among the attractive and even beautiful representatives of their sex, while, on the other hand, the frequency of ugliness, organic infirmities and defects in the lower classes of society does not increase the incidence of neurotic illness amongst them.

The relations existing between self-regard and erotism (libidinal object-cathexes) may be expressed in the following formula: two cases must be distinguished—in the first, the erotic cathexes are "ego-syntonic," *in accordance with the ego-tendencies;* in the second, on the contrary, those cathexes have suffered repression. In the former case (where the path taken by the libido is acceptable to the ego), love takes its place among all the other activities of the ego. Love in itself, in the form of longing and deprivation, lowers the self-regard; whereas to be loved, to have love returned, and to possess the beloved object, exalts it again. When the libido is repressed the erotic cathexis is felt as a severe depletion of the ego, the satisfaction of love is impossible, and the re-enrichment of the ego can be effected only by a withdrawal of the libido from its objects. The return of the libido from the object to the ego and its transformation into narcissism represents, as it were, the restoration of a happy love, and, conversely, an actual happy love corresponds to the primal condition in which object-libido and ego-libido cannot be distinguished.

Perhaps the importance of the subject, and the difficulty in surveying it, may be my excuse for adding a few remarks that are rather loosely strung together.

The development of the ego consists in a departure from the primary narcissism and results in a vigorous attempt to recover it. This departure is brought about by means of the displacement of libido to an ego-ideal imposed from without, while gratification is derived from the attainment of this ideal.

At the same time the ego has put forth its libidinal object-cathexes. It becomes impoverished in consequence both of these cathexes and of the formation of the ego-ideal, and it enriches itself again both by gratification of its object-love and by fulfilling its ideal.

Part of the self-regard is primary—the residue of childish narcissism; another part arises out of such omnipotence as experience corroborates (the fulfilment of the ego-ideal), whilst a third part proceeds from gratification of object-libido.

The ego-ideal has imposed severe conditions upon the gratification of libido through objects, for, by means of its censorship, it rejects some of them as incompatible with itself. Where no such ideal has been formed, the sexual trend in question makes its appearance unchanged in the personality in the form of a perversion. As in childhood, to be his own ideal once more, also where sexual tendencies are concerned, is the happiness that man strives to attain.

The state of being in love consists in a flowing-over of ego-libido to the object. This state has the power to remove repressions and to restore perversions. It exalts the sexual object to the position of sexual ideal. Since, in cases where the love is of the anaclitic or object type, this state results from the fulfilment of infantile conditions of love, we may say that whatever fulfils this condition of love becomes idealized.

The sexual ideal may enter into an interesting auxiliary relation to the ego-ideal. Where narcissistic gratification encounters actual hindrances, the sexual ideal may be used as a substitutive gratification. In such a case a person loves (in conformity with the narcissistic type of object-choice) someone whom he once was and no longer is, or else someone who possesses excellences which he never had at all (cf. *supra*, (*c*)). The parallel formula to that given above runs thus: whoever possesses an excellence which the ego lacks for the attainment of its ideal, becomes loved. This expedient is of special importance for the neurotic, whose ego is depleted by his excessive object-cathexes and who on that account is unable to attain to his ego-ideal. He then seeks a way back to narcissism from his prodigal expenditure of libido upon objects, by choosing a sexual ideal after the narcissistic type which shall possess the excellences to which he cannot attain. This is the cure by love, which he generally prefers to cure by analysis. Indeed, he cannot believe in any other curative mechanism; he usually brings expectations of this sort with him to the treatment and then directs them towards the person of the physician. The patient's incapacity for love, an incapacity resulting from his extensive repressions, naturally stands in the way of such a method of cure. When, by means of the treatment, he has been partially freed from his repressions, we are frequently met by the unintended result that he withdraws from further treatment in order to choose a love-object, hoping that life with the beloved person will complete his recovery. We might be satisfied with this result, if it did not bring with it all the dangers of an overwhelming dependence upon this helper in his need.

The ego-ideal is of great importance for the understanding of group psychology. Besides its individual side, this ideal has a social side; it is also the common ideal of a family, a class or a nation. It not only binds the narcissistic libido, but also a considerable amount of the person's homosexual libido, which in this way becomes turned back into the ego. The dissatisfaction due to the non-fulfilment of this ideal liberates homosexual libido, which is transformed into sense of guilt (dread of the community). Originally this was a fear of punishment by the parents, or, more correctly, the dread of losing their love; later the parents are replaced by an indefinite number of fellow-men. This helps us to understand why it is that paranoia is frequently caused by a wounding of the ego, by a frustration of the gratification desired within the sphere of the ego-ideal, and also to understand the coincidence of ideal-formation and sublimation in the ego-ideal, as well as the demolition of sublimations and possible transformation of ideals in paraphrenic disorders.

IV

Instincts and Their Vicissitudes[1] (1915)

THE VIEW IS OFTEN defended that sciences should be built up on clear and sharply defined basal concepts. In actual fact no science, not even the most exact, begins with such definitions. The true beginning of scientific activity consists rather in describing phenomena and then in proceeding to group, classify and correlate them. Even at the stage of description it is not possible to avoid applying certain abstract ideas to the material in hand, ideas derived from various sources and certainly not the fruit of the new experience only. Still more indispensable are such ideas—which will later become the basal concepts of the science—as the material is further elaborated. They must at first necessarily possess some measure of uncertainty; there can be no question of any clear delimitation of their content. So long as they remain in this condition, we come to an understanding about their meaning by repeated references to the material of observation, from which we seem to have deduced our abstract ideas, but which is in point of fact subject to them. Thus, strictly speaking, they are in the nature of conventions; although everything depends on their being chosen in no arbitrary manner, but determined by the important relations they have to the empirical material—relations that we seem to divine before we can clearly recognize and demonstrate them. It is only after more searching investigation of the field in question that we are able to formulate with increased clarity the scientific concepts underlying it, and progressively so to modify these concepts that they become widely applicable and at the same time consistent logically. Then, indeed, it may be time to immure them in definitions. The progress of science, however, demands a certain elasticity even in these definitions. The science of physics furnishes an excellent illustration of the way in which

[1] First published in *Zeitschrift*, Bd. III., 1915; reprinted in *Sammlung*, Vierte Folge. [Translated by Cecil M. Baines.]

even those "basal concepts" that are firmly established in the form of definitions are constantly being altered in their content.

A conventional but still rather obscure basal concept of this kind, which is nevertheless indispensable to us in psychology, is that of an *instinct*. Let us try to ascertain what is comprised in this conception by approaching it from different angles.

First, from the side of physiology. This has given us the concept of *stimuli* and the scheme of the reflex arc, according to which a stimulus applied *from the outer world* to living tissue (nervous substance) is discharged by action *towards the outer world*. The action answers the purpose of withdrawing the substance affected from the operation of the stimulus, removing it out of range of the stimulus.

Now what is the relation between "instinct" and "stimulus"? There is nothing to prevent our including the concept of "instinct" under that of "stimulus" and saying that an instinct is a stimulus to the mind. But we are immediately set on our guard against treating instinct and mental stimulus as one and the same thing. Obviously, besides those of instinctual origin, there are other stimuli to the mind which behave far more like physiological stimuli. For example, a strong light striking upon the eye is not a stimulus of instinctual origin; it is one, however, when the mucous membrane of the œsophagus becomes parched or when a gnawing makes itself felt in the stomach.[2]

We have now obtained material necessary for discriminating between stimuli of instinctual origin and the other (physiological) stimuli which operate on our minds. First, a stimulus of instinctual origin does not arise in the outside world but from within the organism itself. For this reason it has a different mental effect and different actions are necessary in order to remove it. Further, all that is essential in an external stimulus is contained in the assumption that it acts as a single impact, so that it can be discharged by a single appropriate action—a typical instance being that of motor flight from the source of stimulation. Of course these impacts may

[2] Assuming, of course, that these internal processes constitute the organic basis of the needs described as thirst and hunger.

be repeated and their force may be cumulative, but that makes no difference to our notion of the process and to the conditions necessary in order that the stimulus may be dispelled. An instinct, on the other hand, never acts as a momentary impact but always as a constant force. As it makes its attack not from without but from within the organism, it follows that no flight can avail against it. A better term for a stimulus of instinctual origin is a "need"; that which does away with this need is "satisfaction." This can be attained only by a suitable (adequate) alteration of the inner source of stimulation.

Let us imagine ourselves in the position of an almost entirely helpless living organism, as yet unorientated in the world and with stimuli impinging on its nervous tissue. This organism will soon become capable of making a first discrimination and a first orientation. On the one hand, it will detect certain stimuli which can be avoided by an action of the muscles (flight)—these it ascribes to an outside world; on the other hand, it will also be aware of stimuli against which such action is of no avail and whose urgency is in no way diminished by it—these stimuli are the tokens of an inner world, the proof of instinctual needs. The apperceptive substance of the living organism will thus have found in the efficacy of its muscular activity a means for discriminating between "outer" and "inner."

We thus find our first conception of the essential nature of an instinct by considering its main characteristics, its origin in sources of stimulation within the organism and its appearance as a constant force, and thence we deduce one of its further distinguishing features, namely, that no actions of flight avail against it. Now, in making these remarks, we cannot fail to be struck by a fact which compels us to a further admission. We do not merely accept as basal concepts certain conventions which we apply to the material we have acquired empirically, but we also make use of various complicated postulates to guide us in dealing with psychological phenomena. We have already cited the most important of these postulates; it remains for us expressly to lay stress upon it. It is of a biological nature, and makes use of the concept of "purpose" (one might say, of adaptation of the means to the end) and runs as follows: the nervous system is an apparatus having the function of abolishing stimuli which reach it, or of reducing excitation to the lowest possible level: an apparatus which would even, if this were feasible, maintain itself in an altogether unstimulated condition. Let us for the present not take exception to the indefiniteness of this idea and let us grant that the task of the nervous system is—broadly speaking—*to master stimuli*. We see then how greatly the simple physiological reflex scheme is complicated by the introduction cf instincts. External stimuli impose upon the organism the single task of withdrawing itself from their action: this is accomplished by muscular movements, one of which reaches the goal aimed at and, being the most appropriate to the end in view, is thenceforward transmitted as an hereditary disposition. Those instinctual stimuli which emanate from within the organism cannot be dealt with by this mechanism. Consequently, they make far higher demands upon the nervous system and compel it to complicated and interdependent activities, which effect such changes in the outer world as enable it to offer satisfaction to the internal source of stimulation; above all, instinctual stimuli oblige the nervous system to renounce its ideal intention of warding off stimuli, for they maintain an incessant and unavoidable afflux of stimulation. So we may probably conclude that instincts and not external stimuli are the true motive forces in the progress that has raised the nervous system, with all its incomparable efficiency, to its present high level of development. Of course there is nothing to prevent our assuming that the instincts themselves are, at least in part, the precipitates of different forms of external stimulation, which in the course of phylogenesis have effected modifications in the organism.

Then when we find further that the activity of even the most highly developed mental apparatus is subject to the pleasure-principle, *i.e.* is automatically regulated by feelings belonging to the pleasure-"pain" series, we can hardly reject the further postulate that these feelings reflect the manner in which the process of mastering stimuli takes place. This is certainly so in the sense that "painful" feelings are connected with an increase and pleasurable feelings with a decrease in stimulation. Let us, however, be careful to preserve this assumption in its present highly indefinite form, until we succeed, if that is possible, in discovering what sort of relation exists between pleasure and "pain," on the one hand, and fluctuations in the quantities of stimuli affecting mental life, on the other. It is certain that many kinds of these relations are possible, some of them by no means simple.

If now we apply ourselves to considering mental life from a biological point of view, an "instinct" appears to us as a borderland concept between the mental and the physical, being both the mental representative of the stimuli emanating from within the organism and penetrating to the mind, and at the same time a measure of the demand made upon the energy of the latter in consequence of its connection with the body.

We are now in a position to discuss certain terms used in reference to the concept of an instinct, for example, its impetus, its aim, its object and its source.

By the *impetus* of an instinct we understand its motor element, the amount of force or the measure of the demand upon energy which it represents. The characteristic of impulsion is common to all instincts, is in fact the very essence of them. Every instinct is a form of activity; if we speak loosely of passive instincts, we can only mean those whose aim is passive.

The *aim* of an instinct is in every instance satisfaction, which can only be obtained by abolishing the condition of stimulation in the source of the instinct. But although this remains invariably the final goal of every instinct, there may yet be different ways leading to the same goal, so that an instinct may be found to have various nearer or intermediate aims, capable of combination or interchange. Experience permits us also to speak of instincts which are *inhibited in respect of their aim*, in cases where a certain advance has been permitted in the direction of satisfaction and then an inhibition or deflection has occurred. We may suppose that even in such cases a partial satisfaction is achieved.

The *object* of an instinct is that in or through which it can achieve its aim. It is the most variable thing about an instinct and is not originally connected with it, but becomes attached to it only in consequence of being peculiarly fitted to provide satisfaction. The object is not necessarily an extraneous one: it may be part of the subject's own body. It may be changed any number of times in the course of the vicissitudes the instinct undergoes during life; a highly important part is played by this capacity for displacement in the instinct. It may happen that the same object may serve for the satisfaction of several instincts simultaneously, a phenomenon which Adler calls a "confluence" of instincts. A particularly close attachment of the instinct to its object is distinguished by the term *fixation*: this frequently occurs in early stages of the instinct's development and so puts an end to its mobility, through the vigorous resistance it sets up against detachment.

By the *source* of an instinct is meant that somatic process in an organ or part of the body from which there results a stimulus represented in mental life by an instinct. We do not know whether this process is regularly of a chemical nature or whether it may also correspond with the release of other, *e.g.* mechanical, forces. The study of the sources of instinct is outside the scope of psychology; although its source in the body is what gives the instinct its distinct and essential character, yet in mental life we know it merely by its aims. A more exact knowledge of the sources of instincts is not strictly necessary for purposes of psychological investigation; often the source may be with certainty inferred from the aims.

Are we to suppose that the different instincts which operate upon the mind but of which the origin is somatic are also distinguished by different qualities and act in the mental life in a manner qualitatively different? This supposition does not seem to be justified; we are much more likely to find the simpler assumption sufficient—namely, that the instincts are all qualitatively alike and owe the effect they produce only to the quantities of excitation accompanying them, or perhaps further to certain functions of this quantity. The difference in the mental effects produced by the different instincts may be traced to the difference in their sources. In any event, it is only in a later connection that we shall be able to make plain what the problem of the quality of instincts signifies.

Now what instincts and how many should be postulated? There is obviously a great opportunity here for arbitrary choice. No objection can be made to anyone's employing the concept of an instinct of play or of destruction, or that of a social instinct, when the subject demands it and the limitations of psychological analysis allow of it. Nevertheless, we should not neglect to ask whether such instinctual motives, which are in one direction so highly specialized, do not admit of further analysis in respect of their sources, so that only those primal instincts which are not to be resolved further could really lay claim to the name.

I have proposed that two groups of such primal instincts should be distinguished: the *self-preservative* or *ego*-instincts and the *sexual* instincts. But this proposition has not the weight of a necessary postulate, such as, for instance, our assumption about the biological "purpose" in the mental apparatus (*v. supra*); it is merely an auxiliary construction, to be retained only so long as it proves useful, and it will make little difference to the results of our work of description and classification if we replace it by another. The occasion for it arose in the course of the evolution of psychoanalysis, which was first employed upon the psychoneuroses, actually upon the group designated transference neuroses (hysteria and obsessional neurosis); through them it became plain that at the root of all such affections there lies a conflict between the claims of sexuality and those of the ego. It is always possible that an exhaustive study of the other neurotic affections (especially of the narcissistic psychoneuroses, the schizophrenias) may oblige us to alter this formula and therewith to make a different classification of the primal instincts. But for the present we do not know what this new formula may be, nor have we met with any argument which seems likely to be prejudicial to the contrast between sexual and ego-instincts.

I am altogether doubtful whether work upon psychological material will afford any decisive indication for the distinction and classification of instincts. Rather it would seem necessary to apply to this material certain definite assumptions in order to work upon it, and we could wish that these assumptions might be taken from some other branch of knowledge and transferred to psychology. The contribution of biology on this point certainly does not run counter to the distinction between sexual and ego-instincts. Biology teaches that sexuality is not on a level with the other functions of the individual, for its "purposes" go beyond the individual, their content being the production of new individuals and the preservation of the species. It shows, further, that the relation existing between the ego and sexuality may be conceived of in two ways, apparently equally well justified: in the one, the individual is regarded as of prime importance, sexuality as one of his activities and sexual satisfaction as one of his needs; while in the other the individual organism is looked upon as a transitory and perishable appendage to the quasi-immortal germ-plasm bequeathed to him by the race. The assumption that the sexual function differs from other bodily processes in virtue of special chemical processes is, I understand, also a postulate of the Ehrlich school of biological research.

Since a study of the instincts from the side of consciousness presents almost insuperable difficulties, psychoanalytic investigation of mental disturbances remains the principal source of our knowledge. The development of this line of investigation, however, has necessarily produced hitherto information of a more or less definite nature only in regard to the sexual instincts, for it is this group in particular which can be observed in isolation, as it were, in the psychoneuroses. With the extension of psychoanalysis to other neurotic affections we may be sure that we shall find a basis for our knowledge of the ego-instincts also, though it would be optimistic to expect equally favourable conditions for observation in this further field of research.

An attempt to formulate the general characteristics of the sexual instincts would run as follows: they are numerous, emanate from manifold organic sources, act in the first instance independently of one another and only at a late stage achieve a more or less complete synthesis. The aim which each strives to attain is "organ-pleasure"; only when the synthesis is complete do they enter the service of the function of reproduction, becoming thereby generally recognizable as sexual instincts. At their first appearance they support themselves upon the instincts of self-preservation, from which they only gradually detach themselves; in their choice of object also they follow paths indicated by the ego-instincts. Some of them remain throughout life associated with these latter and furnish them with libidinal components, which with normal functioning easily escape notice and are clearly recognizable only when disease is present. They have this distinctive characteristic—that they have in a high degree the capacity to act vicariously for one another and that they can readily change their objects. In consequence of the last-mentioned properties they are capable of activities widely removed from their original modes of attaining their aims (sublimation).

Our inquiry into the various vicissitudes which instincts undergo in the process of development and in the course of life must be confined to the sexual instincts, for these are the more familiar to us. Observation shows us that an instinct may undergo the following vicissitudes:

> Reversal into its opposite,
> Turning round upon the subject,
> Repression,
> Sublimation.

Since I do not intend to treat of sublimation here and since repression requires a special chapter to itself, it only remains for us to describe and discuss the two first points. Bearing in mind that there are tendencies which are opposed to the instincts pursuing a straightforward course, we may regard these vicissitudes as modes of defence against the instincts.

The *reversal* of an instinct *into its opposite* may on closer scrutiny be resolved into two different processes: a change from active to passive, and a reversal of the content. The two processes, being essentially distinct, must be treated separately.

Examples of the first process are met with in the two pairs of opposites: sadism-masochism and scoptophilia-exhibitionism. The reversal here concerns only the aims of the instincts. The passive aim (to be tortured, or looked at) has been substituted for the active aim (to torture, to look at). Reversal of content is found in the single instance of the change of love into hate.

The *turning round* of an instinct *upon the subject* is suggested to us by the reflection that masochism is actually sadism turned round upon the subject's own ego, and that exhibitionism includes the love of gazing at the subject's own body. Further, analytic observation leaves us in no doubt that the masochist also enjoys the *act* of torturing when this is being applied to himself, and the exhibitionist the exposing of someone in being exposed himself. So the essence of the process is the change of the object, while the aim remains unchanged.

We cannot fail to note, however, that in these examples turning round upon the subject's self and transformation from active to passive coincide or occur in one process. To elucidate the relation between the two processes, a more thorough investigation must be undertaken.

With the pair of opposites sadism-masochism, the process may be represented as follows:

(a) Sadism consists in the exercise of violence or power upon some other person as its object.

(b) This object is abandoned and replaced by the subject's self. Together with the turning round upon the self the change from an active to a passive aim in the instinct is also brought about.

(c) Again another person is sought as object; this person, in consequence of the alteration which has taken place in the aim of the instinct, has to take over the original rôle of the subject.

Case (c) is the condition commonly termed masochism. Satisfaction follows in this case also by way of the original sadism, the passive ego placing itself in phantasy back in its former situation, which, however, has now been given up to another subject outside the self. Whether there is, besides this, a more direct masochistic satisfaction is highly doubtful. A primary masochism not derived in the manner I have described from sadism, does not appear to be met with.[3] That it is not superfluous to make the assumption of stage (b) is quite clear when we observe the behaviour of the sadistic impulse in cases of obsessional neurosis. In these we have the turning upon the subject's self, without the attitude of passivity towards another: the reversal has only reached the second stage. Self-torment and self-punishment have arisen from the desire to torture, but not masochism. The active voice is changed, not into the passive, but into the reflexive middle voice.

[3] *Additional Note*, 1924. In later works (cf. "The Economic Problem of Masochism," 1924, *infra*, pp. 190-201) relating to problems of instinctual life, I have expressed the opposite view.

The conception of sadism is made more complicated by the circumstance that this instinct, side by side with its general aim (or perhaps, rather, within it), seems to press towards a quite special aim:—the infliction of pain, in addition to subjection and mastery of the object. Now psychoanalysis would seem to show that the infliction of pain plays no part in the original aims sought by the instinct: the sadistic child takes no notice of whether or not it inflicts pain, nor is it part of its purpose to do so. But when once the transformation into masochism has taken place, the experience of pain is very well adapted to serve as a passive masochistic aim, for we have every reason to believe that sensations of pain, like other unpleasant sensations, extend into sexual excitation and produce a condition which is pleasurable, for the sake of which the subject will even willingly experience the unpleasantness of pain. Where once the suffering of pain has been experienced as a masochistic aim, it can be carried back into the sadistic situation and result in a sadistic aim of *inflicting pain*, which will then be masochistically enjoyed by the subject while inflicting pain upon others, through his identification of himself with the suffering object. Of course, in either case it is not the pain itself which is enjoyed, but the accompanying sexual excitement, and this is especially easy for the sadist. The enjoyment of pain would thus be a primary masochistic aim, which, however, can then also become the aim of the originally sadistic instinct.

In order to complete my exposition I would add that pity cannot be described as a result of the reversal of the sadistic instinct, but necessitates the conception of a *reaction-formation* against that instinct (for the difference, *v. infra*).

Rather different and simpler results are afforded by the investigation of another pair of opposites, namely, those instincts whose aim is sexual gazing (scoptophilia) and self-display (the "voyeur" and exhibitionist tendencies as they are called in the language of the perversions). Here again we may postulate the same stages as in the previous instance: (*a*) scoptophilia as an activity directed towards an extraneous object; (*b*) abandonment of the object and a turning of the scoptophilic instinct towards a part of the subject's own person; therewith a transformation to passivity and the setting up of a new aim—that of being looked at; (c) the institution of a new subject to whom one displays oneself in order to be looked at. Here too, it is hardly possible to doubt that the active aim appears before the passive, that scoptophilia precedes exhibitionism. But there is an important divergence from what happens in the case of sadism, in that we can recognize in the scoptophilic instinct a yet earlier stage than that described as (a). That is to say, that at the beginning of its activity the scoptophilic instinct is auto-erotic: it has indeed an object, but that object is the subject's own body. It is only later that the instinct comes (by the way of comparison) to exchange this object for the analogous one of the body of another (stage (a)). Now this preliminary stage is interesting because it is the source of both the situations represented in the resulting pair of opposites, according to which element in the original situation is reversed. The following might serve as a scheme for the scoptophilic instinct:

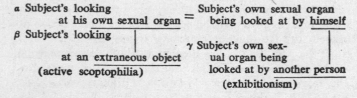

A preliminary stage of this kind is absent in sadism, which from the outset is directed upon an extraneous object, although it might not be altogether unreasonable to regard as such a stage the child's efforts to gain control of his own limbs.[4]

With regard to both these instincts just examined as examples, it must be said that transformation of them by a reversal from active to passive and by a turning round upon the subject never in fact concerns the whole amount of impelling force pertaining to the instinct. To some extent its earlier active direction always persists side by side with the later passive direction, even when the transformation is very extensive. The only correct description of the scoptophilic

[4] Cf. preceding footnote, p. 92.

instinct would be that all phases of its development, the auto-erotic, preliminary phase as well as its final active or passive form, co-exist alongside one another; and the truth of this statement becomes manifest if we base our opinion, not upon the actions which are prompted by the instinct, but upon the mechanism of its satisfaction. Perhaps yet another way of conceiving and representing the matter may be justified. We may split up the life of each instinct into a series of "thrusts," distinct from one another in the time of their occurrence but each homogeneous within its own period, whose relation to one another is comparable to that of successive eruptions of lava. We can then perhaps picture to ourselves that the earliest and most primitive instinct-eruption persists in an unchanged form and undergoes no development at all. The next "thrust" would then from the outset have undergone a change of form, being turned, for instance, from active to passive, and it would then, with this new characteristic, be superimposed upon the earlier layer, and so on. So that, if we take a survey of the instinctual tendency from its beginning up to any given stopping-point, the succession of "thrusts" which we have described would present the picture of a definite development of the instinct.

The fact that, at that later period of development, the instinct in its primary form may be observed side by side with its (passive) opposite deserves to be distinguished by the highly appropriate name introduced by Bleuler: *ambivalence*.

These considerations regarding the developmental history of an instinct and the permanent character of the intermediate stages in it should make instinct-development more comprehensible to us. Experience shows that the degree of demonstrable ambivalence varies greatly in individuals, groups and races. Marked ambivalence of an instinct in a human being at the present day may be regarded as an archaic inheritance, for we have reason to suppose that the part played in the life of the instincts by the active impulses in their original form was greater in primitive times than it is on an average to-day.

We have become accustomed to call the early phase of the development of the ego, during which its sexual instincts find auto-erotic satisfaction, *narcissism*, without having so far entered into any discussion of the relation between auto-erotism and narcissism. It follows that, in considering the preliminary phase of the scoptophilic instinct, when the subject's own body is the object of the scoptophilia, we must place it under the heading of narcissism; it is a narcissistic formation. From this phase the active scoptophilic instinct, which has left narcissism behind, is developed, while the passive scoptophilic instinct, on the contrary, holds fast to the narcissistic object. Similarly, the transformation from sadism to masochism betokens a reversion to the narcissistic object, while in both cases the narcissistic (active) subject is exchanged by identification for another, extraneous ego. Taking into consideration the preliminary narcissistic stage of sadism constructed by us, we approach the more general view that those vicissitudes which consist in the instinct being turned round upon the subject's own ego and undergoing reversal from activity to passivity are dependent upon the narcissistic organization of the ego and bear the stamp of that phase. Perhaps they represent attempts at defence which at higher stages of the development of the ego are effected by other means.

At this point we may remember that so far we have discussed only two pairs of instincts and their opposites: sadism-masochism and scoptophilia-exhibitionism. These are the best-known sexual instincts which appear in ambivalent forms. The other components of the later sexual function are at present too inaccessible to analysis for us to be able to discuss them in a similar way. In general we can assert of them that their activities are auto-erotic, *i.e.* their object becomes negligible in comparison with the organ which is their source, and as a rule the two coincide. The object of the scoptophilic instinct, although it also in the first instance is a part of the subject's own body, nevertheless is not the eye itself; and with sadism the organic source, probably the musculature with its capacity for action, directly presupposes an object other than itself, even though that object be part of the subject's own body. In the auto-erotic instincts, the part played by the organic source is so decisive that, according to a plausible supposition of P. Federn and L. Jekels,[5] the form and function of the organ determine the activity or passivity of the instinct's aim.

The transformation of the "content" of an instinct into its opposite is observed in a single instance only—the changing of *love into hate*. It is particularly common to find both these directed simultaneously towards the same object, and this phenomenon of their co-existence furnishes the most important example of ambivalence of feeling.

The case of love and hate acquires a special interest from the circumstance that it resists classification in our scheme of the instincts. It is impossible to doubt the existence of a most intimate relation between these two contrary feelings and sexual life, but one is naturally unwilling to conceive of love as being a kind of special component-instinct of sexuality in the same way as are the others just discussed. One would prefer to regard loving rather as the expression of the whole sexual current of feeling, but this idea does not clear up our difficulties and we are at a loss how to conceive of an essential opposite to this striving.

Loving admits of not merely one, but of three antitheses. First there is the antithesis of loving—hating; secondly, there is loving—being loved; and, in addition to these, loving and hating together are the opposite of the condition of neutrality or indifference. The second of these two antitheses, loving—being loved, corresponds exactly to the transformation from active to passive and may be traced to a primal situation in the same way as the scoptophilic instinct. This situation is that of *loving oneself*, which for us is the characteristic of narcissism. Then, according to whether the self as object or subject is exchanged for an extraneous one, there results the active aim of loving or the passive one of being loved, the latter remaining nearly related to narcissism.

Perhaps we shall come to a better understanding of the manifold opposites of loving if we reflect that our mental life as a whole is governed by *three polarities*, namely, the following antitheses:

> Subject (ego)—Object (external world),
> Pleasure—Pain,
> Active—Passive.

The antithesis of ego—non-ego (outer), *i.e.* subject—object, is, as we have already said, thrust upon the individual being at an early stage, by the experience that it can abolish external stimuli by means of muscular action but is defenceless against those stimuli that originate in instinct. This antithesis remains sovereign above all in our intellectual activity and provides research with a fundamental situation which no amount of effort can alter. The polarity of pleasure—pain depends upon a feeling-series, the significance of which in determining our actions (will) is paramount and has already been emphasized. The antithesis of active and passive must not be confounded with that of ego-subject—external object. The relation of the ego to the outer world is passive in so far as it receives stimuli from it, active when it reacts to these. Its instincts compel it to a quite special degree of activity towards the outside world, so that, if we wished to emphasize the essence of the matter, we might say that the ego-subject is passive in respect of external stimuli, active in virtue of its own instincts. The antithesis of active—passive coalesces later with that of masculine—feminine, which, until this has taken place, has no psychological significance. The fusion of activity with masculinity and passivity with femininity confronts us, indeed, as a biological fact, but it is by no means so invariably complete and exclusive as we are inclined to assume.

The three polarities within the mind are connected with one another in various highly significant ways. There is a certain primal psychic situation in which two of them coincide. Originally, at the very beginning of mental life, the ego's instincts are directed to itself and it is to some extent capable of deriving satisfaction for them on itself. This condition is known as narcissism and this potentiality for satisfaction is termed auto-erotic.[6] The outside world is at this time, gen-

___

[6] Some of the sexual instincts are, as we know, capable of this auto-erotic satisfaction and so are adapted to be the channel for that development under the sway of the pleasure-principle which we shall describe later. The sexual instincts which from the outset require an object and the needs of the ego-instincts, which are never capable of auto-erotic satisfaction, interfere, of course, with this condition and prepare the way for progress. More, the primal narcissistic condition would not have been able to attain

erally speaking, not cathected with any interest and is indifferent for purposes of satisfaction. At this period, therefore, the ego-subject coincides with what is pleasurable and the outside world with what is indifferent (or even painful as being a source of stimulation). Let us for the moment define loving as the relation of the ego to its sources of pleasure: then the situation in which the ego loves itself only and is indifferent to the outside world illustrates the first of the polarities in which "loving" appeared.

In so far as it is auto-erotic, the ego has no need of the outside world, but, in consequence of experiences undergone by the instincts of self-preservation, it tends to find objects there and doubtless it cannot but for a time perceive inner instinctual stimuli as painful. Under the sway of the pleasure-principle there now takes place a further development. The objects presenting themselves, in so far as they are sources of pleasure, are absorbed by the ego into itself, "introjected" (according to an expression coined by Ferenczi); while, on the other hand, the ego thrusts forth upon the external world whatever within itself gives rise to pain (*v. infra*: the mechanism of projection).

Thus the original *reality-ego*, which distinguished outer and inner by means of a sound objective criterion, changes into a purified *pleasure-ego*, which prizes above all else the quality of pleasure. For this pleasure-ego the outside world is divided into a part that is pleasurable, which it has incorporated into itself, and a remainder that is alien to it. A part of itself it has separated off, and this it projects into the external world and regards as hostile. According to this new arrangement the congruence of the two polarities,

ego-subject with pleasure,

outside world with pain (or earlier with neutrality), is once more established.

When the stage of primary narcissism is invaded by the object, the second contrary attitude to that of love, namely, hate, attains to development.

---

such a development were it not that every individual goes through a period of helplessness and dependence on fostering care, during which his urgent needs are satisfied by agencies outside himself and thereby withheld from developing along their own line.

As we have heard, the ego's objects are presented to it from the outside world in the first instance by the instincts of self-preservation, and it is undeniable also that hate originally betokens the relation of the ego to the alien external world with its afflux of stimuli. Neutrality may be classified as a special case of hate or rejection, after having made its appearance first as the forerunner of hate. Thus at the very beginning, the external world, objects and that which was hated were one and the same thing. When later on an object manifests itself as a source of pleasure, it becomes loved, but also incorporated into the ego, so that for the purified pleasure-ego the object once again coincides with what is extraneous and hated.

Now, however, we note that just as the antithesis love—indifference reflects the polarity ego—external world, so the second antithesis, love—hate, reproduces the polarity pleasure—pain, which is bound up with the former. When the purely narcissistic stage gives place to the object-stage, pleasure and pain denote the relations of the ego to the object. When the object becomes a source of pleasurable feelings, a motor tendency is set up which strives to bring the object near to and incorporate it into the ego; we then speak of the "attraction" exercised by the pleasure-giving object, and say that we "love" that object. Conversely, when the object is the source of painful feelings, there is a tendency which endeavours to increase the distance between object and ego and to repeat in relation to the former the primordial attempt at flight from the external world with its flow of stimuli. We feel a "repulsion" from the object, and hate it; this hate can then be intensified to the point of an aggressive tendency towards the object, with the intention of destroying it.

We might at a pinch say of an instinct that it "loves" the objects after which it strives for purposes of satisfaction, but to say that it "hates" an object strikes us as odd; so we become aware that the attitudes of love and hate cannot be said to characterize the relations of instincts to their objects, but are reserved for the relations of the ego as a whole to objects. But, if we consider a colloquial usage which is certainly full of meaning, we see that there is yet another limitation to the significance of love and hate. We do not say of those objects which serve the interests of self-preservation that we love them; rather we emphasize the fact that we need them, and perhaps add an element of a different kind in our relation to them by words which denote a much lesser degree of love— for example, to be fond of, to like, to find agreeable.

So the word "to love" becomes shifted ever further into the sphere of the pure pleasure-relation existing between the ego and its object and finally attaches itself to sexual objects in the narrower sense and to those which satisfy the needs of sublimated sexual instincts. The discrimination of the ego-instincts from the sexual, a discrimination which we have imposed upon our psychology, is seen, therefore, to be in conformity with the spirit of our speech. Since we do not customarily say that the single sexual component-instinct loves its object, but see the most appropriate case in which to apply the word "love" in the relation of the ego to its sexual object, we learn from this fact that the applicability of the word in this relation begins only with the synthesis of all the component-instincts under the primacy of the genitals and in the service of the function of reproduction.

It is noteworthy that in the use of the word "hate" no such intimate relation to sexual pleasure and the sexual function appears: on the contrary, the painful character of the relation seems to be the sole decisive feature. The ego hates, abhors and pursues with intent to destroy all objects which are for it a source of painful feelings, without taking into account whether they mean to it frustration of sexual satisfaction or of gratification of the needs of self-preservation. Indeed, it may be asserted that the true prototypes of the hate-relation are derived not from sexual life, but from the struggle of the ego for self-preservation and self-maintenance.

So we see that love and hate, which present themselves to us as essentially antithetical, stand in no simple relation to each other. They did not originate in a cleavage of any common primal element, but sprang from different sources and underwent each its own development before the influence of the pleasure-pain relation constituted them antitheses to each other. At this point we are confronted with the task of putting together what we know of the genesis of love and hate.

Love originates in the capacity of the ego to satisfy some

of its instincts auto-erotically through the obtaining of "organ-pleasure." It is primarily narcissistic, is then transferred to those objects which have been incorporated in the ego, now much extended, and expresses the motor striving of the ego after these objects as sources of pleasure. It is intimately connected with the activity of the later sexual instincts and, when these have been completely synthetized, coincides with the sexual trend as a whole. The preliminary stages of love reveal themselves as temporary sexual aims, while the sexual instincts are passing through their complicated development. First amongst these we recognize the phase of incorporating or devouring, a type of love which is compatible with abolition of any separate existence on the part of the object, and which may therefore be designated ambivalent. At the higher stage of the pregenital sadistic-anal organization, the striving after the object appears in the form of an impulsion to mastery, in which injury or annihilation of the object is a matter of indifference. This form and preliminary stage of love is hardly to be distinguished from hate in its behaviour towards the object. Only when the genital organization is established does love become the antithesis of hate.

The relation of hate to objects is older than that of love. It is derived from the primal repudiation by the narcissistic ego of the external world whence flows the stream of stimuli. As an expression of the pain-reaction induced by objects, it remains in constant intimate relation with the instincts of self-preservation, so that sexual and ego-instincts readily develop an antithesis which repeats that of love and hate. When the sexual function is governed by the ego-instincts, as at the stage of the sadistic-anal organization, they impart the qualities of hate to the instinct's aim as well.

The history of the origin and relations of love makes us understand how it is that love so constantly manifests itself as "ambivalent," *i.e.* accompanied by feelings of hate against the same object. This admixture of hate in love is to be traced in part to those preliminary stages of love which have not been wholly outgrown, and in part is based upon reactions of aversion and repudiation on the part of the ego-instincts which, in the frequent conflicts between the interests of the ego and those of love, can claim to be supported by real and actual motives. In both cases, therefore, the admixture of hate may be traced to the source of the self-preservative instincts. When a love-relationship with a given object is broken off, it is not infrequently succeeded by hate, so that we receive the impression of a transformation of love into hate. This descriptive characterization is amplified by the view that, when this happens, the hate which is motivated by considerations of reality is reinforced by a regression of the love to the sadistic preliminary stage, so that the hate acquires an erotic character and the continuity of a love-relation is ensured.

The third antithesis of love, the transformation of loving into being loved, represents the operation of the polarity of active and passive, and is to be judged in the same way as in scoptophilia and sadism. We may sum up by saying that the essential feature in the vicissitudes undergone by instincts is *their subjection to the influences of the three great polarities that govern mental life.* Of these three polarities we might describe that of activity—passivity as the *biological*, that of ego—external world as the *real*, and finally that of pleasure—pain as the *economic* respectively.

That possible vicissitude undergone by an instinct which we call *repression* will form the subject of a further inquiry.

V

Repression[1] (1915)

ONE OF THE VICISSITUDES an instinctual impulse may undergo is to meet with resistances the aim of which is to make the impulse inoperative. Under certain conditions, which we shall presently investigate more closely, the impulse then passes into the state of *repression*. If it were a question of the operation of an external stimulus, obviously flight would be the appropriate remedy; with an instinct, flight is of no avail, for the ego cannot escape from itself. Later on, rejection based on judgement (*condemnation*) will be found to be a good weapon against the impulse. Repression is a preliminary phase of condemnation, something between flight and condemnation; it is a concept which could not have been formulated before the time of psychoanalytic research.

It is not easy in theory to deduce the possibility of such a thing as repression. Why should an instinctual impulse suffer such a fate? For this to happen, obviously a necessary condition must be that attainment of its aim by the instinct should produce "pain" instead of pleasure. But we cannot well imagine such a contingency. There are no such instincts; satisfaction of an instinct is always pleasurable. We should have to assume certain peculiar circumstances, some sort of process which changes the pleasure of satisfaction into "pain."

In order the better to define repression we may discuss some other situations in which instincts are concerned. It may happen that an external stimulus becomes internal, for example, by eating into and destroying a bodily organ, so that a new source of constant excitation and increase of tension is formed. The stimulus thereby acquires a far-reaching similarity to an instinct. We know that a case of this sort is experienced by us as *physical pain*. The aim of this pseudo-instinct, however, is simply the cessation of the change in the

[1] First published in *Zeitschrift*, Bd. III., 1915; reprinted in *Sammlung*, Vierte Folge. [Translated by Cecil M. Baines.]

organ and of the pain accompanying it. There is no other direct pleasure to be attained by cessation of the pain. Further, pain is imperative; the only things which can subdue it are the effect of some toxic agent in removing it and the influence of some mental distraction.

The case of physical pain is too obscure to help us much in our purpose. Let us suppose that an instinctual stimulus such as hunger remains unsatisfied. It then becomes imperative and can be allayed by nothing but the appropriate action for satisfying it; it keeps up a constant tension of need. Anything like a repression seems in this case to be utterly out of the question.

So repression is certainly not an essential result of the tension produced by lack of satisfaction of an impulse being raised to an unbearable degree. The weapons of defence of which the organism avails itself to guard against that situation must be discussed in another connection.

Let us instead confine ourselves to the clinical experience we meet with in the practice of psychoanalysis. We then see that the satisfaction of an instinct under repression is quite possible; further, that in every instance such a satisfaction is pleasurable in itself, but is irreconcilable with other claims and purposes; it therefore causes pleasure in one part of the mind and "pain" in another. We see then that it is a condition of repression that the element of avoiding "pain" shall have acquired more strength than the pleasure of gratification. Psychoanalytic experience of the transference neuroses, moreover, forces us to the conclusion that repression is not a defence-mechanism present from the very beginning, and that it cannot occur until a sharp distinction has been established between what is conscious and what is unconscious: that *the essence of repression lies simply in the function of rejecting and keeping something out of consciousness*. This conception of repression would be supplemented by assuming that, before the mental organization reaches this phase, the other vicissitudes which may befall instincts, *e.g.* reversal into the opposite or turning round upon the subject, deal with the task of mastering the instinctual impulses.

It seems to us now that in view of the very great extent to which repression and the unconscious are correlated, we must defer probing more deeply into the nature of repression until we have learnt more about the structure of the various institutions in the mind—and about what differentiates consciousness from the unconscious. Till we have done this, all we can do is to put together in purely descriptive fashion some characteristics of repression noted in clinical practice, even though we run the risk of having to repeat unchanged much that has been said elsewhere.

Now we have reason for assuming *a primal repression*, a first phase of repression, which consists in a denial of entry into consciousness to the mental (ideational) presentation of the instinct. This is accompanied by a *fixation*; the ideational presentation in question persists unaltered from then onwards and the instinct remains attached to it. This is due to certain properties of unconscious processes of which we shall speak later.

The second phase of repression, *repression proper*, concerns mental derivatives of the repressed instinct-presentation, or such trains of thought as, originating elsewhere, have come into associative connection with it. On account of this association, these ideas experience the same fate as that which underwent primal repression. Repression proper, therefore, is actually an after-expulsion. Moreover, it is a mistake to emphasize only the rejection which operates from the side of consciousness upon what is to be repressed. We have to consider just as much the attraction exercised by what was originally repressed upon everything with which it can establish a connection. Probably the tendency to repression would fail of its purpose if these forces did not co-operate, if there were not something previously repressed ready to assimilate that which is rejected from consciousness.

Under the influence of study of the psychoneuroses, which brings before us the important effects of repression, we are inclined to overestimate their psychological content and to forget too readily that repression does not hinder the instinct-presentation from continuing to exist in the unconscious and from organizing itself further, putting forth derivatives and instituting connections. Really, repression interferes only with the relation of the instinct-presentation to one system of the mind, namely, to consciousness.

Psychoanalysis is able to show us something else which is important for understanding the effects of repression in the psychoneuroses. It shows us, for instance, that the instinct-presentation develops in a more unchecked and luxuriant fashion if it is withdrawn by repression from conscious influence. It ramifies like a fungus, so to speak, in the dark and takes on extreme forms of expression, which when translated and revealed to the neurotic are bound not merely to seem alien to him, but to terrify him by the way in which they reflect an extraordinary and dangerous strength of instinct. This illusory strength of instinct is the result of an uninhibited development of it in phantasy and of the damming-up consequent on lack of real satisfaction. The fact that this last result is bound up with repression points the direction in which we have to look for the true significance of the latter.

In reverting to the contrary aspect, however, let us state definitely that it is not even correct to suppose that repression withholds from consciousness all the derivatives of what was primally repressed. If these derivatives are sufficiently far removed from the repressed instinct-presentation, whether owing to the process of distortion or by reason of the number of intermediate associations, they have free access to consciousness. It is as though the resistance of consciousness against them was in inverse proportion to their remoteness from what was originally repressed. During the practice of the psychoanalytic method, we continually require the patient to produce such derivatives of what has been repressed as, in consequence either of their remoteness or of distortion, can pass the censorship of consciousness. Indeed, the associations which we require him to give, while refraining from any consciously directed train of thought or any criticism, and from which we reconstruct a conscious interpretation of the repressed instinct-presentation, are precisely derivatives of this kind. We then observe that the patient can go on spinning a whole chain of such associations, till he is brought up in the midst of them against some thought-formation, the relation of which to what is repressed acts so intensely that he is compelled to repeat his attempt at repression. Neurotic symptoms, too, must have fulfilled the condition referred to, for they are derivatives of the repressed, which has finally by means of these formations wrested from consciousness the right of way previously denied it.

We can lay down no general rule concerning the degree of distortion and remoteness necessary before the resistance of consciousness is abrogated. In this matter a delicate balancing takes place, the play of which is hidden from us; its mode of operation, however, leads us to infer that it is a question of a definite degree of intensity in the cathexis of the unconscious —beyond which it would break through for satisfaction. Repression acts, therefore, in a *highly specific* manner in each instance; every single derivative of the repressed may have its peculiar fate—a little more or a little less distortion alters the whole issue. In this connection it becomes comprehensible that those objects to which men give their preference, that is, their ideals, originate in the same perceptions and experiences as those objects of which they have most abhorrence, and that the two originally differed from one another only by slight modifications. Indeed, as we found in the origin of the fetish, it is possible for the original instinct-presentation to be split into two, one part undergoing repression, while the remainder, just on account of its intimate association with the other, undergoes idealization.

The same result as ensues from an increase or a decrease in the degree of distortion may also be achieved at the other end of the apparatus, so to speak, by a modification in the conditions producing pleasure and "pain." Special devices have been evolved, with the object of bringing about such changes in the play of mental forces that what usually gives rise to "pain" may on this occasion result in pleasure, and whenever such a device comes into operation the repression of an instinct-presentation that is ordinarily repudiated is abrogated. The only one of these devices which has till now been studied in any detail is that of joking. Generally the lifting of the repression is only transitory: the repression is immediately re-established

Observations of this sort, however, suffice to draw our attention to some further characteristics of repression. Not only is it, as we have just explained, *variable* and *specific*, but it is also exceedingly *mobile*. The process of repression is not to be regarded as something which takes place once for all, the results of which are permanent, as when some living thing has been killed and from that time onward is dead; on the contrary, repression demands a constant expenditure of energy, and if this were discontinued the success of the repression would be jeopardized, so that a fresh act of repression would be necessary. We may imagine that what is repressed exercises a continuous straining in the direction of consciousness, so that the balance has to be kept by means of a steady counter-pressure. A constant expenditure of energy, therefore, is entailed in maintaining a repression, and economically its abrogation denotes a saving. The mobility of the repression, incidentally, finds expression also in the mental characteristics of the condition of sleep which alone renders dream-formation possible. With a return to waking life the repressive cathexes which have been called in are once more put forth.

Finally, we must not forget that after all we have said very little about an instinctual impulse when we state it to be repressed. Without prejudice to the repression such an impulse may find itself in widely different conditions; it may be inactive, *i.e.* cathected with only a low degree of mental energy, or its degree of cathexis (and consequently its capacity for activity) may vary. True, its activity will not result in a direct abrogation of the repression, but it will certainly set in motion all the processes which terminate in a breaking through into consciousness by circuitous routes. With unrepressed derivatives of the unconscious the fate of a particular idea is often decided by the degree of its activity or cathexis. It is an everyday occurrence that such a derivative can remain unrepressed so long as it represents only a small amount of energy, although its content is of such a nature as to give rise to a conflict with conscious control. But the quantitative factor is manifestly decisive for this conflict; as soon as an idea which is fundamentally offensive exceeds a certain degree of strength, the conflict takes on actuality, and it is precisely activation of the idea that leads to its repression. So that, where repression is concerned, an increase in energic cathexis operates in the same way as an approach to the unconscious, while a decrease in that energy operates like distance from the unconscious or like distortion. We understand that the repressing tendencies can find a substitute for repression in a weakening or lessening of whatever is distasteful to them.

In our discussion hitherto we have dealt with the repression of an instinct-presentation, and by that we understood an idea or group of ideas which is cathected with a definite amount of the mental energy (libido, interest) pertaining to an instinct. Now clinical observation forces us further to dissect something that hitherto we have conceived of as a single entity, for it shows us that beside the idea there is something else, another presentation of the instinct to be considered, and that this other element undergoes a repression which may be quite different from that of the idea. We have adopted the term *charge of affect* for this other element in the mental presentation; it represents that part of the instinct which has become detached from the idea, and finds proportionate expression, according to its quantity, in processes which become observable to perception as affects. From this point on, in describing a case of repression, we must follow up the fate of the idea which undergoes repression separately from that of the instinctual energy attached to the idea.

We should be glad enough to be able to give some general account of the outcome of both of these, and when we have taken our bearings a little we shall actually be able to do so. In general, repression of the ideational presentation of an instinct can surely only have the effect of causing it to vanish from consciousness if it had previously been in consciousness, or of holding it back if it is about to enter it. The difference, after all, is not important; it amounts to much the same thing as the difference between ordering an undesirable guest out of my drawing-room or out of my front hall, and refusing to let him cross my threshold once I have recognized him.[2] The fate of the quantitative factor in the instinct-presentation may be one of three, as we see by a cursory survey of the observations made through psychoanalysis: either the instinct is altogether

[2] This metaphor, applicable to the process of repression, may also be extended to include one of the characteristics of repression mentioned earlier. I need only add that I have to place a sentinel to keep constant guard over the door which I have forbidden this guest to pass, lest he should burst it open (*v. supra*).

suppressed, so that no trace of it is found, or it appears in the guise of an affect of a particular qualitative tone, or it is transformed into anxiety. With the two last possibilities we are obliged to focus our attention upon the *transformation* into *affects*, and especially into *anxiety*, of the mental energy belonging to the *instincts*, this being a new possible vicissitude undergone by an instinct.

We recall the fact that the motive and purpose of repression was simply the avoidance of "pain." It follows that the fate of the charge of affect belonging to the presentation is far more important than that of the ideational content of it and is decisive for the opinion we form of the process of repression. If a repression does not succeed in preventing feelings of "pain" or anxiety from arising, we may say that it has failed, even though it may have achieved its aim as far as the ideational element is concerned. Naturally, the case of unsuccessful repression will have more claim on our interest than that of repression which is eventually successful; the latter will for the most part elude our study.

We now wish to gain some insight into the mechanism of the process of repression, and especially we want to know whether it has a single mechanism only, or more than one, and whether perhaps each of the psychoneuroses may be distinguished by a characteristic repression-mechanism peculiar to itself. At the outset of this inquiry, however, we encounter complications. The mechanism of a repression becomes accessible to us only when we deduce it from its final results. If we confine our observations to the results of its effect on the ideational part of the instinct-presentation, we discover that as a rule repression creates a *substitute-formation*. What then is the mechanism of such a substitute-formation, or must we distinguish several mechanisms here also? Further, we know that repression leaves *symptoms* in its train. May we then regard substitute-formation and symptom-formation as coincident processes, and, if this is on the whole possible, does the mechanism of substitute-formation coincide with that of repression? So far as we know at present, it seems probable that the two are widely divergent, that it is not the repression itself which produces substitute-formations and symptoms, but that these latter constitute indications of a *return of the repressed* and owe their existence to quite other processes. It would also seem advisable to examine the mechanisms of substitute- and symptom-formation before those of repression.

Obviously there is no ground here for speculation to explore: on the contrary, the solution of the problem must be found by careful analysis of the results of repression observable in the individual neuroses. I must, however, suggest that we should postpone this task, too, until we have formed reliable conceptions of the relation of consciousness to the unconscious. Only, in order that the present discussion may not be quite unfruitful, I will anticipate by saying: (1) that the mechanism of repression does not in fact coincide with the mechanism or mechanisms of substitute-formation, (2) that there are many different mechanisms of substitute-formation, and (3) that the different mechanisms of repression have at least this one thing in common: *a withdrawal of energic cathexis* (or of *libido*, if it is a question of sexual instincts).

Further, confining myself to the three best-known forms of psychoneurosis, I will show by means of some examples how the conceptions here introduced find application to the study of repression. From *anxiety-hysteria* I will choose an instance which has been subjected to thorough analysis—that of an animal-phobia. The instinctual impulse subjected to repression here is a libidinal attitude towards the father, coupled with dread of him. After repression, this impulse vanishes out of consciousness: the father does not appear in consciousness as an object for the libido. As a substitute for him we find in a corresponding situation some animal which is more or less suited to be an object of dread. The substitute-formation of the ideational element has established itself by way of a displacement along the line of a series of associated ideas which is determined in some particular way. The quantitative element has not vanished, but has been transformed into anxiety. The result is a fear of a wolf, instead of a claim for love from the father. Of course the categories here employed are not enough to supply a complete explanation even of the simplest case of psychoneurosis: there are always other points of view to be taken into account.

Such a repression as that which takes place in an animal-phobia must be described as radically unsuccessful. All that it has done is to remove the idea and set another in its place; it has not succeeded at all in its aim of avoiding "pain." On this account, too, the work of the neurosis, far from ceasing, proceeds into a "second movement," so to speak, which is designed to attain its immediate and more important aim. There follows an attempt at flight, the formation of the *phobia proper*—a number of things have to be *avoided* in order to prevent an outbreak of anxiety. A more particular investigation would enable us to understand the mechanism by which the phobia achieves its aim.

We are led to quite another view of the process of repression when we consider the picture of a true *conversion-hysteria*. Here the salient point is that it is possible to bring about a total disappearance of the charge of affect. The patient then displays towards his symptoms what Charcot called *"la belle indifférence des hystériques."* At other times this suppression is not so completely successful: a part of the sensations of distress attaches to the symptoms themselves, or it has proved impossible entirely to prevent outbreaks of anxiety, and this in its turn sets the mechanism of phobia-formation working. The ideational content of the instinct-presentation is completely withdrawn from consciousness; as a substitute-formation—and concurrently, as a symptom—we have an excessive innervation (in typical cases, a somatic innervation), sometimes of a sensory, sometimes of a motor character, either as an excitation or as an inhibition. The area of over-innervation proves on closer observation to belong to the repressed instinct-presentation itself, and, as if by a process of *condensation*, to have absorbed the whole cathexis. Of course these remarks do not cover the whole mechanism of a conversion-hysteria; the element of *regression* especially, which will be appraised in another connection, has to be taken into account.

In so far as it is rendered possible only by means of extensive substitute-formations, the repression which takes place in hysteria may be pronounced entirely unsuccessful; with reference to mastering the charge of affect, however, which is the real task of repression, it generally betokens a complete success. Again, in conversion-hysteria the process of repression terminates with the formation of the symptom and does not, as in anxiety-hysteria, need to proceed to a "second movement"—or, strictly speaking, an unlimited number of "movements."

A totally different aspect of repression is shown in the third affection to which we are referring for purposes of this comparison: in the *obsessional neurosis*. Here we are at first in doubt what it is that we have to regard as the repressed instinct-presentation—a libidinal or a hostile trend. This uncertainty arises because the obsessional neurosis rests on the premise of a regression by means of which a sadistic trend has been substituted for a tender one. It is this hostile impulse against a loved person which has undergone repression. The effect at an early phase of the work of repression is quite different from that produced later. At first the repression is completely successful, the ideational content is rejected and the affect made to disappear. As a substitute-formation there arises an alteration in the ego, an increased sensitiveness of conscience, which can hardly be called a symptom. Substitute- and symptom-formation do not coincide here. Here, too, we learn something about the mechanism of repression. Repression, as it invariably does, has brought about a withdrawal of libido, but for this purpose it has made use of a *reaction-formation*, by intensifying an antithesis. So here the substitute-formation has the same mechanism as the repression and at bottom coincides with it, while yet chronologically, as well as in its content, it is distinct from the symptom-formation. It is very probable that the whole process is made possible by the ambivalent relation into which the sadistic impulse destined for repression has been introduced.

But the repression, at first successful, does not hold; in the further course of things its failure becomes increasingly obvious. The ambivalence which has allowed repression to come into being by means of reaction-formation also constitutes the point at which the repressed succeeds in breaking through again. The vanished affect is transformed, without any diminution, into dread of the community, pangs of conscience, or self-reproaches; the rejected idea is replaced by a *displacement-substitute*, often by displacement on to something utterly trivial or indifferent. For the most part there is an unmistakable tendency to complete re-establishment of the repressed idea. Failure of repression of the quantitative factor brings into play, by means of various taboos and prohibitions, the same mechanism of flight as we have seen at work in the formation of hysterical phobias. The rejection of the idea from consciousness is, however, obstinately maintained, because it ensures abstention from action, preclusion of the motor expression of an impulse. So the final form of the work of repression in the obsessional neurosis is a sterile and never-ending struggle.

The short series of comparisons which have been presented here may easily convince us that more comprehensive investigations are necessary before we can hope to understand thoroughly the processes connected with repression and the formation of neurotic symptoms. The extraordinary intricacy of all the factors to be taken into consideration leaves us only one way open by which to present them. We must select first one and then another point of view, and follow it up through the material at our disposal as long as application of it seems to prove fruitful. Each separate point so treated will be incomplete in itself and there cannot fail to be obscurities where we touch upon material not previously dealt with; but we may hope that the final synthesis of them all will lead to a good understanding of the subject.

VI

The Unconscious[1] (1915)

PSYCHOANALYSIS has taught us that the essence of the process of repression lies, not in abrogating or annihilating the ideational presentation of an instinct, but in withholding it from becoming conscious. We then say of the idea that it is in a state of "unconsciousness," of being not apprehended by the conscious mind, and we can produce convincing proofs to show that unconsciously it can also produce effects, even of a kind that finally penetrate to consciousness. Everything that is repressed must remain unconscious, but at the very outset let us state that the repressed does not comprise the whole unconscious. The unconscious has the greater compass: the repressed is a part of the unconscious.

How are we to arrive at a knowledge of the unconscious? It is of course only as something conscious that we know anything of it, after it has undergone transformation or translation into something conscious. The possibility of such translation is a matter of everyday experience in psychoanalytic work. In order to achieve this, it is necessary that the person analysed should overcome certain resistances, the very same as those which at some earlier time placed the material in question under repression by rejecting it from consciousness.

1. *Justification for the Conception of the Unconscious*

In many quarters our justification is disputed for assuming the existence of an unconscious system in the mind and for employing such an assumption for purposes of scientific work. To this we can reply that our assumption of the existence of the unconscious is *necessary* and *legitimate*, and that we possess manifold *proofs* of the existence of the unconscious. It is necessary because the data of consciousness are exceedingly

---

[1] First published in *Zeitschrift*, Bd. III., 1915; reprinted in *Sammlung*, Vierte Folge. [Translated by Cecil M. Baines.]

defective; both in healthy and in sick persons mental acts are often in process which can be explained only by presupposing other acts, of which consciousness yields no evidence. These include not only the parapraxes[2] and dreams of healthy persons, and everything designated a mental symptom or an obsession in the sick; our most intimate daily experience introduces us to sudden ideas of the source of which we are ignorant, and to results of mentation arrived at we know not how. All these conscious acts remain disconnected and unintelligible if we are determined to hold fast to the claim that every single mental act performed within us must be consciously experienced; on the other hand, they fall into a demonstrable connection if we interpolate the unconscious acts that we infer. A gain in meaning and connection, however, is a perfectly justifiable motive, one which may well carry us beyond the limitations of direct experience. When, after this, it appears that the assumption of the unconscious helps us to construct a highly successful practical method, by which we are enabled to exert a useful influence upon the course of conscious processes, this success will have won us an incontrovertible proof of the existence of that which we assumed. We become obliged then to take up the position that it is both untenable and presumptuous to claim that whatever goes on in the mind must be known to consciousness.

We can go further and in support of an unconscious mental state allege that only a small content is embraced by consciousness at any given moment, so that the greater part of what we call conscious knowledge must in any case exist for very considerable periods of time in a condition of latency, that is to say, of unconsciousness. of not being apprehended by the mind. When all our latent memories are taken into consideration it becomes totally incomprehensible how the existence of the unconscious can be gainsaid. We then encounter the objection that these latent recollections can no longer be described as mental processes, but that they correspond to residues of somatic processes from which something mental can once more proceed. The obvious answer to this should be that a latent memory is, on the contrary, in-

---

[2] [E.g. slips of the tongue, mislaying of objects, etc.—Trans.]

dubitably a residuum of a mental process. But it is more important to make clear to our own minds that this objection is based on the identification—not, it is true, explicitly stated but regarded as axiomatic—of conscious and mental. This identification is either a *petitio principii* and begs the question whether all that is mental is also necessarily conscious, or else it is a matter of convention, of nomenclature. In this latter case it is of course no more open to refutation than any other convention. The only question that remains is whether it proves so useful that we must needs adopt it. To this we may reply that the conventional identification of the mental with the conscious is thoroughly unpractical. It breaks up all mental continuity, plunges us into the insoluble difficulties of psychophysical parallelism, is open to the reproach that without any manifest grounds it overestimates the part played by consciousness, and finally it forces us prematurely to retire from the territory of psychological research without being able to offer us any compensation elsewhere.

At any rate it is clear that the question—whether the latent states of mental life, whose existence is undeniable, are to be conceived of as unconscious mental states or as physical ones —threatens to resolve itself into a war of words. We shall therefore be better advised to give prominence to what we know with certainty of the nature of these debatable states. Now, as far as their physical characteristics are concerned, they are totally inaccessible to us: no physiological conception nor chemical process can give us any notion of their nature. On the other hand, we know for certain that they have abundant points of contact with conscious mental processes; on being submitted to a certain method of operation they may be transformed into or replaced by conscious processes, and all the categories which we employ to describe conscious mental acts, such as ideas, purposes, resolutions and so forth, can be applied to them. Indeed, of many of these latent states we have to assert that the only point in which they differ from states which are conscious is just in the lack of consciousness of them. So we shall not hesitate to treat them as objects of psychological research, and that in the most intimate connection with conscious mental acts.

The stubborn denial of a mental quality to latent mental processes may be accounted for by the circumstance that most of the phenomena in question have not been objects of study outside psychoanalysis. Anyone who is ignorant of the facts of pathology, who regards the blunders of normal persons as accidental, and who is content with the old saw that dreams are froth[3] need only ignore a few more problems of the psychology of consciousness in order to dispense with the assumption of an unconscious mental activity. As it happens, hypnotic experiments, and especially post-hypnotic suggestion, had demonstrated tangibly even before the time of psycho-analysis the existence and mode of operation of the unconscious in the mind.

The assumption of an unconscious is, moreover, in a further respect a perfectly *legitimate* one, inasmuch as in postulating it we do not depart a single step from our customary and accepted mode of thinking. By the medium of consciousness each one of us becomes aware only of his own states of mind; that another man possesses consciousness is a conclusion drawn by analogy from the utterances and actions we perceive him to make, and it is drawn in order that this behaviour of his may become intelligible to us. (It would probably be psychologically more correct to put it thus: that without any special reflection we impute to everyone else our own constitution and therefore also our consciousness, and that this identification is a necessary condition of understanding in us.) This conclusion—or identification—was formerly extended by the ego to other human beings, to animals, plants, inanimate matter and to the world at large, and proved useful as long as the correspondence with the individual ego was overwhelmingly great; but it became more untrustworthy in proportion as the gulf between the ego and the non-ego widened. To-day, our judgement is already in doubt on the question of consciousness in animals; we refuse to admit it in plants and we relegate to mysticism the assumption of its existence in inanimate matter. But even where the original tendency to identification has withstood criticism—that is,

[3] [*"Träume sind Schäume."*]

when the non-ego is our fellow-man—the assumption of a consciousness in him rests upon an inference and cannot share the direct certainty we have of our own consciousness.

Now psychoanalysis demands nothing more than that we should apply this method of inference to ourselves also—a proceeding to which, it is true, we are not constitutionally disposed. If we do this, we must say that all the acts and manifestations which I notice in myself and do not know how to link up with the rest of my mental life must be judged as if they belonged to someone else and are to be explained by the mental life ascribed to that person. Further, experience shows that we understand very well how to interpret in others (*i.e.* how to fit into their mental context) those same acts which we refuse to acknowledge as mentally conditioned in ourselves. Some special hindrance evidently deflects our investigations from ourselves and interferes with our obtaining true knowledge of ourselves.

Now this method of inference, applied to oneself in spite of inner opposition, does not lead to the discovery of an unconscious, but leads logically to the assumption of another, second consciousness which is united in myself with the consciousness I know. But at this point criticism may fairly make certain comments. In the first place, a consciousness of which its own possessor knows nothing is something very different from that of another person and it is questionable whether such a consciousness, lacking, as it does, its most important characteristic, is worthy of any further discussion at all. Those who have contested the assumption of an unconscious system in the mind will not be content to accept in its place an unconscious consciousness. Secondly, analysis shows that the individual latent mental processes inferred by us enjoy a high degree of independence, as though each had no connection with another, and knew nothing about any other. We must be prepared, it would appear, to assume the existence not only of a second consciousness in us, but of a third and fourth also, perhaps of an infinite series of states of consciousness, each and all unknown to us and to one another. In the third place —and this is the most weighty argument of all—we have to take into account that analytic investigation reveals some of these latent processes as having characteristics and peculiarities which seem alien to us, or even incredible, and running directly counter to the well-known attributes of consciousness. This justifies us in modifying our inference about ourselves and saying that what is proved is not a second consciousness in us, but the existence of certain mental operations lacking in the quality of consciousness. We shall also, moreover, be right in rejecting the term "subconsciousness" as incorrect and misleading. The known cases of *"double conscience"* (splitting of consciousness) prove nothing against our view. They may most accurately be described as cases of a splitting of the mental activities into two groups, whereby a single consciousness takes up its position alternately with either the one or the other of these groups.

In psychoanalysis there is no choice for us but to declare mental processes to be in themselves unconscious, and to compare the perception of them by consciousness with the perception of the outside world through the sense-organs; we even hope to extract some fresh knowledge from the comparison. The psychoanalytic assumption of unconscious mental activity appears to us, on the one hand, a further development of that primitive animism which caused our own consciousness to be reflected in all around us, and, on the other hand, it seems to be an extension of the corrections begun by Kant in regard to our views on external perception. Just as Kant warned us not to overlook the fact that our perception is subjectively conditioned and must not be regarded as identical with the phenomena perceived but never really discerned, so psychoanalysis bids us not to set conscious perception in the place of the unconscious mental process which is its object. The mental, like the physical, is not necessarily in reality just what it appears to us to be. It is, however, satisfactory to find that the correction of inner perception does not present difficulties so great as that of outer perception—that the inner object is less hard to discern truly than is the outside world.

2. *Different Significations of the Term "Unconscious"; the Topographical Aspect*

Before going any further, let us note the important, though inconvenient, fact that unconsciousness is only one attribute of the mental and by no means suffices to describe its character. There are mental acts of very varying values which yet have in common the characteristic of being unconscious. The unconscious comprises, on the one hand, processes which are merely latent, temporarily unconscious, but which differ in no other respect from conscious ones and, on the other hand, processes such as those which have undergone repression, which if they came into consciousness must stand out in the crudest contrast to the rest of the conscious mind. It would put an end to all misunderstandings if, from now on, in describing the various kinds of mental acts we were to pay no attention to whether they were conscious or unconscious, but, when classifying and correlating them, inquired only to which instincts and aims they were related, how they were composed and to which of the systems in the mind that are superimposed one upon another they belonged. This, however, is for various reasons impracticable, and it follows that we cannot escape the imputation of ambiguity in that we use the words conscious and unconscious sometimes in a descriptive and sometimes in a systematic sense, in which latter they signify inclusion in some particular system and possession of certain characteristics. We might still attempt to avoid confusion by employing for the recognized mental systems certain arbitrarily chosen names which have no reference to consciousness. Only we should first have to justify the principles on which we distinguish the systems and we should not be able to ignore the question of consciousness, seeing that it forms the point of departure for all our investigations. Perhaps we may look for some assistance from the proposal to employ, at any rate in writing, the abbreviation Cs for consciousness and the Ucs for the unconscious when we are using the two words in the systematic sense.

To deal with the positive aspects, we now assert on the findings of psychoanalysis that a mental act commonly goes through two phases, between which is interposed a kind of testing process (censorship). In the first phase the mental act is unconscious and belongs to the system Ucs; if upon the scrutiny of the censorship it is rejected, it is not allowed to pass into the second phase; it is then said to be "repressed" and must remain unconscious. If, however, it passes this scrutiny, it enters upon the second phase and thenceforth belongs to the second system, which we will call the Cs. But the fact that it so belongs does not unequivocally determine its relation to consciousness. It is not yet conscious, but it is certainly *capable of entering consciousness,* according to J. Breuer's expression, that is, it can now, without any special resistance and given certain conditions, become the object of consciousness. In consideration of this capacity to become conscious we also call the system Cs the *"preconscious."* If it should turn out that a certain censorship also determines whether the preconscious becomes conscious, we shall discriminate more sharply between the systems Pcs and Cs. For the present let it suffice us to bear in mind that the system Pcs shares the characteristics of the Cs and that the rigorous censorship exercises its office at the point of transition from the Ucs to the Pcs (or Cs).

By accepting the existence of these (two or three) mental systems, psychoanalysis has departed a step further from the descriptive psychology of consciousness and has taken to itself a new problem and a new content. Up till now, it differed from academic (descriptive) psychology mainly by reason of its dynamic conception of mental processes; now we have to add that it professes to consider mental topography also, and to indicate in respect of any given mental operation within what system or between what systems it runs its course. This attempt, too, has won it the name of "depth-psychology." We shall hear that it may be further amplified by yet another aspect of the subject.

If we wish to treat seriously the notion of a topography of mental acts, we must direct our interest to a doubt which arises at this point. When a mental act (let us confine ourselves here to an act of ideation) is transferred from the system Ucs into the system Cs (or Pcs), are we to suppose that this transposition involves a fresh registration comparable to a second record of the idea in question, situated, moreover, in a fresh locality in the mind and side by side with which the original unconscious record continues to exist? Or are we rather to believe that the transformation consists in a change in the state of the idea, involving the same material and occurring in the same locality? This question may appear abstruse, but it must be put if we wish to form a more definite conception of mental topography, of the depth-dimension in the mind. It is a difficult one because it goes beyond pure psychology and touches on the relations of the mental apparatus to anatomy. We know that a rough correlation of this sort exists. Research has afforded irrefutable proof that mental activity is bound up with the function of the brain as with that of no other organ. The discovery of the unequal importance of the different parts of the brain and their individual relations to particular parts of the body and to intellectual activities takes us a step further—we do not know how big a step. But every attempt to deduce from these facts a localization of mental processes, every endeavour to think of ideas as stored up in nerve-cells and of excitations as passing along nerve-fibres, has completely miscarried. The same fate would await any doctrine which attempted to recognize, let us say, the anatomical position of the system Cs—conscious mental activity—in the cortex and to localize the unconscious processes in the subcortical parts of the brain. Here there is an hiatus which at present cannot be filled, nor is it one of the tasks of psychology to fill it. Our mental topography has for the present nothing to do with anatomy; it is concerned not with anatomical locations, but with regions in the mental apparatus, irrespective of their possible situation in the body.

In this respect then our work is untrammelled and may proceed according to its own requirements. It will, moreover, be useful for us to remind ourselves that our hypotheses can in the first instance lay claim only to the value of illustrations. The former of the two possibilities which we considered—namely, that the conscious phase of an idea implies a fresh record of it, which must be localized elsewhere—is doubtless the cruder but also the more convenient. The second assumption—that of a merely functional change of state—is *a priori* more probable, but it is less plastic, less easy to handle. With the first, or topographical, assumption is bound up that of a topographical separation of the systems Cs and Ucs and also the possibility that an idea may exist simultaneously in two parts of the mental apparatus—indeed, that if it is not inhibited by the censorship, it regularly advances from the one position to the other, possibly without its first location or record being abandoned. This may seem odd, but it can be supported by observations from psychoanalytic practice.

If we communicate to a patient some idea which he has at one time repressed but which we have discovered in him, our telling him makes at first no change in his mental condition. Above all, it does not remove the repression nor undo its effects, as might perhaps be expected from the fact that the previously unconscious idea has now become conscious. On the contrary, all that we shall achieve at first will be a fresh rejection of the repressed idea. At this point, however, the patient has in actual fact the same idea in two forms in two separate localities in his mental apparatus: first, he has the conscious memory of the auditory impression of the idea conveyed in what we told him, and, secondly and side by side with this, he has—as we know for certain—the unconscious memory of his actual experience existing in him in its earlier form. Now in reality there is no lifting of the repression until the conscious idea, after overcoming the resistances, has united with the unconscious memory-trace. Only through bringing the latter itself into consciousness is the effect achieved. On superficial consideration this would seem to show that conscious and unconscious ideas are different and topographically separated records of the same content. But a moment's reflection shows that the identity of the information given to the patient with his own repressed memory is only apparent. To have listened to something and to have experienced something are psychologically two different things, even though the content of each be the same.

So for the moment we are not able to decide between the two possibilities that we have discussed. Perhaps later on we shall come upon certain factors which may turn the balance in favour of one or the other. Perhaps we shall discover that our question, as we formulated it, was not sufficiently comprehensive and that the difference between a conscious and an unconscious idea has to be defined quite otherwise.

3. Unconscious Emotions

We limited the foregoing discussion to ideas and may now raise a new question, the answer to which must contribute to the elucidation of our theoretical position. We said that there were conscious and unconscious ideas; but are there also unconscious instinctual impulses, emotions and feelings, or are such constructions in this instance devoid of any meaning?

I am indeed of opinion that the antithesis of conscious and unconscious does not hold for instincts. An instinct can never be an object of consciousness—only the idea that represents the instinct. Even in the unconscious, moreover, it can only be represented by the idea. If the instinct did not attach itself to an idea or manifest itself as an affective state, we could know nothing about it. Though we do speak of an unconscious or a repressed instinctual impulse, this is a looseness of phraseology which is quite harmless. We can only mean an instinctual impulse the ideational presentation of which is unconscious, for nothing else comes into consideration.

We should expect the answer to the question about unconscious feelings, emotions and affects to be just as easily given. It is surely of the essence of an emotion that we should feel it, *i.e.* that it should enter consciousness. So for emotions, feelings and affects to be unconscious would be quite out of the question. But in psychoanalytic practice we are accustomed to speak of unconscious love, hate, anger, etc., and find it impossible to avoid even the strange conjunction, "unconscious consciousness of guilt," or a paradoxical "unconscious anxiety." Is there more meaning in the use of these terms than there is in speaking of "unconscious instincts"?

The two cases are really not on all fours. To begin with it may happen that an affect or an emotion is perceived, but misconstrued. By the repression of its proper presentation it is forced to become connected with another idea, and is now interpreted by consciousness as the expression of this other idea. If we restore the true connection, we call the original affect "unconscious," although the affect was never unconscious but its ideational presentation had undergone repression. In any event, the use of such terms as "unconscious affect and emotion" has reference to the fate undergone, in consequence of repression, by the quantitative factor in the instinctual impulse.[4] We know that an affect may be sub-

---

[4] Cf. the preceding paper on "Repression."

jected to three different vicissitudes: either it remains, wholly or in part, as it is; or it is transformed into a qualitatively different charge of affect, above all into anxiety; or it is suppressed, *i.e.* its development is hindered altogether. (These possibilities may perhaps be studied even more easily in the technique of the dream-work than in the neuroses.) We know, too, that to suppress the development of affect is the true aim of repression and that its work does not terminate if this aim is not achieved. In every instance where repression has succeeded in inhibiting the development of an affect we apply the term "unconscious" to those affects that are restored when we undo the work of repression. So it cannot be denied that the use of the terms in question is logical; but a comparison of the unconscious affect with the unconscious idea reveals the significant difference that the unconscious idea continues, after repression, as an actual formation in the system Ucs, whilst to the unconscious affect there corresponds in the same system only a potential disposition which is prevented from developing further. So that, strictly speaking, although no fault be found with the mode of expression in question, there are no unconscious affects in the sense in which there are unconscious ideas. But there may very well be in the system Ucs affect-formations which, like others, come into consciousness. The whole difference arises from the fact that ideas are cathexes—ultimately of memory-traces—whilst affects and emotions correspond with processes of discharge, the final expression of which is perceived as feeling. In the present state of our knowledge of affects and emotions we cannot express this difference more clearly.

It is of especial interest to us to have established the fact that repression can succeed in inhibiting the transformation of an instinctual impulse into affective expression. This shows us that the system Cs normally controls affectivity as well as access to motility; and this enhances the importance of repression, since it shows us that the latter is responsible, not merely when something is withheld from consciousness, but also when affective development and the inauguration of muscular activity is prevented. Conversely, too, we may say that as long as the system Cs controls activity and motility, the mental condition of the person in question may be called normal. Nevertheless, there is an unmistakable difference in the relation of the controlling system to the two allied processes of discharge.[5] Whereas the control of the system Cs over voluntary motility is firmly rooted, regularly withstands the onslaught of neurosis and only breaks down in psychosis, the control of the Cs over affective development is less firmly established. Even in normal life we can recognize that a constant struggle for primacy over affectivity goes on between the two systems Cs and Pcs, that certain spheres of influence are marked off one from another and that the forces at work tend to mingle.

The importance of the system Cs (Pcs) for the avenues of affective and motor discharge enables us to understand also the rôle which falls to substitutive ideas in determining the form of a disease. It is possible for affective development to proceed directly from the system Ucs; in this case it always has the character of anxiety, the substitute for all "repressed" affects. Often, however, the instinctual impulse has to wait until it has found a substitutive idea in the system Cs. Affective development can then proceed from this conscious substitute, the nature of which determines the qualitative character of the affect. We have asserted that, under repression, a severance takes place between the affect and the idea to which it belongs, and that each then fulfils its separate destiny. For purposes of description this is incontrovertible; in actuality, however, the affect does not as a rule arise until it has succeeded in penetrating into the Cs in attachment to some new substitutive idea.

4. Topography and Dynamics of Repression

So far we have gathered from our discussion that repression is essentially a process affecting ideas, on the border between the systems Ucs and Pcs (Cs), and we can now make a fresh attempt to describe this process more minutely. It must be a matter of withdrawal of cathexis; but the question is, in what

[5] Affectivity manifests itself essentially in motor (*i.e.* secretory and circulatory) discharge resulting in an (internal) alteration of the subject's own body without reference to the outer world; motility, in actions designed to effect changes in the outer world.

system does the withdrawal take place and to which system does the cathexis withdrawn belong?

In the Ucs the repressed idea remains capable of action and must therefore have retained its cathexis. So it must be something else which has been withdrawn. Let us take the case of repression proper ("after-expulsion") as it affects an idea which is preconscious or even has already entered consciousness. Repression can consist here only in the withdrawal from the idea of the (pre)conscious cathexis which belongs to the system Pcs. The idea then remains without cathexis, or receives cathexis from the Ucs, or retains the unconscious cathexis which it previously had. We have, therefore, withdrawal of the preconscious, retention of the unconscious, or substitution of an unconscious for a preconscious, cathexis. We notice, moreover, that we have unintentionally, as it were, based these reflections upon the assumption that the transition from the system Ucs to the system nearest to it is not effected through the making of a new record but through a change in its state, an alteration in its cathexis. The functional hypothesis has here easily routed the topographical.

But this process of withdrawal of libido does not suffice to make comprehensible to us another characteristic of repression. It is not clear why the idea which has retained its cathexis or has received cathexis from the Ucs should not, in virtue of its cathexis, renew the attempt to penetrate into the system Pcs. The withdrawal of libido would then have to be repeated, and the same performance would recur interminably, but the result would not be repression. In the same way the mechanism just discussed of withdrawal of preconscious cathexis would fail to explain the process of primal repression; for here we have to consider an unconscious idea which as yet has received no cathexis from the Pcs and therefore cannot be deprived of it.

What we are looking for, therefore, is another process which maintains the repression in the first case and, in the second, ensures its being established and continued; and this other process we can only find in the assumption of an *anti-cathexis*, by means of which the system Pcs guards itself against the intrusion of the unconscious idea. We shall see from clinical examples how such an anti-cathexis established in the system Pcs manifests itself. This it is which represents the continuous effort demanded by a primal repression but also guarantees its persistence. The anti-cathexis is the sole mechanism of primal repression; in the case of repression proper ("after-expulsion") there is in addition withdrawal of the preconscious cathexis. It is quite possible that the cathexis withdrawn from the idea is the very one used for anti-cathexis.

We see how we have gradually been led to introduce a third point of view into the scheme of mental phenomena—beside the dynamic and the topographical, we take the *economic* standpoint, one from which we try to follow out the fate of given volumes of excitation and to achieve, at least relatively, some assessment of it. It will be only right to give a special name to the way of regarding things which is the final result of psychoanalytic research. I propose that, when we succeed in describing a mental process in all its aspects, dynamic, topographic and economic, we shall call this a *metapsychological* presentation. We must say beforehand that in the present state of our knowledge we shall succeed in this only at isolated points.

Let us make a tentative effort to give a metapsychological description of the process of repression in the three transference neuroses, which are familiar to us. Here we may substitute for the term "cathexis" that of "libido," because, as we know, in this case it is the fates of sexual impulses with which we are dealing.

In anxiety-hysteria a preliminary phase of the process is frequently overlooked, perhaps indeed is really omitted; on careful observation, however, it can be clearly discerned. It consists in anxiety appearing without the subject knowing what he is afraid of. We must suppose that there was present in the Ucs some love-impulse which demanded to be translated into the system Pcs; the preconscious cathexis, however, recoiled from it in the manner of an attempt at flight, and the unconscious libidinal cathexis of the rejected idea was discharged in the form of anxiety. Then at some repetition of this process a first step was taken in the direction of mastering this distressing development of anxiety. The fugitive cathexis attached itself to a substitutive idea which, on the one hand, was connected by association with the rejected idea, and, on the other, escaped repression by reason of its remoteness from that idea (displacement-substitute), and which permitted of a rationalization of the still uncontrollable outbreak of anxiety. The substitutive idea now plays the part of an anti-cathexis for the system Cs (Pcs) by securing that system against an emergence into consciousness of the repressed idea; on the other hand, it is, or acts as if it were, the point at which the anxiety-affect, which is now all the more uncontrollable, may break out and be discharged. Clinical observation shows, for instance, that when a child suffers from an animal-phobia he experiences anxiety under two kinds of conditions: in the first place, when the repressed love-impulse becomes intensified, and, in the second, when the child perceives the animal it is afraid of. The substitutive idea acts in the one instance as a conductor from the system Ucs to the system Cs; in the other instance, as an independent source for the release of anxiety. The extending control on the part of the system Cs usually manifests itself by a tendency for the substitutive idea to be aroused more easily as time goes on in the second rather than the first way. Perhaps the child ends by behaving as though he had no liking at all for his father but had become quite free from him, and as though the fear of the animal were the real fear. Only that this fear of the animal, fed as such a fear is from the springs of unconscious instinct, proves obdurate and extravagant in the face of all influences brought to bear from the system Cs, and thereby betrays its origin in the system Ucs.

In the second phase of anxiety-hysteria, therefore, the anti-cathexis from the system Cs has led to substitute-formation. Soon the same mechanism is applied in a fresh direction. The process of repression, as we know, is not yet terminated, and finds a further aim in the task of inhibiting the outbreak of anxiety started by the substitute. This happens in the following manner: all the associations in the neighbourhood of the substitutive idea become endowed with a peculiar intensity of cathexis, so that they may display a high degree of sensibility to excitation. Excitation at any point of this protective structure must, on account of its connection with the substitutive idea, give rise to a slight degree of development of anxiety, which is then used as a signal to inhibit, by means of a fresh flight on the part of the cathexis, any further development of anxiety. The further the sensitive and vigilant anti-cathexis becomes extended round the substitute which is feared, the more exactly can the mechanism function which is designed to isolate the substitutive idea and to protect it from fresh excitation. Naturally these precautions guard only against excitations approaching the substitutive idea from without through perception, never against instinctual excitation which encounters the substitutive idea from the direction of its connection with the repressed idea. So they begin to operate only when the substitute has successfully taken over representation of what has been repressed, and they can never operate with complete security. With each increase of instinctual excitation the protecting rampart round the substitutive idea must be shifted a little further outwards. The whole construction, which is produced in analogous fashion in the other neuroses, is termed a phobia. The avoidances, renunciations and prohibitions by which we recognize anxiety-hysteria are the manifestations of flight from conscious cathexis of the substitutive idea. Surveying the whole process, we may say that the third phase has repeated and amplified the work of the second. The system Cs now protects itself by an anti-cathexis of its surrounding associations against the activation of the substitutive idea, just as previously that system secured itself by cathexis of the substitutive idea against the emergence of the repressed idea. Substitute-formation by the way of displacement has thus proceeded in its course. We must also add that the system Cs had formerly only one little point at which the repressed instinctual impulse could break through, namely, the substitutive idea; but that ultimately the whole protective structure of the phobia corresponds to a "salient" of unconscious influence of this kind. Further, we may lay stress on the interesting point of view that by the whole defence-mechanism thus set in action a projection outwards of the menace from the instinct has been achieved. The ego behaves as if the danger of an outbreak of anxiety threatened it not from the direction of an instinct but from the direction of perception: this enables the ego to react against this external danger with the attempts at flight consisting of the avoidances characteristic of a phobia. In this process repression succeeds in one particular: the discharge of anxiety may be to some extent dammed up, but only at a heavy sacrifice of personal freedom. Attempts at flight from the claims of instinct are, however, in general useless, and the result of the flight by means of a phobia remains still unsatisfactory.

A great deal of what we have recognized as true of anxiety-hysteria holds good for the two other neuroses also, so that we can confine our discussion to the points of difference and the part played by the anti-cathexis. In conversion-hysteria the instinctual cathexis of the repressed idea is transformed into the innervation necessary for the symptom. How far and in what circumstances the unconscious idea discharges its cathexis through this outlet towards innervation, so that it can relinquish its pressure towards the system Cs—these and similar questions had better be reserved for a special investigation of hysteria. In conversion-hysteria the part played by the anti-cathexis proceeding from the system Cs (Pcs) is clear and becomes manifest in the symptom-formation. It is the anti-cathexis that decides upon what part of the instinct-presentation the whole cathexis may be concentrated. The part thus selected to form a symptom fulfils the condition of expressing the aim of the instinctual impulse no less than the defensive or punishing endeavour of the system Cs; so it achieves hyper-cathexis and is maintained from both directions like the substitutive idea in anxiety-hysteria. From this circumstance we may conclude without much more ado that the degree of expenditure in repression put forth by the system Cs need not be commensurate with the energic cathexis of the symptom; for the strength of the repression is measured by the anti-cathexis put forth, and the symptom is supported not only by this anti-cathexis but also by the instinctual cathexis from the system Ucs which is interwoven with it.

With reference to the obsessional neurosis, we need only add to the observations brought forward in the preceding paper[6] that here the anti-cathexis of the system Cs comes most noticeably into the foreground. It is this that brings about the first repression, in the shape of a reaction-formation, and later it is the point at which the repressed idea breaks

[6] P. 114.

through. We may find room for the supposition that, if the work of repression seems far less successful in anxiety-hysteria and in the obsessional neurosis than in conversion-hysteria, it is because the anti-cathexis is so prominent and all outlet is lacking.

5. Special Characteristics of the System Ucs

The differentiation we have drawn between the two systems within the mind receives fresh significance when we observe that processes in the one system, Ucs, show characteristics which are not again met with in the system immediately above it.

The kernel of the system Ucs consists of instinct-presentations whose aim is to discharge their cathexis; that is to say, they are wish-impulses. These instinctual impulses are co-ordinate with one another, exist independently side by side, and are exempt from mutual contradiction. When two wishes whose aims must appear to us incompatible become simultaneously active, the two impulses do not detract one from the other or cancel each other, but combine to form an intermediate aim, a compromise.

There is in this system no negation, no dubiety, no varying degree of certainty: all this is only imported by the work of the censorship which exists between the Ucs and the Pcs. Negation is, at a higher level, a substitute for repression. In the Ucs there are only contents more or less strongly cathected.

Intensity of cathexis is mobile in a far greater degree in this than in the other systems. By the process of displacement one idea may surrender to another the whole volume of its cathexis; by that of condensation it may appropriate the whole cathexis of several other ideas. I have proposed to regard these two processes as distinguishing marks of the so-called *primary process* in the mind. In the system Pcs the *secondary process*[7] holds sway; where a primary process is allowed to take its course in connection with elements belonging to the system Pcs, it appears "comic" and excites laughter.

---

[7] Cf. Section VII. of *Die Traumdeutung*, which is based upon ideas developed by J. Breuer in *Studien über Hysterie*.

The processes of the system Ucs are timeless; *i.e.* they are not ordered temporally, are not altered by the passage of time, in fact bear no relation to time at all. The time-relation also is bound up with the work of the system Cs.

The processes of the Ucs are just as little related to reality. They are subject to the pleasure-principle; their fate depends only upon the degree of their strength and upon their conformity to regulation by pleasure and pain.

Let us sum up: *exemption from mutual contradiction, primary process* (motility of cathexis), *timelessness,* and *substitution of psychic for external reality*—these are the characteristics which we may expect to find in processes belonging to the system Ucs.[8]

Unconscious processes can only be observed by us under the conditions of dreaming and of neurosis; that is to say, when the processes of the higher system Pcs revert to an earlier level by a certain process of degradation (regression). Independently they are unrecognizable, indeed cannot exist, for the system Ucs is at a very early stage overlaid by the system Pcs which has captured the means of access to consciousness and to motility. The means of discharge for the system Ucs is by means of physical innervation leading to development of affect, but even this outlet is, as we have seen, contested by the system Pcs. Left to itself, the system Ucs would not in normal conditions be able to bring about any purposive muscular acts, with the exception of those already organized as reflexes.

In order to grasp the full significance of the characteristics of the system Ucs described above, we should have to contrast and compare them with those of the system Pcs. But this would take us so far afield that I propose that we should once more call a halt and not undertake the comparison of the two till we can do so in connection with our discussion of the higher system: only the most pressing points of all shall be mentioned at this stage.

The processes of the system Pcs display, no matter whether they are already conscious or only capable of becoming con-

---

[8] We are reserving for a different context the mention of another notable privilege of the system Ucs.

scious, an inhibition of the tendency of cathected ideas towards discharge. When a process moves over from one idea to another, the first retains a part of its cathexis and only a small part undergoes displacement. Displacement and condensation after the mode of the primary process are excluded or very much restricted. This circumstance caused Breuer to assume the existence of two different stages of cathectic energy in mental life: one in which that energy is tonically "bound" and the other in which it moves freely and presses towards discharge. I think that this discrimination represents the deepest insight we have gained up to the present into the nature of nervous energy, and I do not see how we are to evade such a conclusion. A metapsychological presentation most urgently calls for further discussion at this point, though perhaps that would still be too daring an undertaking.

Further, it devolves upon the system Pcs to make communication possible between the different ideational contents so that they can influence one another, to give them a relation to time, to set up the censorship or censorships, and to establish the institution of "testing reality" and the reality-principle. Conscious memory, too, seems to depend wholly on the Pcs and should be clearly distinguished from the memory-traces in which the experiences of the Ucs become fixed; it probably corresponds with the making of a special record—a conception which we tried to employ as explaining the relation of conscious to unconscious ideas, but which we have already discarded. In this connection also we shall find the means to put an end to our uncertainty regarding the name of the higher system which at present we vaguely call sometimes the Pcs and sometimes the Cs.

Here, too, it will be as well to utter a warning against overhasty generalizations about what we have brought to light in regard to apportioning the various mental activities to one or other of the two systems. We are describing the state of affairs as it appears in the adult human being, in whom the system Ucs in the strict sense functions only as a stage preliminary to the higher organization. The content and connections of this system as the individual develops, the significance it possesses in the case of animals—these are points on which no conclusion can be deduced from our description: they must be investigated independently. Moreover, in the human being we must be prepared to find possible pathological conditions under which the two systems alter, or even exchange, both their content and their characteristics.

6. *Communication between the Two Systems*

It would certainly be wrong to imagine that the Ucs remains at rest while the whole work of the mind is performed by the Pcs, that the Ucs is something finished with, a vestigial organ, a residuum from the process of evolution; wrong also to assume that communication between the two systems is confined to the act of repression, the Pcs casting everything which disturbs it into the abyss of the Ucs. On the contrary, the Ucs is living and capable of development and maintains a number of other relations to the Pcs, amongst them that of co-operation. To sum up, we must say that the Ucs is continued into its so-called derivatives, is accessible to the influence of life, perpetually acts upon the Pcs, and even is, on its part, capable of influence by the latter system.

Study of the derivatives of the Ucs will altogether disappoint our expectations of a schematically clear division of the one mental system from the other. This circumstance will certainly give rise to dissatisfaction with our results and will probably be used to cast doubts upon the value of our way of distinguishing the two groups of mental processes. Our answer is, however, that we have no other aim but that of translating into theory the results of observation, and we shall deny that there is any obligation on us to achieve at our very first attempt a theory that commends itself by its simplicity, in which all is plain sailing. We defend its complexities so long as we find that they fit in with the results of observation, and we do not abandon our expectation of being guided in the end by those very complexities to recognition of a state of affairs that is at once simple in itself and at the same time answers to all the complications of reality.

Amongst the derivatives of the unconscious instinctual impulses, the character of which we have just described, there are some which unite in themselves opposite features. On the one hand, they are highly organized, exempt from self-contradictoriness, have made use of every acquisition of the system Cs, and would hardly be distinguished by our ordinary judgement from the formations of that system. On the other hand, they are unconscious and are incapable of becoming conscious. Thus they belong according to their qualities to the system Pcs, but in actual fact to the Ucs. Their origin remains decisive for the fate they will undergo. We may compare them with those human half-breeds who, taken all round, resemble white men, but betray their coloured descent by some striking feature or other, on account of which they are excluded from society and enjoy none of the privileges of white people. Of such a nature are the *phantasy-formations* of normal persons as well as of neurotics, which we have recognized as preliminary phases in the formation both of dreams and of symptoms, and which, in spite of their high degree of organization, remain repressed and therefore cannot become conscious. They draw near to consciousness and remain undisturbed so long as they do not become strongly cathected, but as soon as a certain degree of this is exceeded they are thrust back. Substitute-formations are similar, more highly organized derivatives of the Ucs; but these succeed in breaking through into consciousness, thanks to some favourable relation, as, for example, when they coincide with a preconscious anti-cathexis.

When, on another occasion, we examine more closely the way in which entry into consciousness is conditioned, we shall be able to find a solution for some of the difficulties arising here. At this point it seems a good plan to contrast with the foregoing points of view, which take their rise in consideration of the Ucs, one which presents itself from the direction of consciousness. Consciousness regards the whole sum of mental processes as belonging to the realm of the preconscious. A very great part of this preconscious material originates in the unconscious, has the characteristics of derivatives of the unconscious, and is subject to a censorship before it can pass into consciousness. Another part of the Pcs can become conscious without any censorship. Here we light upon a contradiction of an earlier assumption: from the point of view of repression we were obliged to place the censorship which is decisive for consciousness between the systems Ucs and Pcs. Now it becomes probable to us that there is a censorship between the Pcs and the Cs. But we shall do well not to regard this complication as a difficulty, but to assume that to every transition from one system to that immediately above it (that is, every advance to a higher stage of mental organization) there corresponds a new censorship. As a corollary, we shall have, it is true, to discard the assumption of a continuous laying down of new records.

The reason for all these difficulties is that consciousness, the only characteristic of mental processes directly available to us, is in no wise suited to serve as a criterion for the erection of systems. Apart from the circumstance that what belongs to consciousness is not always in consciousness but can also be temporarily latent, observation has shown that much which shares the attributes of the system Pcs does not become conscious; and, further, we shall find that the entry into consciousness is circumscribed by certain dispositions of attention. Hence consciousness stands in no simple relation either to the different systems or to the process of repression. The truth is that it is not only what is repressed that remains alien to consciousness, but also some of the impulses which dominate our ego and which therefore form the strongest functional antithesis to what is repressed. In proportion as we try to win our way to a metapsychological view of mental life, we must learn to emancipate ourselves from our sense of the importance of that symptom which consists in "being conscious."

So long as we still cling to this we see our generalizations regularly invaded by exceptions. We see that derivatives of the Pcs enter consciousness as substitute-formations and as symptoms, generally after undergoing great distortion in contrast to the Ucs, although often many characteristics inviting repression have been retained. We find that many preconscious formations remain unconscious, though, to judge by their nature, we should suppose that they might very well become conscious. Probably in their case the stronger attraction of the Ucs asserts itself. We are led to look for the more important difference, not between the conscious and the preconscious, but between the preconscious and the unconscious. On the border of the Pcs the censorship thrusts back the Ucs, but its derivatives can circumvent this censorship, achieve a high degree of organization, and in the Pcs reach a certain intensity of cathexis; when, however, this is exceeded and they try to force themselves into consciousness, they are recognized as derivatives of the Ucs, and are repressed afresh at the new frontier by the censorship between the Cs and the Pcs. Thus the former censorship is exercised against the Ucs itself, and the latter against its preconscious derivatives. We might suppose that in the course of individual development the censorship had been advanced a step.

In psychoanalytic treatment the existence of the second censorship, located between the systems Pcs and Cs, is proved beyond question. We require the patient to produce freely derivatives of the Ucs, we pledge him to overcome the objections of the censorship against these preconscious formations becoming conscious, and, by overthrowing this censorship, we open up the way to abrogating the repression accomplished by the earlier one. To this let us add that the existence of the censorship between the Pcs and the Cs teaches us that becoming conscious is no mere act of perception, but is probably also a *hyper-cathexis*, a further advance in the mental organization.

Let us turn our attention to the communications existing between the unconscious and the other systems, not so much with a view to establishing any fresh fact as in order to avoid omitting the most prominent features. At the roots of instinctual activity the systems communicate with one another in the freest possible way: some of the processes here set in motion pass through the Ucs, as through a preparatory stage, and reach the highest mental development in the Cs, whilst some are retained as the Ucs. But the Ucs is also affected by experiences originating in outer perception. Normally all the paths from perception to the Ucs remain open; only those leading out from the Ucs are barred by repression.

It is very remarkable that the Ucs of one human being can react upon that of another, without the Cs being implicated at all. This deserves closer investigation, especially with a view to finding out whether preconscious activity can be excluded as a factor in bringing this about; but for purposes of description the fact is incontestable.

The content of the system Pcs (or Cs) is derived partly from the instinctual life (through the medium of the Ucs), and partly from perception. It is doubtful how far the processes of this system can exert a direct influence on the Ucs; examination of pathological cases often reveals an almost incredible independence and lack of susceptibility to influence on the part of the Ucs. A complete divergence of their tendencies, a total dissociation of the two systems, is a general characteristic of disease. Yet psychoanalytic treatment is based upon influence by the Cs on the Ucs, and shows at any rate that, though laborious, this is not impossible. The derivatives of the Ucs which act as intermediaries between the two systems open the way, as we have already said, towards accomplishing this. But we may well suppose that a spontaneously effected alteration in the Ucs from the side of the Cs is a difficult and slow process.

Co-operation between a preconscious and an unconscious impulse, even when the latter is subject to very strong repression, may be established if the situation permits of the unconscious impulse operating in harmony with one of the controlling tendencies. The repression is removed for the occasion, the repressed activity being admitted as a reinforcement of the one intended by the ego. In respect of this single constellation the unconscious becomes ego-syntonic, falls into line with the ego, without any change taking place in the repression otherwise. The effect of the Ucs in this co-operation is unmistakable; the reinforced tendencies reveal themselves as, in spite of all, different from the normal—they make possible achievements of special perfection, and they manifest a resistance in the face of opposition similar to that of obsessional symptoms.

The content of the Ucs may be compared with a primitive population in the mental kingdom. If inherited mental formations exist in the human being—something analogous to instinct in animals—these constitute the nucleus of the Ucs. Later there is added all that is discarded as useless during childhood development, and this need not differ in its nature from what is inherited. A sharp and final division between the content of the two systems, as a rule, takes place only at puberty.

7. Recognition of the Unconscious

So long as we derive our ideas of the Ucs only from our knowledge of dream-life and the transference neuroses, all that we can predicate of that system is probably represented in the foregoing remarks. It is certainly not much, and at some points it gives an impression of obscurity and confusion; especially do we look in vain for the possibility of bringing the Ucs into any connection, or classifying it under any heading, with which we are already familiar. Analysis of one of those affections called narcissistic psychoneuroses alone promises to furnish us with conceptions through which the enigmatic Ucs will be brought within our reach in a tangible fashion.

Since the publication of a work by Abraham (1908)—attributed by its conscientious author to my instigation—we have been trying to define Kraepelin's dementia praecox (Bleuler's schizophrenia) on the basis of its relation to that pair of opposites consisting of the ego and its object. In the transference neuroses (anxiety- and conversion-hysteria and the obsessional neurosis) there was nothing to give special prominence to these opposites. We knew, indeed, that frustration from the side of the object occasioned the outbreak of neurosis and that neurosis involved abandonment of the real object; also that the libido withdrawn from the real object reverted first to an object in phantasy and then to one that had been repressed (introversion). But object-cathexis in general is in such cases retained with great energy, and more minute examination of the processes of repression has forced us to assume that object-cathexis persists in the system Ucs in spite of—or rather in consequence of—the repression. Indeed the capacity for transference, of which we make use for therapeutic purposes in these affections, presupposes unimpaired object-cathexis.

In schizophrenia, on the other hand, we have been obliged to assume that after the process of repression the withdrawn libido does not seek a new object, but retreats into the ego; that is to say, that here the object-cathexes are given up and a primitive objectless condition of narcissism is re-established. The incapacity of these patients for transference—so far as the process of disease extends—their consequent inaccessibility to therapeutic efforts, the repudiation of the outer world characteristic of them, the manifestations of hyper-cathexis of their ego, the final outcome in complete apathy—all these clinical features seem to accord excellently with the assumption that object-cathexes are relinquished. As regards the relation of the two psychical systems to each other, all observers have been struck by the fact that in schizophrenia a great deal is consciously expressed which in the transference neuroses can be demonstrated to exist in the Ucs only by means of psychoanalysis. But at the beginning we were not able to establish any intelligible connection between the ego-object relation and the relationships of consciousness.

In the following unexpected way we seem to arrive at what we are seeking. In schizophrenics we observe—especially in the earlier stages which are so instructive—a number of changes in *speech*, some of which deserve to be regarded from a particular point of view. The patient often devotes peculiar care to his way of expressing himself, which becomes "precious" and "elaborate." The construction of the sentences undergoes a peculiar disorganization, making them so incomprehensible to us that the patient's remarks seem nonsensical. Often some relation to bodily organs or innervations is prominent in the content of these utterances. This may be correlated with another observation, namely, that, in such symptoms of schizophrenia as are comparable with the substitute-formations of hysteria or the obsessional neurosis, the relation between the substitute and the repressed material nevertheless displays peculiarities which would surprise us in these two forms of neurosis.

Dr. Viktor Tausk of Vienna has placed at my disposal some observations that he has made in the initial stages of schizophrenia, which are particularly valuable in that the patient herself was anxious to explain her utterances further. I will take two of his examples to illustrate the thesis I wish to defend, and I have no doubt that every observer could easily produce plenty of such material.

One of Tausk's patients, a girl who was brought to the

clinic after a quarrel with her lover, complained that *her eyes were not right, they were twisted*. This she herself explained by uttering in properly constructed sentences a series of reproaches against her lover. "She could not understand him at all, he looked different every time; he was a shammer, an eye-twister,[9] he had twisted her eyes; now they were not her eyes any more; now she saw the world with different eyes."

The patient's remarks about her first incomprehensible utterance have the value of an analysis, for they contain the equivalent of the original words expressed in a generally comprehensible form; at the same time they explain the meaning and the genesis of speech-formation in schizophrenia. In agreement with Tausk, I would here lay stress on the point that the relation to the bodily organ (the eye) has usurped the place of the whole content of the thought. The schizophrenic speech displays a hypochondriac trait: it has become "organ-speech."

A second remark of the same patient's runs: "She was standing in church, suddenly she felt a jerk, she had to *change her position*, as though somebody put her into a position, as though she were *placed in a certain position*."

There follows the analysis by means of a fresh series of reproaches against her lover: "he was common, he had made her common, too, though she was naturally refined; he had made her like himself by leading her to think that he was superior to her; now she had become like him, because she thought she would be better if she were like him; he had *given a false impression of his own position*,[10] now she was just like him (identification!), he had *changed her position*."[11]

The movement by which she "changed her position," Tausk remarks, stood for the idea of "misrepresenting her position" and for the identification with the lover. Again I would call attention to the manner in which the whole train of thought is dominated by that element which has for its content a bodily

---

[9] [*Augenverdreher*, used in German to mean a *deceiver.*—Trans.]

[10] *Sich verstellen* = to feign, disguise oneself.

[11] *Verstellen* = to change the place of. [As with *Augenverdreher*, there is again a play on words, the concrete meaning of the word replacing its metaphorical sense.—Trans.]

innervation (or, rather, the sensation of it). An hysteric would, in the first case, have convulsively rolled her eyes, and, in the second, have given actual jerks, instead of having the impulse to jerk or the sensation of being jerked; and in neither case would this have been accompanied by any conscious thoughts, nor would she afterwards have been able to express any such thoughts.

So far these two observations illustrate what we have called hypochondriac language or "organ-speech." But they also point to something which seems to us more important, namely, to another state of things of which we have innumerable instances (for example, in the cases quoted in Bleuler's monograph) and which may be reduced to a definite formula. In schizophrenia *words* are subject to the same process as that which makes dream-images out of dream-thoughts, the one we have called the primary mental process. They undergo condensation, and by means of displacement transfer their cathexes to one another without remainder; the process may extend so far that a single word, which on account of its manifold relations is specially suitable, can come to represent a whole train of thought. The works of Bleuler, Jung and their pupils have yielded abundant material precisely in support of this very proposition.[12]

Before we draw any conclusion from impressions such as these, let us consider further the distinctions between the substitutive idea in schizophrenia and in hysteria and the obsessional neurosis—nice distinctions, it is true, yet producing a very strange effect. A patient whom I have at present under observation has let himself withdraw from all the interests of life on account of the unhealthy condition of the skin of his face. He declares that he has blackheads and that there are deep holes in his face which everyone notices. Analysis shows that he is working out his castration complex upon his skin. At first he busied himself with these blackheads without any misgivings; and it gave him great pleasure to squeeze them out, because, as he said, something spurted out when he did so. Then he began to think that there was a deep cavity

---

[12] The dream-work, too, occasionally treats words like things, and then creates very similar "schizophrenic" utterances or neologisms.

wherever he had got rid of a blackhead and he reproached himself most vehemently with having ruined his skin for ever by "constantly fiddling at it with his hand." Pressing out the content of the blackheads is clearly to him a substitute for onanism. The cavity which then appears in consequence of his guilty act is the female genital, *i.e.* stands for the fulfilment of the threat of castration (or the phantasy representing it) called forth by onanism. This substitute-formation has, in spite of its hypochondriacal character, considerable resemblance to an hysterical conversion; and yet we have the feeling that there must be something different in it, that we cannot believe such a substitute-formation possible in a case of hysteria, even before we can say in what the difference consists. A tiny little hole such as a pore of the skin will hardly be used by an hysteric as a symbol for the vagina, which otherwise he will compare with every imaginable object capable of enclosing a space. Besides, we should think that the multiplicity of these little cavities would prevent him from using them as a substitute for the female genital. The same applies to the case of a young patient reported by Tausk some years ago to the Vienna Psycho-Analytical Society. This patient behaved in other respects exactly as though suffering from an obsessional neurosis; he took hours to dress, and so on. The striking feature of the case, however, was that he was able to tell the meaning of his inhibitions without any resistance. For example, in pulling on his stockings he was disturbed by the idea that he must draw apart the knitted stitches, *i.e.* the holes, and every hole was for him a symbol of the female genital aperture. This again is a thing with which we cannot credit a patient suffering from obsessional neurosis; a patient of this kind observed by R. Reitler (one who suffered from the same lingering over putting on his stockings), after overcoming the resistances, found the explanation that his foot symbolised the penis, putting on the stocking stood for an onanistic act, and that he had constantly to pull the stocking off and on, partly in order to complete the representation of onanism, and partly in order to undo the act.

If we ask ourselves what it is that gives the character of strangeness to the substitute-formation and the symptom in schizophrenia, we come at last to understand that it is the predominance of the word-relation over that of the thing. There is only a very slight similarity between the squeezing out of a blackhead and an ejaculation from the penis, still less similarity between the countless little pores of the skin and the vagina; but in the former case there *is*, in both instances, a spurting out, while in the latter the cynical saying, "a hole is a hole," is *literally* true. The identity of the two when expressed in *words,* not the resemblance of the objects designated, has dictated the substitution. Where the two—word and thing— do not coincide, the substitute-formation in schizophrenia deviates from that in the transference neuroses.

Let us bring these considerations into connection with the conclusion that in schizophrenia the object-cathexes are relinquished. We must then modify this assumption and say: the cathexis of the ideas of the words corresponding to the objects is retained. What we could permissibly call the conscious idea of the object can now be split up into the *idea of the word* (verbal idea) and the *idea of the thing* (concrete idea); the latter consists in the cathexis, if not of the direct memory-images of the thing, at least of remoter memory-traces derived from these. It strikes us all at once that now we know what is the difference between a conscious and an unconscious idea. The two are not, as we supposed, different records of the same content situate in different parts of the mind, nor yet different functional states of cathexis in the same part; but the conscious idea comprises the concrete idea plus the verbal-idea corresponding to it, whilst the unconscious idea is that of the thing alone. The system Ucs contains the thing-cathexes of the objects, the first and true object-cathexes; the system Pcs originates in a hyper-cathexis of this concrete idea by a linking up of it with the verbal ideas of the words corresponding to it. It is such hyper-cathexes, we may suppose, that bring about higher organization in the mind and make it possible for the primary process to be succeeded by the secondary process which dominates Pcs. Now, too, we are in a position to state precisely what it is that repression denies to the rejected idea in the transference neuroses—namely, translation of the idea into words which are to remain attached to the object. The idea which is not put into words or the mental act which has not received hyper-cathexis then remains in the unconscious in a state of repression.

I may call attention to the fact that already very early we possessed the insight which to-day enables us to understand one of the most striking characteristics of schizophrenia. The last pages of *Die Traumdeutung*, published in 1900, expound the thesis that thought-processes, *i.e.* those cathected mental acts which are more remote from perception, are in themselves devoid of quality and are unconscious, deriving their capacity to enter consciousness only from association with the residues of word-perceptions. The verbal ideas, for their part, are derived from sense-perceptions in the same way as concrete ideas are; so that the question might be raised why ideas of objects cannot become conscious through the agency of their own residues of perceptions. But possibly thought proceeds in systems that are so far remote from the original residues of perception that they have no longer retained anything of the qualities of these residues, so that in order to become conscious the content of the thought-systems needs to be reinforced by new qualities. Besides, linking them up with words may impart quality even to cathexes to which, representing as they do only relations between the ideas of objects, no quality could accrue from the perceptions themselves. Such relations, comprehensible only through words, form one of the most important parts of our thought-processes. We understand that linking them up with verbal ideas is still not identical with actually becoming conscious, but only with the potentiality of this; it is therefore characteristic of the system Pcs and of that only. Now, however, we note that with these discussions we have departed from our real theme and find ourselves in the midst of problems concerning the preconscious and the conscious, which for good reasons we are reserving for separate treatment.

In considering schizophrenia, which, to be sure, we only touch on here so far as seems indispensable for general knowledge of the Ucs, the doubt must occur to us whether the process here termed repression has anything at all in common with the repression which takes place in the transference neuroses. The formula that repression is a process which occurs between the systems Ucs and Pcs (or Cs), and results in withholding the repressed material from consciousness, must in any event be modified, in order to embrace the case of dementia praecox and other narcissistic affections. But the ego's attempt at flight, expressing itself in withdrawal of conscious cathexis, nevertheless remains a common factor. The most superficial reflection shows us how much more radically and thoroughly this attempt at flight, this flight of the ego, is carried out in the narcissistic neuroses.

If, in schizophrenia, this flight consists in withdrawal of instinctual cathexis from those points which represent the unconscious idea of the object, it may seem strange that that part of the same idea which belongs to the system Pcs—the verbal ideas corresponding to it—should, on the contrary, undergo a more intense cathexis. We might rather expect that the verbal idea, being the preconscious part, would have to sustain the first impact of the repression and that it would be wholly insusceptible of cathexis after the repression had proceeded as far as the unconscious concrete ideas. This is certainly difficult to understand. The solution suggests itself that the cathexis of the verbal idea is not part of the act of repression, but represents the first of the attempts at recovery or cure which so conspicuously dominate the clinical picture of schizophrenia. These endeavours are directed towards regaining the lost objects, and it may well be that to achieve this purpose their path to the object must be by way of the word belonging to it; they then have, however, to content themselves with words in the place of things. Our mental activity moves, generally speaking, in one of two opposite directions: either it starts from the instincts and passes through the system Ucs to conscious mentation, or, on excitation from without, it passes through the systems Cs and Pcs till it reaches the unconscious cathexes of the ego and of its objects. This second way must, in spite of the repression which has taken place, have remained clear, and for some distance there is nothing to block the endeavours of the neurosis to regain its objects. When we think in abstractions there is a danger that we may neglect the relations of words to unconscious concrete ideas, and it must be confessed that the expression and content of our philosophizing begins to acquire an unwelcome resemblance to the schizophrenic's way of thinking. We may, on the other hand, attempt a characterization of the schizophrenic's mode of thought by saying that he treats concrete things as though they were abstract.

If we have really recognized the nature of the Ucs and have correctly defined the difference between an unconscious and a preconscious idea, then researches starting from many other points may be expected to bring us back to the same conclusions.

VII

Metapsychological Supplement to the Theory of Dreams[1] (1916)

WE ARE ABLE to learn in various ways how advantageous it is for our researches to institute comparisons with certain states and phenomena which may be conceived of as *normal prototypes* of morbid affections. Among these we may include such affective conditions as grief or mourning and the state of being in love, but also the state of sleep and the phenomenon of dreaming.

We are not accustomed to expend much thought on the fact that every night human beings lay aside the garments they pull over their skin, and even also other objects which they use to supplement their bodily organs (so far as they have succeeded in making good their deficiencies by substitutes)— for instance, their spectacles, false hair or teeth, and so on. In addition to this, when they go to sleep they perform a perfectly analogous dismantling of their minds—they lay aside most of their mental acquisitions; thus both physically and mentally approaching remarkably close to the situation in which they began life. Somatically, sleep is an act which reproduces intra-uterine existence, fulfilling the conditions of repose, warmth and absence of stimulus; indeed, in sleeping, many people resume the foetal position. The feature characterizing the mind of a sleeping person is an almost complete withdrawal from the surrounding world and the cessation of all interest in it.

[1] First published in *Zeitschrift*, Bd. IV., 1916–1918; reprinted in *Sammlung*, Vierte Folge. [Translated by Cecil M. Baines.]

This and the following paper are taken from a collection which I originally intended to publish in book form, under the title "Preliminary Material for a Metapsychological Theory." They follow on certain papers which appeared in *Zeitschrift*, Bd. III.: "Instincts and their Vicissitudes," "Repression," and "The Unconscious." The series is designed to clarify and subject to a more profound study the theoretical assumptions upon which a psychoanalytic system could be based.

When we investigate psychoneurotic conditions, we find in each of them occasion to comment upon a so-called *temporal regression,* i.e. the particular extent to which each of them retraces the stages of its evolution. We distinguish two such regressions—one in the development of the ego and the other in that of the libido. In sleep, the latter is carried to the point of restoring the primitive narcissism, while the former goes back to the state of hallucinatory wish-fulfilment.

It is, of course, the study of dreams which has taught us what we know of the mental characteristics of sleep. It is true that dreams only show us the dreamer in so far as he is not asleep; nevertheless they are bound to reveal to us characteristics of sleep itself at the same time. We have learnt from observation some peculiarities of dreams which at first we could not understand, but can now easily fit into a scheme. Thus, we know that dreams are absolutely egoistic and that the person who plays the chief part in their scenes is always to be recognized as the dreamer. We now readily understand that this is due to the narcissism of sleep. Narcissism and egoism are indeed one and the same; the word "narcissism" is only employed to emphasize that this egoism is a libidinal phenomenon as well; or, to put it in another way, narcissism may be described as the libidinal complement of egoism. The "diagnostic" capacity of dreams becomes equally comprehensible, too—a phenomenon which is universally acknowledged but regarded as so puzzling; in dreams incipient physical disease is often detected earlier and more clearly than in waking life, and all the current bodily sensations assume gigantic proportions. This magnifying process is hypochondriacal in character; it follows from the withdrawal of all mental cathexes from the outer world back to the ego, and it makes possible early recognition of bodily changes which in waking life would still for a time have remained unnoticed.

A dream indicates that something was going on which tended to disturb sleep, and it enables us to understand the way in which this disturbance can be warded off. The final outcome is that the sleeper has dreamed and is able to go on sleeping; the inner claim which wanted to absorb him has been replaced by an outer experience, the claim of which he has succeeded in discharging. A dream is, therefore, among other things, a *projection*: an externalization of an internal process. We remember that we have already met with projection elsewhere among the means adopted for defence. The mechanism of an hysterical phobia, too, culminated in the substitution of an outer danger, from which the person might strive to protect himself by flight, for an inner instinctual claim. We will, however, reserve detailed treatment of projection till we come to analyse that narcissistic affection in which this mechanism plays the most striking part.

But now, how can it happen that the intention to sleep becomes disturbed? The disturbance may proceed from an inner excitation or from an outer stimulus. Let us first consider the more obscure and more interesting case of the disturbance from within. Experience shows us that dreams are excited by residues from the previous day, cathected thoughts, which have not submitted to the general withdrawal of cathexes, but have retained in spite of it a certain degree of libidinal or other interest. So the narcissism of sleep has here from the outset had to admit an exception, and therewith dream-formation begins. In analysis we learn to recognize these day-residues as latent dream-thoughts, which, both by reason of their nature and of the whole situation, must be regarded as preconscious ideas, belonging to the system Pcs.

Before we can explain dream-formation further, certain difficulties have to be overcome. The narcissism of sleep does indeed signify the withdrawal of cathexis from all ideas of objects, both from the unconscious and the preconscious parts of them. If then certain "day-residues" have retained their cathexis, we hesitate to assume that they acquire so much energy at night as to compel attention on the part of consciousness; we are inclined rather to assume that the cathexis they have retained is far weaker than that which they possessed during the day. Here analysis saves us further speculations, for it shows us that these day-residues have to receive reinforcement from unconscious instinctual impulses if they are to act as shapers of dreams. This hypothesis at first presents no difficulties, for we must believe that in sleep the censorship between the Pcs and the Ucs is greatly weakened, communication between the two systems being thus made easier.

But there is another ground for misgiving, which we must not pass over in silence. If the narcissistic state of sleep has resulted in withdrawal of all cathexes belonging to the systems Ucs and Pcs, then there can no longer be any possibility of the preconscious day-residue being reinforced by unconscious instinctual impulses, which have themselves surrendered their cathexes to the ego. Here the theory of dream-formation ends in a contradiction, unless we can rescue it by modifying our assumption of the narcissism of sleep.

Such a reservation is, as we shall discover later, necessary in the theory of dementia praecox as well. Our modified hypothesis must run as follows: that part of the system Ucs which is under repression does not comply with the ego's desire for sleep, but retains its cathexes in whole or in part, and in general has acquired, in consequence of repression, a certain measure of independence of the ego. To correspond with this, some amount of the expenditure on repression (anti-cathexis) would have to be maintained throughout the night, in order to meet the menace from the instincts, though the blocking of all paths to affective discharge and to motility may considerably diminish the degree of anti-cathexis necessary. So we should picture the situation which leads to dream-formation something as follows: the desire for sleep endeavours to call in all the cathexes put forth by the ego and to establish an absolute narcissism. This can only partly succeed, for the repressed material in the system Ucs does not yield to the desire for sleep. Part of the anti-cathexis has to be maintained, therefore, and the censorship between the Ucs and the Pcs must remain operative, even if not in full force. So far as the control of the ego extends, all the systems are emptied of cathexes. The stronger the instinctual unconscious cathexes, the more unstable is the sleep. We know, too, the extreme case in which the ego gives up the desire to sleep because it feels unable to inhibit the repressed impulses set free during sleep—in other words, when sleep is abandoned because of the fear of dreams.

Later on we shall learn to appreciate the weighty consequences of this conclusion regarding the insubordination of repressed impulses. For the present let us follow out the situation in dream-formation.

The possibility mentioned above—that some of the preconscious thoughts of the day also prove refractory and retain a part of their cathexis—must be recognized as a second kind of interference with the narcissism. Fundamentally the two cases may be identical: the resistance of the day-residues may originate in a connection with unconscious tendencies already in existence during waking life; or the process may be less simple, and the day-residues which have not been wholly deprived of cathexis may establish a connection with the repressed material only in sleep, when there is greater facility of communication between the Pcs and the Ucs. In either case there follows the same decisive step in dream-formation: the preconscious dream-wish is formed, which *expresses the unconscious impulse in the material of the preconscious day-residues*. This dream-wish must be sharply distinguished from the day-residues; it need not have existed in waking life; it may already display the irrational character noticeable in all that is unconscious when we come to translate it into terms of consciousness. Nor must the dream-wish be confounded with the wish-impulses that are, perhaps, but by no means necessarily, to be found amongst the preconscious (latent) dream-thoughts. If, however, such preconscious wishes do exist, the dream-wish allies itself with them, acting as the most effective reinforcement of them.

We now have to consider the further vicissitudes undergone by this wish-impulse, which essentially represents an unconscious instinctual demand and in the Pcs has taken on the guise of a dream-wish, a wish-fulfilling phantasy. Reflection tells us that this wish-impulse may be dealt with in three different ways. It may be the way that would be normal in waking life, by penetrating from the Pcs into consciousness; or it may circumvent the Cs and find direct motor discharge; or it may take the unsuspected way that observation nevertheless leads us to follow up. In the first case, it would become a *delusion* having as content the fulfilment of the wish; but in sleep this never happens. (With our scanty knowledge of the metapsychological conditions of mental processes, we may perhaps see in this fact a hint that complete absence of cathexes in a system renders it less susceptible to stimulation.) The second case, that of direct motor discharge, should be excluded by the same principle, for access to motility is normally yet a step further off from the censorship of consciousness; but we do meet with exceptional instances of this sort in the form of somnambulism. We do not know what conditions this phenomenon, or why it is not of more frequent occurrence. What actually happens in dream-formation constitutes a very remarkable and quite unforeseen solution. The process begun in the Pcs and reinforced by the Ucs pursues a retrogressive course, through the Ucs, to perception, which forces itself upon consciousness. This *regression* is the third phase of dream-formation. To realize the whole process, let us recapitulate the two former phases: reinforcement of the preconscious day-residues by the Ucs—activation of the dream-wish.

We call this kind of regression a *topographical* one, to distinguish it from the previously mentioned temporal or developmental regression. The two do not necessarily always coincide, but they do so in the particular example before us. The reversion in its course of the excitation from the Pcs through the Ucs to perception is at the same time a return to the primitive level of hallucinatory wish-fulfilment.

We have already, in the *Traumdeutung*, described the way in which the regression of the preconscious day-residues proceeds in dream-formation. In this process thoughts are transformed into images, mainly visual; that is to say, verbal ideas are reduced to the ideas of the corresponding things, on the whole as if the process were controlled by considerations of *suitability for plastic representation*. When regression is complete, there remains a series of cathexes in the system Ucs, cathexes of the memory-traces of things, upon which the primary mental process works till, by means of condensation of them and displacement of their respective cathexes, it has shaped the manifest dream-content. Only where the verbal ideas in the day-residues are recent, actual fragments of perceptions, and not the expression of thoughts, are they treated like concrete ideas, becoming subject to the influence of condensation and displacement. Hence the rule laid down in the *Traumdeutung*, and since confirmed beyond all doubt, that words and speeches in the dream-content are not new formations, but are imitated from speeches from the day preceding the dream (or from other recent impressions, such as from something read). It is very remarkable how little the dream-work adheres to verbal ideas; it is always ready to exchange one word for another till it finds the expression most favourable for plastic representation.[2]

Now it is in this respect that the essential difference between the dream-work and schizophrenia becomes clear. In the latter, the actual language in which the preconscious thought was expressed becomes the subject of elaboration by the primary process; in dreams, it is not the words, but the concrete ideas into which the words have been resolved. A topographical regression takes place in dreams, but not in schizophrenia; in dreams there is free communication between (pcs) word-cathexes and (ucs) thing-cathexes, while it is characteristic of schizophrenia that this communication is cut off. The impression this difference makes on one is lessened precisely by the dream-interpretations we essay in psychoanalytic practice. For as the work of interpretation traces the course taken by the dream-work, follows the paths which lead from the latent thoughts to the dream-elements, exhausts the possible meanings of verbal ambiguities and points out the words that act as bridges between different groups of material, we receive an impression now of a joke,

---

[2] I also ascribe to the consideration of suitability for plastic representation the fact (which is insisted on and perhaps over-estimated by Silberer) that some dreams admit of two simultaneous, and yet essentially different, interpretations, one of which he calls the analytic and the other the "anagogic." When this happens, we are invariably concerned with thoughts of a very abstract nature which must have made representation in the dream very difficult. We might compare the task of representing pictorially a leading article in a political paper. In such cases, the dream-work must first replace the text of abstract thought by one more concrete, connected with the former in some way—by comparison, symbolism, allegorical allusion, or, best of all, genetically—so that the more concrete text then becomes material for the dream-work instead of the abstract. The abstract thoughts yield the so-called anagogic interpretation, which, when we unravel the meaning of the dream, we discover more easily than the true analytic one. Otto Rank has justly remarked that certain dreams of patients undergoing analytic treatment are the best models of these dreams with more than one interpretation.

now of schizophrenia, and are apt to forget that for a dream all operations with words are merely preparatory to regression to concrete ideas.

The dream-process is completed by the thought-content (transformed by regression and worked over into a wish-phantasy) entering consciousness as a sense-perception, undergoing, as it does so, the secondary elaboration to which every perceptual content is subject. We say that the dream-wish is converted into an *hallucination* and as such commands belief in the reality of its fulfilment. It is just round this concluding piece of dream-formation that the gravest uncertainties centre, to explain which we have set out to compare with dreams the pathological states allied to them.

The formation of the wish-phantasy and its regression to hallucination are the most essential parts of the dream-work, but they do not belong exclusively to dreams. On the contrary, they are found similarly in two morbid states: in acute hallucinatory confusion (Meynert's "amentia"), and in the hallucinatory phase of schizophrenia. The hallucinatory delirium of amentia is a clearly recognizable wish-phantasy, often perfectly framed like a beautiful day-dream. One might speak in quite general terms of an *hallucinatory wish-psychosis*, ascribing it equally to dreams and to amentia. There are dreams, too, which consist of nothing but undistorted wish-phantasies, very rich in content. The hallucinatory phase of schizophrenia has been less thoroughly studied; it seems generally to be of a composite nature, but in its essence it might well correspond to a fresh attempt at restitution, designed to restore to the ideas of objects their libidinal cathexis.[3] I cannot extend the comparison to the other hallucinatory states in various pathological affections, because in their case I neither have experience of my own upon which to draw, nor can I utilize that of others.

Let us be clear that the hallucinatory wish-psychosis—in dreams or elsewhere—performs two by no means identical functions. Not only does it bring into consciousness hidden or repressed wishes, but it also represents them as fulfilled, and

---

[3] We met with the first attempt of this sort—the hyper-cathexis of verbal ideas—in the paper on "The Unconscious." See p. 135.

that in such a way as to command entire belief. It is important to understand this conjunction. It by no means necessarily follows that unconscious wishes must be regarded as realities when once they have entered consciousness; for, as we know, our judgement is very well able to distinguish realities from ideas and wishes, however intense. On the other hand, it seems justifiable to assume that belief in reality is bound up with sense-perception. When once a thought has succeeded in regressing as far as to the unconscious memory-traces of objects and thence to perception, that perception presents itself to us as real. So hallucination brings belief in reality with it. We now have to ask what conditions the forming of an hallucination. The first answer would be regression, and this would replace the question concerning the formation of hallucinations by one concerning the mechanism of regression. We do not need to wait long for an answer to this latter question where dreams are concerned. The regression of the preconscious dream-thoughts to the memory-pictures of things is clearly the result of the attraction exercised by these unconscious instinct-presentations—*e.g.* repressed recollections of experiences—upon the thoughts expressed in words. Only we soon perceive that we are on a false scent. If the secret of hallucination is nothing else than that of regression, every regression of sufficient intensity would produce an hallucination with belief in its reality. But we are quite familiar with situations in which a process of regressive reflection brings to consciousness very clear visual memory-pictures, though we do not on that account for a single moment take them for actual perceptions. Again, we could very well imagine cases in which the dream-work penetrated to such memory-pictures, made conscious what was previously unconscious, and mirrored to us a wish-phantasy which roused our longing but would not present itself to us as the actual fulfilment of the wish. Hallucination must therefore be something more than the regressive revival of memory-images in themselves unconscious.

Let us, moreover, bear in mind the great practical importance there is in the capacity to distinguish perceptions from mental images, however intensively recalled. Our whole attitude to the outer world, to reality, depends on this capacity so to distinguish. We have posited that this capacity did not always exist, and that at the beginning of our mental life we really hallucinated the satisfying object when we felt the need of it. But even so, satisfaction remained lacking, and this failure must very soon have moved us to create some "faculty" to help us to distinguish such a wish-perception from an actual fulfilment and to avoid it for the future. In other words, we gave up hallucinatory gratification of our wishes at a very early period and established a kind of *"testing"* of reality. The question now arises in what this testing of reality consisted, and how the hallucinatory wish-psychosis of dreams and amentia, and such conditions, succeeds in abolishing it and in re-establishing the old mode of gratification.

The answer suggests itself if we now proceed to define somewhat more precisely the third of our mental systems, the system Cs, which hitherto we have not sharply distinguished from Pcs. Already in *Die Traumdeutung* it became necessary to decide upon regarding conscious perception as the function of a special system, to which we have ascribed certain remarkable properties and shall be justified in attributing other characteristics as well. This system, there called Pcpt (perception), we now identify with the system Cs, upon which normally the operation of becoming conscious depends. But the fact of something becoming conscious is still not wholly identical with that of its belonging to a particular system, for we have learnt that sensorial memory-pictures can be observed to which we could not possibly accord a mental location in the systems Cs or Pcpt.

However, we must put off discussing this difficulty till we can focus our interest upon the system Cs itself. In the present connection we may be allowed to assume that hallucination consists in a cathexis of the system Cs (Pcpt), which, however, does not proceed—as normally—from without, but from within, the condition being that regression shall be carried far enough to reach this system itself and thus to pass beyond the testing of reality.[4]

---

[4] To supplement the above, I will add that any attempt to explain hallucination would have to be made from the starting-point of a *negative* hallucination, rather than of a positive one.

In an earlier passage[5] we claimed that the still helpless organism had the capacity for making a first orientation in the world by means of its perceptions, distinguishing both "outer" and "inner" according to their relation to actions of the muscles. A perception which is made to disappear by motor activity is recognized as external, as reality; where such activity makes no difference, the perception originates within the subject's own body—it is not real. To be thus able not only to recognize, but at the same time to rid himself of, reality is of great value to the individual, and he would wish to be equipped with a similar weapon against the often merciless claims of his instincts. That is why he takes such pains to *project, i.e.* to transfer outwards, all that becomes troublesome to him from within.

This function of orientating the individual in the world by discrimination between inner and outer must now, after detailed dissection of the mental apparatus, be ascribed to the system Cs (Pcpt) alone. Cs must have at its command motor innervation which determines whether the perception can be made to disappear or whether it proves persistent. The capacity for testing reality need be nothing more than this function.[6] We can say nothing more precise on this point, for we know as yet too little of the nature and mode of operation of the system Cs. We shall place the testing of reality, as one of the great *institutions of the ego,* alongside the *censorships* which we have come to recognize between the psychic systems, and we shall expect that analysis of the narcissistic affections will help to reveal other similar institutions.

On the other hand, we can already learn from pathology how the testing of reality may be abolished or put out of action; this will be clearer in the wish-psychosis, amentia, than in dreams. Amentia is the reaction to a loss which reality affirms, but which the ego tries to deny, since it finds it insupportable. Thereupon the ego breaks off its relation to reality; it withdraws the cathexis from the perceptual system Cs—or perhaps better, one cathexis, the peculiar nature of which may be the subject of further inquiry. With this turning

[5] See "Instincts and their Vicissitudes," p. 84.
[6] Cf. a later passage on the distinction between the testing of reality and of actuality.

away from reality the testing of reality is done away with, the (unrepressed, completely conscious) wish-phantasies can penetrate into consciousness and thence be regarded as a more desirable reality. Such a withdrawal may be co-ordinated with the processes of repression; amentia presents the interesting spectacle of a breach between the ego and one of its organs which had perhaps served it most faithfully and was most closely related to it.[7]

The function performed by this "aversion" in amentia is performed in dreams by voluntary renunciation. Sleep desires to know nothing of the outer world, nor is it interested in reality, or only so far as abandoning the state of sleep—waking up—comes into account. Hence sleep withdraws cathexes from the system Cs as well as from the other systems, Pcs and Ucs, in so far as the libido-positions contained in them obey the sleep-wish. When the system Cs is thus devoid of cathexis, the possibility of a testing of reality is abandoned; and those excitations which have, independently of the state of sleep, entered on the path of regression will find it clear as far as the system Cs, where they will count as undisputed reality.[8] Where the hallucinatory psychosis of dementia praecox is concerned, we shall infer from our discussion that hallucination cannot be amongst the initial symptoms of the affection. It becomes possible only when the patient's ego is so far disintegrated that the testing of reality no longer stands in the way of it.

To our psychology of dream-processes we contribute this conclusion: that all essential characteristics of dreams are

[7] At this point we may venture to suggest that the toxic hallucinations, too, e.g. alcoholic delirium, are to be understood in analogous fashion. The unbearable loss imposed by reality would be just that of alcohol. If the latter is supplied, the hallucinations cease.

[8] The principle of the insusceptibility to excitation of uncathected systems here appears to be invalidated in the case of the system Cs (Pcpt). But it can be a question only of the partial abolition of cathexis, and particularly for this perceptual system we must assume many conditions of excitation, very different from those of other systems.—Of course we should not attempt to disguise or gloss over the uncertain and tentative character of these metapsychological discussions. Only deeper investigation can lead to a certain degree of probability being attained.

determined by the factor which conditions sleep. Aristotle of old is altogether right in his modest pronouncement that dreams are the mental activity of the sleeper. We might complete his statement by saying: they are remnants of mental activity made possible by the imperfect extent to which the narcissistic state of sleep has been achieved. This does not sound very different from what psychologists and philosophers have always said, but it is based on views concerning the structure and function of the mental apparatus that diverge entirely from the earlier ones and have this advantage over them—that they have enabled us also to approach an understanding of all the details of dreams.

Finally, let us once more glance at the significance the *topography* of the process of repression has for our insight into the mechanism of mental disturbances. In dreams the withdrawal of cathexis (libido, interest) affects all systems equally; in the transference neuroses, the preconscious cathexis is withdrawn; in schizophrenia, that of the Ucs; in amentia, that of the Cs.

VIII

Mourning and Melancholia[1] (1917)

NOW THAT DREAMS have proved of service to us as the normal prototypes of narcissistic mental disorders, we propose to try whether a comparison with the normal emotion of grief, and its expression in mourning, will not throw some light on the nature of melancholia. This time, however, we must make a certain prefatory warning against too great expectations of the result. Even in descriptive psychiatry the definition of melancholia is uncertain; it takes on various clinical forms (some of them suggesting somatic rather than psychogenic affections) that do not seem definitely to warrant reduction to a unity. Apart from those impressions which every observer may gather, our material here is limited to a small number of cases the psychogenic nature of which was indisputable. Any claim to general validity for our conclusions shall be forgone at the outset, therefore, and we will console ourselves by reflecting that, with the means of investigation at our disposal to-day, we could hardly discover anything that was not typical, at least of a small group if not of a whole class of disorders.

A correlation of melancholia and mourning seems justified by the general picture of the two conditions.[2] Moreover, wherever it is possible to discern the external influences in life which have brought each of them about, this exciting cause proves to be the same in both. Mourning is regularly the reaction to the loss of a loved person, or to the loss of some abstraction which has taken the place of one, such as fatherland, liberty, an ideal, and so on. As an effect of the same influences, melancholia instead of a state of grief develops in some people, whom we consequently suspect of a morbid pathological disposition. It is also well worth notice that, al-

[1] First published in Zeitschrift, Bd. IV., 1916–18; reprinted in Sammlung, Vierte Folge. [Translated by Joan Riviere.]

[2] Abraham, to whom we owe the most important of the few analytic studies on this subject, also took this comparison as his starting-point. (Zentralblatt, Bd. II., 1912.)

though grief involves grave departures from the normal attitude to life, it never occurs to us to regard it as a morbid condition and hand the mourner over to medical treatment. We rest assured that after a lapse of time it will be overcome, and we look upon any interference with it as inadvisable or even harmful.

The distinguishing mental features of melancholia are a profoundly painful dejection, abrogation of interest in the outside world, loss of the capacity to love, inhibition of all activity, and a lowering of the self-regarding feelings to a degree that finds utterance in self-reproaches and self-revilings, and culminates in a delusional expectation of punishment. This picture becomes a little more intelligible when we consider that, with one exception, the same traits are met with in grief. The fall in self-esteem is absent in grief; but otherwise the features are the same. Profound mourning, the reaction to the loss of a loved person, contains the same feeling of pain, loss of interest in the outside world—in so far as it does not recall the dead one—loss of capacity to adopt any new object of love, which would mean a replacing of the one mourned, the same turning from every active effort that is not connected with thoughts of the dead. It is easy to see that this inhibition and circumscription in the ego is the expression of an exclusive devotion to its mourning, which leaves nothing over for other purposes or other interests. It is really only because we know so well how to explain it that this attitude does not seem to us pathological.

We should regard it as a just comparison, too, to call the temper of grief "painful." The justification for this comparison will probably prove illuminating when we are in a position to define pain in terms of the economics of the mind.[8]

Now in what consists the work which mourning performs? I do not think there is anything far-fetched in the following representation of it. The testing of reality, having shown that the loved object no longer exists, requires forthwith that all the libido shall be withdrawn from its attachments to this

[8] [The words "painful" and "pain" in this paragraph represent the German *Schmerz* (*i.e.* the ordinary connotation of *pain* in English) and not *Unlust*, the mental antithesis of pleasure, also technically translated "pain."—*Trans.*]

object. Against this demand a struggle of course arises—it may be universally observed that man never willingly abandons a libido-position, not even when a substitute is already beckoning to him. This struggle can be so intense that a turning away from reality ensues, the object being clung to through the medium of a hallucinatory wish-psychosis.[4] The normal outcome is that deference for reality gains the day. Nevertheless its behest cannot be at once obeyed. The task is now carried through bit by bit, under great expense of time and cathectic energy, while all the time the existence of the lost object is continued in the mind. Each single one of the memories and hopes which bound the libido to the object is brought up and hyper-cathected, and the detachment of the libido from it accomplished. Why this process of carrying out the behest of reality bit by bit, which is in the nature of a compromise, should be so extraordinarily painful is not at all easy to explain in terms of mental economics. It is worth noting that this pain[5] seems natural to us. The fact is, however, that when the work of mourning is completed the ego becomes free and uninhibited again.

Now let us apply to melancholia what we have learnt about grief. In one class of cases it is evident that melancholia too may be the reaction to the loss of a loved object; where this is not the exciting cause one can perceive that there is a loss of a more ideal kind. The object has not perhaps actually died, but has become lost as an object of love (*e.g.* the case of a deserted bride). In yet other cases one feels justified in concluding that a loss of the kind has been experienced, but one cannot see clearly what has been lost, and may the more readily suppose that the patient too cannot consciously perceive what it is he has lost. This, indeed, might be so even when the patient was aware of the loss giving rise to the melancholia, that is, when he knows whom he has lost but not *what* it is he has lost in them. This would suggest that melancholia is in some way related to an unconscious loss of a love-object, in contradistinction to mourning, in which there is nothing unconscious about the loss.

[4] Cf. the preceding paper.
[5] [Cf. footnote three. The German here is *Schmerz-unlust*, a combination of the two words for *pain*.—Trans.]

loss of interest was fully accounted for by the absorbing work of mourning. The unknown loss in melancholia would also result in an inner labour of the same kind and hence would be responsible for the melancholic inhibition. Only, the inhibition of the melancholiac seems puzzling to us because we cannot see what it is that absorbs him so entirely. Now the melancholiac displays something else which is lacking in grief —an extraordinary fall in his self-esteem, an impoverishment of his ego on a grand scale. In grief the world becomes poor and empty; in melancholia it is the ego itself. The patient represents his ego to us as worthless, incapable of any effort and morally despicable; he reproaches himself, vilifies himself and expects to be cast out and chastised. He abases himself before everyone and commiserates his own relatives for being connected with someone so unworthy. He does not realize that any change has taken place in him, but extends his self-criticism back over the past and declares that he was never any better. This picture of delusional belittling—which is predominantly moral—is completed by sleeplessness and refusal of nourishment, and by an overthrow, psychologically very remarkable, of that instinct which constrains every living thing to cling to life.

Both scientifically and therapeutically it would be fruitless to contradict the patient who brings these accusations against himself. He must surely be right in some way and be describing something that corresponds to what he thinks. Some of his statements, indeed, we are at once obliged to confirm without reservation. He really is as lacking in interest, as incapable of love and of any achievement as he says. But that, as we know, is secondary, the effect of the inner travail consuming his ego, of which we know nothing but which we compare with the work of mourning. In certain other self-accusations he also seems to us justified, only that he has a keener eye for the truth than others who are not melancholic. When in his exacerbation of self-criticism he describes himself as petty, egoistic, dishonest, lacking in independence, one whose sole aim has been to hide the weaknesses of his own nature, for all we know it may be that he has come very near to self-knowledge; we only wonder why a man must become ill before he can discover truth of this kind. For there can be no doubt that whoever holds and expresses to others such an opinion of himself—one that Hamlet harboured of himself and all men[6]—that man is ill, whether he speaks the truth or is more or less unfair to himself. Nor is it difficult to see that there is no correspondence, so far as we can judge, between the degree of self-abasement and its real justification. A good, capable, conscientious woman will speak no better of herself after she develops melancholia than one who is actually worthless; indeed, the first is more likely to fall ill of the disease than the other, of whom we too should have nothing good to say. Finally, it must strike us that after all the melancholiac's behaviour is not in every way the same as that of one who is normally devoured by remorse and self-reproach. Shame before others, which would characterize this condition above everything, is lacking in him, or at least there is little sign of it. One could almost say that the opposite trait of insistent talking about himself and pleasure in the consequent exposure of himself predominates in the melancholiac.

The essential thing, therefore, is not whether the melancholiac's distressing self-abasement is justified in the opinion of others. The point must be rather that he is correctly describing his psychological situation in his lamentations. He has lost his self-respect and must have some good reason for having done so. It is true that we are then faced with a contradiction which presents a very difficult problem. From the analogy with grief we should have to conclude that the loss suffered by the melancholiac is that of an object; according to what he says the loss is one in himself.

Before going into this contradiction, let us dwell for a moment on the view melancholia affords of the constitution of the ego. We see how in this condition one part of the ego sets itself over against the other, judges it critically, and, as it were, looks upon it as an object. Our suspicion that the critical institution in the mind which is here split off from the ego might also demonstrate its independence in other circumstances will be confirmed by all further observations. We shall really find justification for distinguishing this institution from

[6] "Use every man after his desert, and who should 'scape whipping?" (Act II. Sc. 2).

the rest of the ego. It is the mental faculty commonly called conscience that we are thus recognizing; we shall count it, along with the censorship of consciousness and the testing of reality, among the great institutions of the ego and shall also find evidence elsewhere showing that it can become diseased independently. In the clinical picture of melancholia dissatisfaction with the self on moral grounds is far the most outstanding feature; the self-criticism much less frequently concerns itself with bodily infirmity, ugliness, weakness, social inferiority; among these latter ills that the patient dreads or asseverates the thought of poverty alone has a favoured position.

There is one observation, not at all difficult to make, which supplies an explanation of the contradiction mentioned above. If one listens patiently to the many and various self-accusations of the melancholiac, one cannot in the end avoid the impression that often the most violent of them are hardly at all applicable to the patient himself, but that with insignificant modifications they do fit someone else, some person whom the patient loves, has loved or ought to love. This conjecture is confirmed every time one examines the facts. So we get the key to the clinical picture—by perceiving that the self-reproaches are reproaches against a loved object which have been shifted on to the patient's own ego.

The woman who loudly pities her husband for being bound to such a poor creature as herself is really accusing her husband of being a poor creature in some sense or other. There is no need to be greatly surprised that among those transferred from him some genuine self-reproaches are mingled: they are allowed to obtrude themselves since they help to mask the others and make recognition of the true state of affairs impossible; indeed, they derive from the "for" and "against" contained in the conflict that has led to the loss of the loved object. The behaviour of the patients too becomes now much more comprehensible. Their complaints are really "plaints" in the legal sense of the word; it is because everything derogatory that they say of themselves at bottom relates to someone else that they are not ashamed and do not hide their heads. Moreover, they are far from evincing towards those around them the attitude of humility and submission that alone would befit such worthless persons; on the contrary, they give a great deal of trouble, perpetually taking offence and behaving as if they had been treated with great injustice. All this is possible only because the reactions expressed in their behaviour still proceed from an attitude of revolt, a mental constellation which by a certain process has become transformed into melancholic contrition.

Once this is recognized there is no difficulty in reconstructing this process. First there existed an object-choice, the libido had attached itself to a certain person; then, owing to a real injury or disappointment concerned with the loved person, this object-relationship was undermined. The result was not the normal one of withdrawal of the libido from this object and transference of it to a new one, but something different for which various conditions seem to be necessary. The object-cathexis proved to have little power of resistance, and was abandoned; but the free libido was withdrawn into the ego and not directed to another object. It did not find application there, however, in any one of several possible ways, but served simply to establish an *identification* of the ego with the abandoned object. Thus the shadow of the object fell upon the ego, so that the latter could henceforth be criticized by a special mental faculty like an object, like the forsaken object. In this way the loss of the object became transformed into a loss in the ego, and the conflict between the ego and the loved person transformed into a cleavage between the criticizing faculty of the ego and the ego as altered by the identification.

Certain things may be directly inferred with regard to the necessary conditions and effects of such a process. On the one hand, a strong fixation to the love-object must have been present; on the other hand, in contradiction to this, the object-cathexis can have had little power of resistance. As Otto Rank has aptly remarked, this contradiction seems to imply that the object-choice had been effected on a narcissistic basis, so that when obstacles arise in the way of the object-cathexis it can regress into narcissism. The narcissistic identification with the object then becomes a substitute for the erotic cathexis, the result of which is that in spite of the conflict with the loved person the love-relation need not be given up. This kind of substitution of identification for object-love is an important mechanism in the narcissistic affections; Karl Landauer has lately been able to point to it in the process of recovery in schizophrenia.[7] It of course represents a regression from one type of object-choice to the primal narcissism. We have elsewhere described how object-choice develops from a preliminary stage of identification, the way in which the ego first adopts an object and the ambivalence in which this is expressed. The ego wishes to incorporate this object into itself, and the method by which it would do so, in this oral or cannibalistic stage, is by devouring it. Abraham is undoubtedly right in referring to this connection the refusal of nourishment met with in severe forms of melancholia.

The conclusion which our theory would require, namely, that the disposition to succumb to melancholia—or some part of it—lies in the narcissistic type of object-choice, unfortunately still lacks confirmation by investigation. In the opening remarks of this paper I admitted that the empirical material upon which this study is founded does not supply all we could wish. On the assumption that the results of observation would accord with our inferences, we should not hesitate to include among the special characteristics of melancholia a regression from object-cathexis to the still narcissistic oral phase of the libido. Identifications with the object are by no means rare in the transference-neuroses too; indeed, they are a well-known mechanism in symptom-formation, especially in hysteria. The difference, however, between narcissistic and hysterical identification may be perceived in the object-cathexis, which in the first is relinquished, whereas in the latter it persists and exercises an influence, usually confined to certain isolated actions and innervations. Nevertheless, even in the transference-neuroses identification is the expression of a community which may signify love. The narcissistic identification is the older, and it paves the way to comprehension of the hysterical form, which has been less thoroughly studied.

Some of the features of melancholia, therefore, are borrowed from grief, and the others from the process of regression from narcissistic object-choice to narcissism. On the one hand, like mourning, melancholia is the reaction to a real loss of a loved object; but, over and above this, it is bound to a condition which is absent in normal grief or which, if it supervenes, transforms the latter into a pathological variety. The loss of a love-object constitutes an excellent opportunity for the ambivalence in love-relationships to make itself felt and come to the fore. Consequently where there is a disposition to obsessional neurosis the conflict of ambivalence casts a pathological shade on the grief, forcing it to express itself in the form of self-reproaches, to the effect that the mourner himself is to blame for the loss of the loved one, *i.e.* desired it. These obsessional states of depression following upon the death of loved persons show us what the conflict of ambivalence by itself can achieve, when there is no regressive withdrawal of libido as well. The occasions giving rise to melancholia for the most part extend beyond the clear case of a loss by death, and include all those situations of being wounded, hurt, neglected, out of favour, or disappointed, which can import opposite feelings of love and hate into the relationship or reinforce an already existing ambivalence. This conflict of ambivalence, the origin of which lies now more in actual experience, now more in constitution, must not be neglected among the conditioning factors in melancholia. If the object-love, which cannot be given up, takes refuge in narcissistic identification, while the object itself is abandoned, then hate is expended upon this new substitute-object, railing at it, depreciating it, making it suffer and deriving sadistic gratification from its suffering. The self-torments of melancholiacs, which are without doubt pleasurable, signify, just like the corresponding phenomenon in the obsessional neurosis, a gratification of sadistic tendencies and of hate,[8] both of which relate to an object and in this way have both been turned round upon the self. In both disorders the sufferers usually succeed in the end in taking revenge, by the circuitous path of self-punishment, on the original objects and in tormenting them by means of the illness, having developed the latter so as to avoid the necessity of openly expressing their hostility against the loved ones. After all, the person who has occasioned the injury to the patient's feelings, and against whom his illness is aimed, is

---

[8] For the distinction between the two, see the paper entitled "Instincts and their Vicissitudes," p. 93.

usually to be found among those in his near neighbourhood. The melancholiac's erotic cathexis of his object thus undergoes a twofold fate: part of it regresses to identification, but the other part, under the influence of the conflict of ambivalence, is reduced to the stage of sadism, which is nearer to this conflict.

It is this sadism, and only this, that solves the riddle of the tendency to suicide which makes melancholia so interesting—and so dangerous. As the primal condition from which instinct-life proceeds we have come to recognize a self-love of the ego which is so immense, in the fear that rises up at the menace of death we see liberated a volume of narcissistic libido which is so vast, that we cannot conceive how this ego can connive at its own destruction. It is true we have long known that no neurotic harbours thoughts of suicide which are not murderous impulses against others re-directed upon himself, but we have never been able to explain what interplay of forces could carry such a purpose through to execution. Now the analysis of melancholia shows that the ego can kill itself only when, the object-cathexis having been withdrawn upon it, it can treat itself as an object, when it is able to launch against itself the animosity relating to an object—that primordial reaction on the part of the ego to all objects in the outer world.[9] Thus in the regression from narcissistic object-choice the object is indeed abolished, but in spite of all it proves itself stronger than the ego's self. In the two contrasting situations of intense love and of suicide the ego is overwhelmed by the object, though in totally different ways.

We may expect to find the derivation of that one striking feature of melancholia, the manifestations of dread of poverty, in anal erotism, torn out of its context and altered by regression.

Melancholia confronts us with yet other problems, the answer to which in part eludes us. The way in which it passes off after a certain time has elapsed without leaving traces of any gross change is a feature it shares with grief. It appeared that in grief this period of time is necessary for detailed carrying out of the behest imposed by the testing of reality, and

[9] Cf. "Instincts and their Vicissitudes," p. 86.

that by accomplishing this labour the ego succeeds in freeing its libido from the lost object. We may imagine that the ego is occupied with some analogous task during the course of a melancholia; in neither case have we any insight into the economic processes going forward. The sleeplessness characteristic of melancholia evidently testifies to the inflexibility of the condition, the impossibility of effecting the general withdrawal of cathexes necessary for sleep. The complex of melancholia behaves like an open wound, drawing to itself cathectic energy from all sides (which we have called in the transference-neuroses "anti-cathexes") and draining the ego until it is utterly depleted; it proves easily able to withstand the ego's wish to sleep. The amelioration in the condition that is regularly noticeable towards evening is probably due to a somatic factor and not explicable psychologically. These questions link up with the further one, whether a loss in the ego apart from any object (a purely narcissistic wound to the ego) would suffice to produce the clinical picture of melancholia and whether an impoverishment of ego-libido directly due to toxins would not result in certain forms of the disease.

The most remarkable peculiarity of melancholia, and one most in need of explanation, is the tendency it displays to turn into mania accompanied by a completely opposite symptomatology. Not every melancholia has this fate, as we know. Many cases run their course in intermittent periods, in the intervals of which signs of mania may be entirely absent or only very slight. Others show that regular alternation of melancholic and manic phases which has been classified as circular insanity. One would be tempted to exclude these cases from among those of psychogenic origin, if the psychoanalytic method had not succeeded in effecting an explanation and therapeutic improvement of several cases of the kind. It is not merely permissible, therefore, but incumbent upon us to extend the analytic explanation of melancholia to mania.

I cannot promise that this attempt will prove entirely satisfying; it is much more in the nature of a first sounding and hardly goes beyond that. There are two points from which one may start: the first is a psychoanalytic point of view, and the second one may probably call a matter of general observation in mental economics. The psychoanalytic point is one which several analytic investigators have already formulated in so many words, namely, that the content of mania is no different from that of melancholia, that both the disorders are wrestling with the same "complex," and that in melancholia the ego has succumbed to it, whereas in mania it has mastered the complex or thrust it aside. The other point of view is founded on the observation that all states such as joy, triumph, exultation, which form the normal counterparts of mania, are economically conditioned in the same way. First, there is always a long-sustained condition of great mental expenditure, or one established by long force of habit, upon which at last some influence supervenes making it superfluous, so that a volume of energy becomes available for manifold possible applications and ways of discharge,—for instance, when some poor devil, by winning a large sum of money, is suddenly relieved from perpetual anxiety about his daily bread, when any long and arduous struggle is finally crowned with success, when a man finds himself in a position to throw off at one blow some heavy burden, some false position he has long endured, and so on. All such situations are characterized by high spirits, by the signs of discharge of joyful emotion, and by increased readiness to all kinds of action, just like mania, and in complete contrast to the dejection and inhibition of melancholia. One may venture to assert that mania is nothing other than a triumph of this sort, only that here again what the ego has surmounted and is triumphing over remains hidden from it. Alcoholic intoxication, which belongs to the same group of conditions, may be explained in the same way —in so far as it consists in a state of elation; here there is probably a relaxation produced by toxins of the expenditure of energy in repression. The popular view readily takes for granted that a person in a maniacal state finds such delight in movement and action because he is so "cheery." This piece of false logic must of course be exploded. What has happened is that the economic condition described above has been fulfilled, and this is the reason why the maniac is in such high spirits on the one hand and is so uninhibited in action on the other.

If we put together the two suggestions reached, we have the following result. When mania supervenes, the ego must have surmounted the loss of the object (or the mourning over the loss, or perhaps the object itself), whereupon the whole amount of anti-cathexis which the painful suffering of melancholia drew from the ego and "bound" has become available. Besides this, the maniac plainly shows us that he has become free from the object by whom his suffering was caused, for he runs after new object-cathexes like a starving man after bread.

This explanation certainly sounds plausible, but in the first place it is too indefinite, and, secondly, it gives rise to more new problems and doubts than we can answer. We will not evade a discussion of them, even though we cannot expect it to lead us to clear understanding.

First, then: in normal grief too the loss of the object is undoubtedly surmounted, and this process too absorbs all the energies of the ego while it lasts. Why then does it not set up the economic condition for a phase of triumph after it has run its course or at least produce some slight indication of such a state? I find it impossible to answer this objection off-hand. It reminds us again that we do not even know by what economic measures the work of mourning is carried through; possibly, however, a conjecture may help us here. Reality passes its verdict—that the object no longer exists— upon each single one of the memories and hopes through which the libido was attached to the lost object, and the ego, confronted as it were with the decision whether it will share this fate, is persuaded by the sum of its narcissistic satisfactions in being alive to sever its attachment to the non-existent object. We may imagine that, because of the slowness and the gradual way in which this severance is achieved, the expenditure of energy necessary for it becomes somehow dissipated by the time the task is carried through.[10]

It is tempting to essay a formulation of the work performed during melancholia on the lines of this conjecture concerning the work of mourning. Here we are met at the outset by an uncertainty. So far we have hardly considered the topographi-

[10] The economic point of view has up till now received little attention in psychoanalytic researches. I would mention as an exception a paper by Viktor Tausk, "Compensation as a Means of Discounting the Motive of Repression," *International Journal of Psycho-Analysis*, vol. v. (*Zeitschrift*, Bd. I., 1913.)

cal situation in melancholia, nor put the question in what systems or between what systems in the mind the work of melancholia goes on. How much of the mental processes of the disease is still occupied with the unconscious object-cathexes that have been given up and how much with their substitute, by identification, in the ego?

Now, it is easy to say and to write that "the unconscious (thing-)presentation of the object has been abandoned by the libido." In reality, however, this presentation is made up of innumerable single impressions (unconscious traces of them), so that this withdrawal of libido is not a process that can be accomplished in a moment, but must certainly be, like grief, one in which progress is slow and gradual. Whether it begins simultaneously at several points or follows some sort of definite sequence is not at all easy to decide; in analyses it often becomes evident that first one, then another memory is activated and that the laments which are perpetually the same and wearisome in their monotony nevertheless each time take their rise in some different unconscious source. If the object had not this great significance, strengthened by a thousand links, to the ego, the loss of it would be no meet cause for either mourning or melancholia. This character of withdrawing the libido bit by bit is therefore to be ascribed alike to mourning and to melancholia; it is probably sustained by the same economic arrangements and serves the same purposes in both.

As we have seen, however, there is more in the content of melancholia than in that of normal grief. In melancholia the relation to the object is no simple one; it is complicated by the conflict of ambivalence. This latter is either constitutional, *i.e.* it is an element of every love-relation formed by this particular ego, or else it proceeds from precisely those experiences that involved a threat of losing the object. For this reason the exciting causes of melancholia are of a much wider range than those of grief, which is for the most part occasioned only by a real loss of the object, by its death. In melancholia, that is, countless single conflicts in which love and hate wrestle together are fought for the object; the one seeks to detach the libido from the object, the other to uphold this libido-position against assault. These single conflicts cannot be located in any system but the Ucs, the region of memory-traces of things (as contrasted with word-cathexes). The efforts to detach the libido are made in this system also during mourning; but in the latter nothing hinders these processes from proceeding in the normal way through the Pcs to consciousness. For the work of melancholia this way is blocked, owing perhaps to a number of causes or to their combined operation. Constitutional ambivalence belongs by nature to what is repressed, while traumatic experiences with the object may have stirred to activity something else that has been repressed. Thus everything to do with these conflicts of ambivalence remains excluded from consciousness, until the outcome characteristic of melancholia sets in. This, as we know, consists in the libidinal cathexis that is being menaced at last abandoning the object, only, however, to resume its occupation of that place in the ego whence it came. So by taking flight into the ego love escapes annihilation. After this regression of the libido the process can become conscious; it appears in consciousness as a conflict between one part of the ego and its self-criticizing faculty.

That which consciousness is aware of in the work of melancholia is thus not the essential part of it, nor is it even the part which we may credit with an influence in bringing the suffering to an end. We see that the ego debases itself and rages against itself, and as little as the patient do we understand what this can lead to and how it can change. We can more readily credit such an achievement to the unconscious part of the work, because it is not difficult to perceive an essential analogy between the work performed in melancholia and in mourning. Just as the work of grief, by declaring the object to be dead and offering the ego the benefit of continuing to live, impels the ego to give up the object, so each single conflict of ambivalence, by disparaging the object, denigrating it, even as it were by slaying it, loosens the fixation of the libido to it. It is possible, therefore, for the process in the Ucs to come to an end, whether it be that the fury has spent itself or that the object is abandoned as no longer of value. We cannot tell which of these two possibilities is the regular or more usual one in bringing melancholia to an end, nor what influence this termination has on the future condition of the case.

The ego may enjoy here the satisfaction of acknowledging itself as the better of the two, as superior to the object.

Even if we accept this view of the work of melancholia, it still does not supply an explanation of the one point upon which we hoped for light. By analogy with various other situations we expected to discover in the ambivalence prevailing in melancholia the economic condition for the appearance of mania when the melancholia has run its course. But there is one fact to which our expectations must bow. Of the three conditioning factors in melancholia—loss of the object, ambivalence, and regression of libido into the ego—the first two are found also in the obsessional reproaches arising after the death of loved persons. In these it is indubitably the ambivalence that motivates the conflict, and observation shows that after it has run its course nothing in the nature of a triumph or a manic state of mind is left. We are thus directed to the third factor as the only one that can have this effect. That accumulation of cathexis which is first of all "bound" and then, after termination of the work of melancholia, becomes free and makes mania possible must be connected with the regression of the libido into narcissism. The conflict in the ego, which in melancholia is substituted for the struggle surging round the object, must act like a painful wound which calls out unusually strong anti-cathexes. Here again, however, it will be well to call a halt and postpone further investigations into mania until we have gained some insight into the economic conditions, first, of bodily pain, and then of the mental pain[11] which is its analogue. For we know already that, owing to the interdependence of the complicated problems of the mind, we are forced to break off every investigation at some point until such time as the results of another attempt elsewhere can come to its aid.[12]

[11] [Schmerz.]
[12] Additional Note, 1924. Cf. the continued discussion of this problem in Group Psychology and the Analysis of the Ego.

IX

The Libido Theory (1923)

LIBIDO IS A TERM used in the theory of the instincts for describing the dynamic manifestation of sexuality. It was already used in this sense by Moll (1898) and was introduced into psychoanalysis by the present writer. What follows is limited to a description of the developments which the theory of the instincts has passed through in psychoanalysis—developments which are still proceeding.

Contrast between Sexual Instincts and Ego Instincts.— Psychoanalysis early became aware that all mental occurrences must be regarded as built upon a basis of the interplay of the forces of the elementary instincts. This, however, led to a difficult predicament, since psychology included no theory of the instincts. No one could say what an instinct really was, the question was left entirely to individual caprice, and every psychologist was in the habit of postulating any instincts in any number that he chose. The first sphere of phenomena to be studied by psychoanalysis comprised what are known as the transference neuroses (hysteria and obsessional neurosis). It was found that their symptoms came about by sexual instinctual impulses being rejected (repressed) by the subject's personality (his ego) and then finding expression by circuitous paths through the unconscious. These facts could be met by drawing a contrast between the sexual instincts and ego instincts (*instincts of self-preservation*), which was in line with the popular saying that hunger and love are what make the world go round: libido was the manifestation of the force of love in the same sense as was hunger of the self-preservative instinct. The nature of the ego instincts remained for the time being undefined and, like all the other characteristics of the ego, inaccessible to analysis. There was no means of deciding whether, and if so what, qualitative differences were to be assumed to exist between the two classes of instincts.

Primal Libido.—C. G. Jung attempted to resolve this obscurity along speculative lines by assuming that there was only a single primal libido which could be either sexualized or desexualized and which therefore coincided in its essence with mental energy in general. This innovation was methodologically disputable, caused a great deal of confusion, reduced the term "libido" to the level of a superfluous synonym and was still confronted in practice with the necessity for distinguishing between sexual and asexual libido. The difference between the sexual instincts and instincts with other aims was not to be got rid of by means of a new definition.

Sublimation.—An attentive examination of the sexual impulses, which were accessible only to psychoanalysis, had meanwhile led to some remarkable detailed findings. What is described as the sexual instinct turns out to be of a highly composite nature and is liable to disintegrate once more into its component instincts. Each component instinct is unalterably characterized by its *source*, that is, by the region or zone of the body from which its excitation is derived. Each has furthermore as distinguishable features an *object* and an *aim*. The aim is always discharge accompanied by satisfaction, but it is capable of being changed from activity to passivity. The object is less closely attached to the instinct than was at first supposed; it is easily exchanged for another one, and moreover, an instinct which had an external object can be turned round upon the subject's own self. The separate instincts can either remain independent of one another or—in what is still an inexplicable manner—can be combined and merged into one another to perform work in common. They are also able to replace one another and to transfer their libidinal cathexis to one another, so that the satisfaction of one instinct can take the place of the satisfaction of others. The most important vicissitude which an instinct can undergo seems to be *sublimation;* here both object and aim are changed, so that what was originally a sexual instinct finds satisfaction in some achievement which is no longer sexual but has a higher social or ethical valuation. These different features do not as yet combine to form an integral picture.

Narcissism.—A decisive advance was made when the analysis of dementia praecox and other psychotic disorders was ventured upon and thus the examination of the ego itself was begun, which had so far been known only as the agency of repression and opposition. It was found that the pathogenic process in dementia praecox is the withdrawal of the libido from objects and its introduction into the ego, while the clamorous symptoms of the disease arise from the vain struggles of the libido to find a pathway back to objects. It thus turned out to be possible for object-libido to change into cathexis of the ego and *vice versa*. Further reflection showed that this process must be presumed to occur on the largest scale and that the ego is to be regarded as a great reservoir of libido from which libido is sent out *to* objects and which is always ready to absorb libido flowing back *from* objects. Thus the instincts of self-preservation were also of a libidinal nature: they were sexual instincts which, instead of external objects, had taken the subject's own ego as an object. Clinical experience had made us familiar with people who behaved in a striking fashion as though they were in love with themselves and this perversion had been given the name of *narcissism*. The libido of the self-preservative instincts was now described as *narcissistic libido* and it was recognized that a high degree of this self-love constituted the primary and normal state of things. The earlier formula laid down for the transference neuroses consequently required to be modified, though not corrected. It was better, instead of speaking of a conflict between sexual instincts and ego instincts, to speak of a conflict between object-libido and ego-libido, or, since the nature of these instincts was the same, between the object-cathexes and the ego.

Apparent Approach to Jung's Views.—It thus seemed on the face of it as though the slow process of psychoanalytic research was following in the steps of Jung's speculation about a primal libido, especially because the transformation of object-libido into narcissism necessarily carries along with it a certain degree of desexualization, or abandonment of the specifically sexual aims. Nevertheless, it has to be borne in mind that the fact that the self-preservative instincts of the ego are recognized as libidinal does not necessarily prove that there are no other instincts operating in the ego.

The Herd Instinct.—It has been maintained in many quarters that there is a special innate and not further analysable "herd instinct," which determines the social behaviour of human beings and impels individuals to come together into larger communities. Psychoanalysis finds itself in contradiction to this view. Even if the social instinct is innate, it may without any difficulty be traced back to what were originally libidinal object-cathexes and may have developed in the childhood of the individual as a reaction-formation against hostile attitudes of rivalry. It is based upon a peculiar kind of identification with other people.

Aim-inhibited Sexual Impulses.—The social instincts belong to a class of instinctual impulses which need not be described as sublimated, though they are closely related to these. They have not abandoned their directly sexual aims, but they are held back by internal resistances from attaining them; they rest content with certain approximations to satisfaction and for that very reason lead to especially firm and permanent attachments between human beings. To this class belong in particular the affectionate relations between parents and children, which were originally fully sexual, feelings of friendship, and the emotional ties in marriage which had their origin in sexual attraction.

Recognition of Two Classes of Instincts in Mental Life.— Though psychoanalysis endeavours as a rule to develop its theories as independently as possible from those of other sciences, it is nevertheless obliged to seek a basis for the theory of the instincts in biology. On the ground of a far-reaching consideration of the processes which go to make up life and which lead to death, it becomes probable that we should recognize the existence of two classes of instincts, corresponding to the contrary processes of construction and dissolution in the organism. On this view, the one set of instincts, which work essentially in silence, would be those which follow the aim of leading the living creature to death and therefore deserve to be called the *"death instincts"*; these would be directed outwards as the result of the combination of numbers of unicellular elementary organisms, and would manifest themselves as *destructive* or *aggressive* impulses. The other set of instincts would be those which are better known to us in analysis, the libidinal, sexual or life instincts, which are best comprised under the name of *Eros*; their purpose would be to form living substance into ever greater unities, so that life may be prolonged and brought to higher development. The erotic instincts and the death instincts would be present in living beings in regular mixtures and fusions; but defusions would also be liable to occur. Life would consist in the manifestations of the conflict or interaction between the two classes of instincts; death would mean for the individual the victory of the destructive instincts but reproduction would mean for him the victory of Eros.

The Nature of the Instincts.—This view would enable us to characterize instincts as tendencies inherent in living substance towards restoring an earlier state of things: that is to say, they would be historically determined and of a conservative nature and, as it were, the expression of an inertia or elasticity present in what is organic. Both classes of instincts, Eros as well as the death instinct, would, on this view, have been in operation and working against each other from the first origin of life.

X

Neurosis and Psychosis[1] (1924)

IN MY BOOKLET *Das Ich und das Es,*[2] which appeared recently, I suggested that the mental apparatus should be subdivided in such a way as to allow of a series of relationships being represented in a simple and synoptic fashion. In other matters—for instance, concerning the origin and function of the super-ego—a good deal remained insufficiently elucidated. Now one may reasonably expect that a proposition of the kind should prove itself useful and helpful in other directions as well, even if it only enables us to see from another angle what we already know, to group it differently and to describe it more convincingly. By applying it in this way we might also reap the advantage of turning away from the greyness of theory back to the ever-green realm of observation.

The essay referred to describes the various allegiances the ego owes, its mediate position between the outer world and the *id*, and its struggles to serve all its masters at one and the same time. Now it so happened that a train of thought suggested elsewhere, which had to do with the causes giving rise to the psychoses and with prevention of them, furnished me with a simple formula concerning what is perhaps the most important genetic difference between neurosis and psychosis: *Neurosis is the result of a conflict between the ego and its* id, *whereas psychosis is the analogous outcome of a similar disturbance in the relation between the ego and its environment (outer world).*

To be suspicious of such simple solutions of problems is undoubtedly a piece of justifiable caution. Moreover, the most that we should expect from it would not be more than that

---

[1] First published in *Zeitschrift,* Bd. X., 1924. [Translated by Joan Riviere.]

[2] [*The Ego and the Id.* To translate the German *"es,"* which means *"it"* and thus implies the *impersonality* of the mind apart from its ego, the Latin *"id"* has been selected.]

this formula should prove itself correct in rough outline. But even that would be something. Also one recalls immediately a whole series of conclusions and discoveries which seem to support our proposition. All our analyses go to show that the transference neuroses originate from the ego's refusing to accept a powerful instinctual impulse existing in its *id* and denying it motor discharge, or disputing the object towards which it is aimed. The ego then defends itself against the impulse by the mechanism of repression; the repressed impulse struggles against this fate, and finds ways which the ego cannot control to create for itself substitutive gratification (a symptom), which is forced upon the ego in the form of a compromise; the ego finds its unity menaced and injured by this interloper, pursues against the symptom the struggle it had formerly maintained against the original impulse, and all this together produces the clinical picture of a neurosis. It is no matter that in undertaking the repression the ego is at bottom following the dictates of its super-ego, which dictates originated in influences of the same kind from the real environment that subsequently found representation in the super-ego. The fact remains that the ego takes sides with these powers that be, that their demands are stronger in it than the claims of instinct from the *id*, and that the force which sets repression to work against that part of the *id* and fortifies it by the anti-cathexis of resistance is the ego. In the service of its super-ego and of reality the ego has come into conflict with its *id*, and this state of affairs is found in all the transference neuroses.

It is just as easy, on the other hand, from what we already know of the mechanism of the psychoses, to quote examples from them pointing to a disturbance in the relation between the ego and its environment. In Meynert's amentia,[8] the acute hallucinatory confusion which is perhaps the most extreme and striking form of psychosis, the outer world is either not perceived in the very least or else any perception of it remains absolutely without effect. Normally, indeed, the outer world commands the ego in two ways: first, by current perceptions which it is constantly able to engender afresh, and secondly,

---

[8] [To be distinguished, of course, from the common English use of the term, meaning feeble-mindedness.]

by the store of memories of former perceptions which, as its "inner world," has become the possession and a constituent part of the ego. Now in amentia not only is acceptance denied to fresh perceptions, but the importance (cathexis) of the inner world—that inner world which formerly reflected the outer world as an image of it—is withdrawn too; the ego creates for itself in a lordly manner a new outer and inner world; and there is no doubt about two facts, that this new world is constructed after the pattern of the impulses in the *id*, and that the motive of this collapse of the ego's relation with the outer world is a severe frustration by reality of a wish, a frustration which seemed too unendurable to be borne. The close affinity of this psychosis with normal dreams is unmistakable. A pre-condition of dreaming, however, is a state of sleep, and complete abandonment of perceptive capacity and of the outer world is one of the features of sleep.

We know that other forms of psychosis, the schizophrenias, incline to end in affective hebetude, that is, to lose all interest in the outer world. In regard to the genesis of delusions, a number of analyses have taught us that the delusion is found like a patch on the spot where originally there was a rent in the relation between ego and outer world. If the condition of a conflict with the outer world is not still more striking than it seems to us now, this is due to the fact that in the clinical picture of the psychoses manifestations of the pathogenic process are often overlaid by those resulting from an attempt at cure or at reconstruction.

There always remains as a common feature in the aetiology both of the psychoneuroses and the psychoses the factor of frustration—the lack of fulfilment of one of those eternal uncontrollable childhood's wishes that are so deeply rooted in our composition, phylogenetically fore-ordained as it is. In the last resort this frustration is always an outer one; in the individual case it may proceed from that internal institution (in the super-ego) which has taken over the part played by the demands of reality. Now the pathogenic effect depends on whether, in the tension of such a conflict, the ego remains true in its allegiance to the outer world and endeavours to subjugate the *id*, or whether it allows itself to be overwhelmed by the *id* and thus torn away from reality. In this apparently simple situation, however, a complication is introduced by the existence of the super-ego, which, in some connection not yet clear to us, combines in itself influences from the *id* as well as from the outer world, and is to some extent an ideal prototype of that state towards which all the ego's endeavours are bending, a reconciliation of its manifold allegiances. The attitude of the super-ego should be taken into account, as has not hitherto been done, in all forms of mental disorder. For the moment, however, we can postulate that there must be diseases founded on a conflict between ego and super-ego. Analysis gives us the right to infer that melancholia is the model of this group, and then we should put in a claim for the name of "narcissistic psychoneuroses" for these disorders. It does not fit in badly with our impressions if we find reasons for distinguishing conditions such as melancholia from the other psychoses. We then observe, however, that we were able to complete our simple genetic formula without abandoning it. A transference neurosis corresponds to a conflict between ego and *id*, a narcissistic neurosis to that between ego and super-ego, and a psychosis to that between ego and outer world. To be sure, we can hardly say at a glance whether this really represents new knowledge or is merely an addition to our list of formulas; but I think that after all its capacity for application must give us courage to keep in mind this dissection of the mental apparatus that I have proposed, namely, into ego, super-ego and *id*.

The proposition that neuroses and psychoses originate in the ego's conflicts with the various powers ruling it, that is, that they correspond with a failure in the function of the ego, which after all is straining to reconcile all these different claims with one another, requires supplementing in a further point. One would like to know in what circumstances and by what means the ego succeeds in surviving such conflicts, which are undoubtedly always present, without falling ill. Now this is a new field for research in which the most various factors will certainly demand consideration. Two of them, however, can be indicated at once. The outcome of such situations will assuredly depend upon economic conditions, upon the relative strength of the forces striving with one another. And further, it is always possible for the ego to avoid a rupture in any of its relations by deforming itself, submitting to forfeit something of its unity, or in the long run even to being gashed and rent. Thus the illogicalities, eccentricities and follies of mankind would fall into a category similar to their sexual perversions, for by accepting them they spare themselves repressions.

In conclusion there remains to be considered the question what that mechanism analogous to repression may be by which the ego severs itself from the outer world. This is not to be answered, in my opinion, without fresh investigations, but, like repression, the content of this mechanism must include a withdrawal of the cathexes emanating from the ego.

XI

The Economic Problem in Masochism[1]
(1924)

WE HAVE A RIGHT to describe the existence of the masochistic trend in the life of the human instincts as from the economic point of view mysterious. For if mental processes are governed by the pleasure-principle, so that avoidance of "pain" and obtaining pleasure is their first aim, masochism is incomprehensible. If physical pain and feelings of distress[2] can cease to be signals of danger and be ends in themselves, the pleasure-principle is paralysed, the watchman of our mental life is to all intents and purposes himself drugged and asleep.

In this light, masochism appears to us as a great danger, which is in no way true of sadism, its counterpart. We feel tempted to call the pleasure-principle the watchman of our lives, instead of only the watchman of our mental life. But then the question of the relation of the pleasure-principle to the two varieties of instincts that we have distinguished, the death-instincts and the erotic (libidinal) life-instincts, demands investigation, and we can reach no further conclusion about the problem of masochism till we have answered this call.

As will be remembered,[3] we have conceived the principle which governs all mental processes as a special case of Fechner's *tendency to stability*, and consequently have ascribed to the mental apparatus the aim of extinguishing, or at least of maintaining at as low a level as possible, the quantities of excitation flowing into it. For this tendency that has been presumed by us Barbara Low has suggested the name Nirvana-principle, which we accept. But we have unquestioningly identified the pleasure-pain-principle with this Nirvana-

---

[1] First published in *Zeitschrift*, Bd. X., 1924. [Translated by Joan Riviere.]

[2] [*Unlust*, usually translated by "pain."—*Trans.*]

[3] Freud, *Beyond the Pleasure-Principle.*

principle. From this it would follow that every "pain" coincides with a heightening, every pleasure with a lowering, of the stimulus-tension existing in the mind; the Nirvana-principle (and the pleasure-principle which is assumed to be identical with it) would be entirely in the service of the death-instincts (the aim of which is to lead our throbbing existence into the stability of an inorganic state) and would have the function of warning us against the claims of the life-instinct, of the libido, which tries to disturb the course life endeavours to take. Unfortunately, this view cannot be correct. It seems that we experience the ebb and flow of quantities of stimuli directly in perceptions of tension which form a series, and it cannot be doubted that there is such a thing as both pleasurable tension and "painful" lowering of tension. The condition of sexual excitement is the most striking example of a pleasurable increase in tension of this kind, but it is certainly not the only one. Pleasure and "pain" cannot, therefore, be referred to a quantitative increase or decrease of something which we call stimulus-tension, although they clearly have a great deal to do with this factor. It seems as though they do not depend on this quantitative factor, but on some peculiarity in it which we can only describe as qualitative. We should be much farther on with psychology if we knew what this qualitative peculiarity was. Perhaps it is something rhythmic, the periodical duration of the changes, the risings and fallings of the volume of stimuli; we do not know.

Whatever it is, we must perceive that the Nirvana-principle, which belongs to the death-instincts, underwent a modification in the living organism through which it became the pleasure-principle, and henceforth we shall avoid regarding the two principles as one. It is not difficult to infer what force it was that effected this modification, that is, if one has any interest at all in following this argument. It can only be the life-instinct, the libido, which has thus wrested a place for itself alongside the death-instinct in regulating the processes of life. In this way we obtain a series, a small but an interesting one: the *Nirvana*-principle expresses the tendency of the death-instincts, the *pleasure*-principle represents the claims of the libido and that modification of it, the *reality*-principle, the influence of the outer world.

None of these three principles can actually be put out of action by another. As a rule they know how to tolerate one another, although conflicts must occasionally arise from the various aims towards which each strives—a quantitative reduction of the stimulus-pressure on one side, on another side some qualitative feature in it, and lastly a postponement of the discharge of tension and a temporary acquiescence in "painful" tension.

The conclusion to be derived from these considerations is that a description of the pleasure-principle as the watchman over our lives cannot be altogether put aside.

Let us return to masochism. It comes under our observation in three shapes: as a condition under which sexual excitation may be roused; as an expression of feminine nature; and as a norm of behaviour. According to this one may distinguish an *erotogenic*, a *feminine*, and a *moral* type of masochism. The first, the erotogenic masochism, the lust of pain, is also to be found at bottom in the other forms; the concept of it can be supported on biological and constitutional grounds; it remains incomprehensible unless one can bring oneself to make certain assumptions about matters that are wrapt in obscurity. The third, in certain respects the most important form in which masochism appears, has only lately, as a sense of guilt that is for the most part unconscious, been properly appreciated by psychoanalysis; it already admits, however, of full explanation and of co-ordination into our previous knowledge. Feminine masochism, on the other hand, is the form most accessible to observation, least mysterious, and is comprehensible in all its relations. We may begin our discussion with it.

In men (to whom for reasons connected with the material I shall limit my remarks) we know this kind of masochism sufficiently well from the phantasies of masochistic persons, who are often in consequence impotent; their phantasies either terminate in an onanistic act or else themselves constitute the sexual gratification. These phantasies are in complete accord with the real conditions sought by masochistic perverts, whether these situations are enacted as an end in themselves or serve to induce potency and lead up to sexual intercourse. In both cases—for the real situations are in fact only a kind of make-believe performance of the phantasies—

the manifest content is of being pinioned, bound, beaten painfully, whipped, in some way mishandled, forced to obey unconditionally, defiled, degraded. Far more rarely some kind of mutilation is also included in their content, but then only in a very restricted manner. The obvious interpretation, which is easily arrived at, is that the masochist wants to be treated like a little, helpless, dependent child, but especially like a naughty child. It is unnecessary to adduce case-material in this connection, for it is all so very much alike and is accessible to any observer, even to non-analysts. But if one has an opportunity of studying cases in which the masochistic phantasies have undergone specially rich elaboration, one easily discovers that in them the subject is placed in a situation characteristic of womanhood, *i.e.* they mean that he is being castrated, is playing the passive part in coitus, or is giving birth. For this reason I have called this form of masochism *a potiori* feminine, although so many of its features point to childish life. This stratification in superimposed layers of the infantile and the feminine will later find a simple explanation. Castration, or the blinding which represents it, often leaves a negative trace in these phantasies by the condition that just the genitals or the eyes are not to be injured in any way. (Incidentally, masochistic tortures seldom convey an impression of such seriousness as the brutalities—phantasied or actual—of sadists.) Moreover, in the manifest content of the masochistic phantasies a feeling of guilt comes to expression, it being assumed that the subject has committed some crime (the nature of which is left uncertain) which is to be expiated by his undergoing the pain and torture. This looks like a superficial rationalization of the masochistic content of the phantasy, but behind it there lies a relation to infantile masturbation. On the other hand, this element of guilt takes us to the third, the moral type of masochism.

The feminine type of masochism described is based entirely on the primary erotogenic type, on the "lust of pain," which cannot be explained without going very far back.

In my *Drei Abhandlungen zur Sexualtheorie,* in the section on the sources of infantile sexuality, I put forward the proposition that sexual excitation arises as an accessory effect of a large series of internal processes as soon as the intensity of these processes has exceeded certain quantitative limits; indeed, that perhaps nothing very important takes place within the organism without contributing a component to the excitation of the sexual instinct. According to this, an excitation of physical pain and feelings of distress would surely also have this effect. This libidinal sympathetic excitation accompanying the tension of physical pain and feelings of distress would be an infantile physiological mechanism which ceases to operate later on. It would reach a varying degree of development in different sexual constitutions; in any case it would provide the physiological foundation on which the structure of erotogenic masochism is subsequently erected in the mind.

The inadequacy of this explanation is seen, however, in that it throws no light on the regular and close connection of masochism with sadism, its counterpart in the life of the instincts. If we go a step further back to our hypothesis of the two varieties of instincts which we believe to be active in animate beings, we come to another conclusion which, however, does not contradict the one just mentioned. In the multicellular living organism the libido meets the death or destruction instinct which holds sway there, and which tries to disintegrate this cellular being and bring each elemental primary organism into a condition of inorganic stability (though this again may be but relative). To the libido falls the task of making this destructive instinct harmless, and it manages to dispose of it by directing it to a great extent and early in life—with the help of a special organic system, the musculature—towards the objects of the outer world. It is then called the instinct of destruction, of mastery, the will to power. A section of this instinct is placed directly in the service of the sexual function, where it has an important part to play: this is true sadism. Another part is not included in this displacement outwards; it remains within the organism and is "bound" there libidinally with the help of the accompanying sexual excitation mentioned above: this we must recognize as the original erotogenic masochism.

We are entirely without any understanding of the physiological ways and means by which this subjugation of the death-instinct by the libido can be achieved. In the psychoanalytical world of ideas we can only assume that a very extensive coalescence and fusion, varying according to conditions, of the two instincts takes place, so that we never have to deal with pure life-instincts and death-instincts at all, but only with combinations of them in different degrees. Corresponding with the fusion of instincts there may under certain influences occur a *"defusion"* of them. How large a part of the death-instincts may refuse to be subjugated in this way by becoming attached to libidinal quantities is at present not possible to ascertain.

If one is willing to disregard a certain amount of inexactitude, it might be said that the death-instinct active in the organism—the primal sadism—is identical with masochism. After the chief part of it has been directed outwards towards objects, there remains as a residuum within the organism the true erotogenic masochism, which on the one hand becomes a component of the libido and on the other still has the subject itself for an object. So that this masochism would be a witness and a survival of that phase of development in which the amalgamation, so important for life afterwards, of death-instinct and Eros took place. We should not be astonished to hear that under certain conditions the sadism or destruction instinct which has been directed outwards can be introjected, turned inward again, regressing in this way to its earlier condition. It then provides that secondary masochism which supplements the original one.

The erotogenic type of masochism passes through all the developmental stages of the libido, and from them it takes the changing shapes it wears in the life of the mind. The fear of being devoured by the totem-animal (father) is derived from the primitive oral stage of libido-organization; the desire to be beaten by the father from the next-following sadistic-anal stage; castration, although it is subsequently denied, enters into the content of masochistic phantasies as a residue from the phallic stage;[4] and from the final genital stage are derived of course the situations characteristic of womanhood, namely, the passive part in coitus and the act of giving birth. The part played by the nates in masochism is also easily intelligible,

---

[4] See "The Infantile Genital Organization of the Libido," *Sexuality and the Psychology of Love*, Collier Books edition BS 192V.

apart from its obvious foundation in reality. The nates are the special erotogenic bodily regions which have preference in the sadistic-anal stage, as the nipple in the oral stage and the penis in the genital stage.

The third form of masochism, the moral type, is chiefly remarkable for having loosened its connection with what we recognize to be sexuality. To all other masochistic sufferings there still clings the condition that it should be administered by the loved person; it is endured at his command; in the moral type of masochism this limitation has been dropped. It is the suffering itself that matters; whether the sentence is cast by a loved or by an indifferent person is of no importance; it may even be caused by impersonal forces or circumstances, but the true masochist always holds out his cheek wherever he sees a chance of receiving a blow. One is much tempted, in explaining this attitude, to leave the libido out of account and to confine oneself to an assumption that here the instinct of destruction is again turned inwards and is now raging against the self; yet there should be some meaning in the usage of speech, which has not ceased to connect this norm of behaviour in life with erotism and calls these maimers of themselves masochists too.

True to a habit which has grown out of our technique, let us first consider the extreme, undeniably pathological form of this masochism. I have described elsewhere[5] how in analytic treatment we come across patients whose behaviour in regard to the effects of the analysis compels us to ascribe to them an "unconscious" feeling of guilt. I there mentioned the trait by which these people are recognized (the "negative therapeutic reaction"), and I did not conceal the fact that a strong feeling of this kind amounts to one of the most difficult resistances and the greatest menace to the success of our medical or educative aims. The gratification of this unconscious sense of guilt is perhaps the strongest item in the whole "advantage through illness" (which is as a rule composed of many different gains), *i.e.* in the sum-total of the forces which oppose the cure and struggle against relinquishing the neurosis; the suffering that the neurosis involves is the very element which

[5] *Das Ich und das Es.*

makes it of value to the masochistic trend. It is instructive, too, to find, against all theory and expectation, that a neurosis which has defied every therapeutic effort may vanish when the person has become involved in the misery of an unhappy marriage, has lost his fortune, or has developed a dangerous organic disease. The one form of suffering has then given way to another, and all that mattered, as we see, was that a certain level of suffering should be maintained.

Patients do not easily believe what we tell them about an unconscious sense of guilt. They know well enough by what torments (pangs of conscience) a conscious feeling of guilt, the consciousness of guilt, can express itself, and so they cannot admit that they could harbour entirely analogous feelings in themselves without observing a trace of them. I think we may meet their objection by abandoning the term "unconscious feeling of guilt," which is in any case an incorrect one psychologically, and substitute for it a "need for punishment" which describes the state of things observed just as aptly. We cannot, however, let ourselves be prevented from judging and localizing this unconscious feeling of guilt in the same way as we do the conscious variety.

We have ascribed to the super-ego the function of the conscience and have recognized the consciousness of guilt as an expression of a tension between ego and super-ego. The ego reacts with feelings of anxiety (pangs of conscience) to the perception that it has failed to perform the behests of its ideal, the super-ego. Now we want to know how the super-ego came to play this exacting part and why the ego has to fear a difference of opinion with its ideal.

We have said that the function of the ego consists in uniting with one another the claims of the three powers it serves, in reconciling them; and we can add that it has in the super-ego a model for this which it can strive to emulate. This super-ego is in fact just as much a representative of the *id* as of the outer world. It originated through the introjection into the ego of the first objects of the libidinal impulses in the *id*, namely, the two parents, by which process the relation to them was desexualized, that is, underwent a deflection from direct sexual aims. Only in this way was it possible for the child to overcome the Oedipus-complex. Now the super-ego has retained essential features of the introjected persons, namely, their power, their severity, their tendency to watch over and to punish. As has been set forth elsewhere,[6] it is quite conceivable that this severity becomes intensified through the "defusion" of the instincts which takes place along with this incorporation into the ego. The super-ego, the conscience at work in it, can then become harsh, cruel and inexorable against the ego which is in its charge. The categorical imperative of Kant is thus a direct inheritance from the Oedipus-complex.

These same persons, however, whose effect persists as the power of conscience after they have ceased to be objects of libidinal impulses in the *id*, belong also to the real outer world. This is where they came from; their power, behind which lie concealed all the influences of the past and of tradition, was one of the most acutely-felt manifestations of reality. In virtue of their coincidence the super-ego, which replaces the Oedipus-complex, becomes also a representative of the real outer world and is thus a model for the ego's endeavours.

In this way the Oedipus-complex proves itself, as has already been suggested on an historical basis,[7] to be the origin of morality in each one of us. In the course of development through childhood which brings about an ever-increasing severance from the parents, their personal significance for the super-ego recedes. To the imagos they leave behind are then linked on the influences of teachers, authorities, of self-chosen models and heroes venerated by society; these persons need no longer be introjected by the ego, which has now become much more resistant. The last figure in the series beginning with the parents is that dark supremacy of Fate, which only the fewest among us are able to conceive of impersonally. Little can be said against the Dutch writer, Multatuli,[8] when he substitutes the divine pair *Logos kai Ananke* for the *Moira* of the Greeks; but all those who transfer the guidance of the world to Providence, to God, or to God and Nature, rouse a suspicion that they still look upon these farthest and remotest

[6] *Das Ich und das Es.*
[7] Freud, *Totem und Tabu,* Abschnitt IV.
[8] Ed. Douwes Dekker (1820–1887).

powers as a parent-couple—mythologically—and imagine themselves linked to them by libidinal bonds. In *Das Ich und das Es* I have made an attempt to derive the objective fear of death in mankind also from the same sort of parental conception of Fate. It seems to be very difficult to free oneself from it.

After these preliminaries we can return to our consideration of the moral type of masochism. We said that the persons in question, by their behaviour—in the treatment and in their lives—make the impression of being morally inhibited to an excessive degree, of being dominated by an especially sensitive conscience, although they are not at all conscious of any such ultra-morality. On close inspection we can surely see the distinction which divides this kind of unconscious development of morality from the moral type of masochism. In the first, the accent falls on the heightened sadism of the super-ego to which the ego subjects itself; in the last, it falls instead on the masochism in the ego itself, which seeks punishment, whether from the super-ego within or from parental authorities without. It may be excused us that we confounded them to begin with, for in both cases it is a question of a relation between the ego and the super-ego or the powers equivalent to it; in both cases there is a craving which is satisfied by punishment and suffering. It is hardly an insignificant detail then that the sadism of the super-ego is for the most part acutely perceived consciously, while the masochistic impulse of the ego as a rule remains hidden from the person and must be inferred from his behaviour.

The unconsciousness of the moral form of masochism guides us to a near clue. We have translated the words "unconscious feeling of guilt" as meaning a need for punishment by some parental authority. Now we know that the wish to be beaten by the father, which is so common, is closely connected with the other wish, to have some passive (feminine) sexual relations with him, and is only a regressive distortion of the latter. If we introduce this explanation into the content of moral masochism, its hidden meaning becomes clear to us. Conscience and morality arose through overcoming, desexualizing, the Oedipus-complex; in moral masochism morality becomes sexualized afresh, the Oedipus-complex is reactivated, a regression from morality back to the Oedipus-complex is under way. This is to the advantage neither of the person concerned nor of morality. An individual may, it is true, preserve the whole or a certain amount of his morality alongside his masochism, but, on the other hand, a good part of his conscience may become swallowed up by his masochism. Further, the masochism in him creates a temptation to "sinful acts" which must then be expiated by the reproaches of the sadistic conscience (as in so many Russian character-types) or by chastisement from the great parental authority of Fate. In order to provoke punishment from this last parent-substitute the masochist must do something inexpedient, act against his own interests, ruin the prospects which the real world offers him, and possibly destroy his own existence in the world of reality.

The revulsion of sadism against the self regularly occurs under the condition of civilized suppression of the instincts, which withholds a great part of the destructive instinctual components from being exercised in life. One can imagine that this backward-flowing part of the instinct of destruction comes to expression in the ego as an intensified masochism. The manifestations of conscience allow us to infer, however, that the destructiveness rebounding from the outer world is also absorbed by the super-ego without any such transformation and increases its sadism against the ego. The sadism of the super-ego and the masochism of the ego supplement each other and combine to produce the same effects. In my opinion it is only in this way possible to understand how it is that a feeling of guilt ensues—frequently or even quite generally—from a suppression of instinct and how it is that the more anyone refrains from aggressiveness towards others the more strict and sensitive his conscience becomes. One might expect that a person who knows himself to be in the habit of avoiding aggressions that are regarded as undesirable by civilization would have a good conscience as a result and would therefore watch over his ego less suspiciously. The situation is generally represented as though the requirements of social life came first and the instinctual renunciation were its consequence. The origin of morality remains then unexplained. The actual state of things seems to be a reversal of this: the first renunciation of instinctual gratification is enforced by external powers, and it is this that creates morality, which expresses itself in conscience and exacts a further renunciation of instinct.

Moral masochism thus becomes the classical piece of evidence for the existence of "instinctual fusion." Its dangerousness lies in its origin in the death-instinct and represents that part of the latter which escaped deflection on to the outer world in the form of an instinct of destruction. But since, on the other hand, it has the value of an erotic component, even the destruction of anyone by himself cannot occur without gratification of the libido.

XII

The Loss of Reality in Neurosis and Psychosis[1] (1924)

I HAVE RECENTLY[2] defined as follows one of the features distinguishing the neuroses from the psychoses: in the former the ego, in virtue of its allegiance to reality, suppresses a part of the *id* (the life of instinct), whereas in the psychoses the same ego, in the service of the *id*, withdraws itself from a part of reality. According to this, the excessive power of the influence of reality is decisive for neurosis, and for psychosis that of the *id*. A loss of reality must be an inherent element in psychosis; while in neurosis, one would suppose, it would be avoided.

But now, this does not at all agree with experience, which shows us all that every neurosis in some way interferes with the patient's situation in life, that it serves him as a means whereby he can withdraw from his real situation and that in its severe forms it signifies directly a flight from real life. This contradiction appears to give grounds for thought; it is, however, easily removed, and an explanation of it will but advance our comprehension of neurosis.

The contradiction exists only so long as we keep in mind merely the situation at the outbreak of the neurosis, when the ego undertakes, in the service of reality, to repress an instinctual impulse. This is not yet the neurosis itself, however. The latter consists much more in those processes which render compensation for the damage done to a part of the *id*, *i.e.* in the reaction to the repression and in a miscarriage of it. The loosening of the relation to reality is then a consequence of this second step in the formation of a neurosis, and we should not be surprised if close investigation showed that the loss of

[1] First published *Collected Papers,* Volume II, Basic Books, New York, 1959. [Translated by Joan Riviere.]

[2] "Neurosis and Psychosis," *supra,* p. 185.

reality concerned precisely that very part of reality which demanded the instinctual repression.

It is nothing new to characterize neurosis as the outcome of a repression which has miscarried. We have always said this, and only because of the new connection it has come into was it necessary to repeat it.

Incidentally, the same doubts arise again in a specially impressive manner when the neurosis in question is a case in which the exciting cause ("the traumatic scene") is known, and in which one can see how the person averts himself from the experience and consigns it to an amnesia. I will take, for instance, a case analysed many years ago,[3] in which a young woman who was in love with her brother-in-law, and whose sister lay dying, was horrified at the thought, "Now he is free and can marry me!" This scene was instantly forgotten, and thus the process of repression which led to the hysterical pains was set in motion. It is instructive to see precisely in such a case, however, the way in which a neurosis attempts to solve the conflict. It discounts the change in reality, by repressing the claim of the instinct in question, the love for the brother-in-law. The psychotic reaction would have been a denial of the fact of the sister's death.

Now one might expect that when a psychosis breaks out something analogous to the process in a neurosis happens, though of course between different institutions in the mind; that is, that two steps may be discernible in a psychosis also, the first of which tears the ego away from reality, while the second tries to make good the damage done and re-establish the relation to reality at the expense of the id. And something of the kind can really be observed in a psychosis; there are indeed two stages in it, the second of which bears the character of a reparation—but then the analogy gives way to a far more extensive similarity in the two processes. The second step in a psychosis is also an attempt to make good the loss of reality, not, however, at the expense of a restriction laid on the id—as in neurosis at the expense of the relation with reality—but in another, a more lordly manner, by creating a new reality which is no longer open to objections like that which

[3] Breuer und Freud, *Studien über Hysterie*, 1895.

has been forsaken. The second step, therefore, in both neurosis and psychosis is induced by the same tendencies; in both it serves the struggle for power on the part of the *id* which will not allow reality to dictate to it. Neurosis and psychosis are both of them an expression of the rebellion of the *id* against the outer world, of its "pain," unwillingness to adapt itself to necessity—to *ananke̅,* or, if one prefers, of its incapacity to do so. They are far more distinguishable from each other in the reaction at the outbreak than in the attempt at reparation which follows it.

The difference at the beginning comes to expression at the end in this way: in neurosis a part of reality is avoided by a sort of flight, but in psychosis it is remodelled. Or one may say that in psychosis flight at the beginning is succeeded by an active phase of reconstruction, while in neurosis obedience at the beginning is followed by a subsequent attempt at flight. Or, to express it in yet another way, neurosis does not deny the existence of reality, it merely tries to ignore it; psychosis denies it and tries to substitute something else for it. A reaction which combines features of both these is the one we call normal or "healthy"; it denies reality as little as neurosis, but then, like a psychosis, is concerned with effecting a change in it. This expedient normal attitude leads naturally to some active achievement in the outer world and is not content, like a psychosis, with establishing the alteration within itself; it is no longer *auto-plastic* but *allo-plastic.*

In a psychosis the remodelling of reality is effected by means of the residues in the mind of former relations with reality; that is, it concerns the memory-traces, ideas and judgements which have previously been formed about reality and by which reality was represented in the life of the mind. But this relation was never a final and complete one; it was perpetually being enriched and altered by new perceptions. Thus to a psychosis also there falls the task of creating perceptions of a kind corresponding with the new reality, which is accomplished most effectually by way of hallucinations. Now the falsifications of memory, the delusional systems and hallucinations in so many cases and forms of psychosis are of a most distressing character and are bound up with a development of dread, which is surely a sign that the whole process of remodelling reality is conducted in the face of most strenuous opposition. We may, for our own purposes, reconstruct the process on the model of a neurosis, which is more familiar to us. Here we see that a reaction of anxiety takes place every time the repressed instinct makes a move forward, and that the result of the conflict is after all but a compromise and as a satisfaction is incomplete. Probably in a psychosis the rejected part of reality re-asserts its claim, just as in neurosis the repressed instinct does; hence the consequences in both are the same. Elucidation of the various mechanisms in the psychoses by which the turning from reality and reconstruction of it is effected, and also of the degree of success they are able to achieve, is a task for special psychiatry which has not yet been undertaken.

There exists, therefore, a further analogy between neurosis and psychosis in that the task undertaken in the second step of each to some extent miscarries; for the repressed instinct (in neurosis) cannot create for itself a completely satisfying substitute, and the presentations of reality do not permit of being re-cast into entirely satisfying moulds (not, at least, in all forms of mental disorder). But the accent falls differently in the two cases. In a psychosis it falls exclusively on the first step, which is pathological in itself and can only lead to disease; in neurosis, on the contrary, it falls on the second step, the miscarriage of repression, whereas the first step may succeed and does succeed on innumerable occasions within the bounds of health—even though it is not achieved free of cost and without leaving traces of the necessary expenditure of mental energy. These differences, and perhaps many others too, are the consequence of the topographical difference in the original situation at the outbreak of the pathogenic conflict—whether in this conflict the ego surrenders to its dependence on the real world or to its allegiance to the *id*.

A neurosis usually contents itself with avoiding the part of reality in question and protecting itself against coming into contact with it. The sharp distinction between neurosis and psychosis is modified, however, by the circumstance that neurosis, too, does not fail to make attempts to substitute a reality more in accord with its desires for the unsatisfactory real one. The way in which this becomes possible is through the *world of phantasy*, a realm that, at the time when the activity of the reality-principle first set in, became distinguished from the real outer world, and later on was excluded from the demands of necessity, like a kind of "reservation," and which, though not inaccessible to the ego, is only loosely attached to it. It is from this world of phantasy that neurosis draws the material for re-creating the world afresh according to its desires, and it finds this material there, as a rule, by way of a regression to an earlier period in real life.

It is hardly possible to doubt that the world of phantasy plays the same part in a psychosis, that for it, too, this world represents the store-chamber from which the materials or the design for constructing a new reality are obtained. But the new phantastic outer world of a psychosis attempts to set itself in place of external reality. That of neurosis, on the contrary, is glad to attach itself, like a children's game, to a part of reality—some other part than the one against which it must protect itself; it endows it with a special meaning and a secret significance which we, not always quite correctly, call *symbolical*. Thus we see that there arises both in neurosis and in psychosis the question not only of the *loss of reality*, but of a *substitute for reality* too.

XIII

A Note upon the "Mystic Writing-Pad"[1]
(1925)

IF I DISTRUST my memory—neurotics, as we know, do so to a remarkable extent, but normal people have every reason for doing so as well—I am able to supplement and guarantee its working by making a note in writing. In that case the surface upon which this note is preserved, the pocket-book or sheet of paper, is as it were a materialized portion of my mnemic apparatus, the rest of which I carry about with me invisible. I have only to bear in mind the place where this "memory" has been deposited and I can then "reproduce" it at any time I like, with the certainty that it will have remained unaltered and so have escaped the possible distortions to which it might have been subjected in my actual memory.

If I want to make full use of this technique for improving my mnemic function, I find that there are two different procedures open to me. On the one hand, I can choose a writing-surface which will preserve intact any note made upon it for an indefinite length of time—for instance, a sheet of paper which I can write upon in ink. I am then in possession of a "permanent memory-trace." The disadvantage of this procedure is that the receptive capacity of the writing-surface is soon exhausted. The sheet is filled with writing, there is no room on it for any more notes, and I find myself obliged to bring another sheet into use, that has not been written on. Moreover, the advantage of this procedure, the fact that it provides a "permanent trace," may lose its value for me if after a time the note ceases to interest me and I no longer want to "retain it in my memory." The alternative procedure avoids both of these disadvantages. If, for instance, I write

[1] ["Notiz über den 'Wunderblock.'" First published simultaneously in *Int. Z. Psychoanal.*, 11 (1925), 1, and in *Ges. Schr.*, 6, 415; reprinted *Ges. W.*, 14, 3. Translation, reprinted from *Int. J. Psycho-Anal.*, 21 (1940), 469, by James Strachey.]

with a piece of chalk upon a slate, I have a receptive surface which retains its receptive capacity for an unlimited time and the notes upon which can be destroyed as soon as they cease to interest me, without any need for throwing away the writing-surface itself. Here the disadvantage is that I cannot preserve a permanent trace. If I want to put some fresh notes upon the slate, I must first wipe out the ones which cover it. Thus an unlimited receptive capacity and a retention of permanent traces seem to be mutually exclusive properties in the apparatus which we use as substitutes for our memory: either the receptive surface must be renewed or the note must be destroyed.

All the forms of auxiliary apparatus which we have invented for the improvement or intensification of our sensory functions are built on the same model as the sense organs themselves or portions of them: for instance, spectacles, photographic cameras, ear-trumpets. Measured by this standard, devices to aid our memory seem particularly imperfect, since our mental apparatus accomplishes precisely what they cannot: it has an unlimited receptive capacity for new perceptions and nevertheless lays down permanent—even though not unalterable—memory-traces of them. As long ago as in 1900 I gave expression in *The Interpretation of Dreams*[2] to a suspicion that this unusual capacity was to be divided between two different systems (or organs of the mental apparatus). According to this view, we possess a system Pcpt.-Cs., which receives perceptions but retains no permanent trace of them, so that it can react like a clean sheet to every new perception; while the permanent traces of the excitations which have been received are preserved in "mnemic systems" lying behind the perceptual system. Later, in *Beyond the Pleasure Principle*

[2] [Cf. the English translation (Revised Edition, 1932), 497f. The translation of the decisive sentence, however, is misleading: "for consciousness memory and quality are mutually exclusive in the ψ-systems" should read "memory and the quality of being conscious are mutually exclusive in the ψ-systems." As Freud mentions in *Beyond the Pleasure Principle* (1920; trans., 1922, 27n.; new trans., 1950, 28n.), this distinction had already been drawn by Breuer in his theoretical section of *Studien über Hysterie* (1895, 164, footnote).]

(1920),[3] I added a remark to the effect that the inexplicable phenomenon of consciousness arises in the perceptual system *instead* of the permanent traces.

Some time ago there came upon the market, under the name of the Mystic Writing-Pad,[4] a small contrivance that promises to perform more than the sheet of paper or the slate. It claims to be nothing more than a writing-tablet from which notes can be erased by an easy movement of the hand. But if it is examined more closely it will be found that its construction shows a remarkable agreement with my hypothetical structure of our perceptual apparatus and that it can in fact provide both an ever-ready receptive surface and permanent traces of the notes that have been made upon it.

The Mystic Pad is a slab of dark brown resin or wax with a paper edging; over the slab is laid a thin transparent sheet, the top end of which is firmly secured to the slab while its bottom end rests upon it without being fixed to it. This transparent sheet is the more interesting part of the little device. It itself consists of two layers, which can be detached from each other except at their two ends. The upper layer is a transparent piece of celluloid; the lower layer is made of thin translucent waxed paper. When the apparatus is not in use, the lower surface of the waxed paper adheres lightly to the upper surface of the wax slab.

To make use of the Mystic Pad, one writes upon the celluloid portion of the covering-sheet which rests upon the wax slab. For this purpose no pencil or chalk is necessary, since the writing does not depend on material being deposited upon the receptive surface. It is a return to the ancient method of writing upon tablets of clay or wax: a pointed stilus scratches the surface, the depressions upon which constitute the "writ-

[3] [English translation, 1922, 28, where, once more, the original meaning is unfortunately missed: "consciousness arises *in the place of* the memory trace" should read *"instead of."* (The mistake is corrected in the new translation, 1950, 29.) So too in *The Interpretation of Dreams* (Revised Edition, 1932, 49n.): "consciousness occurs actually *in the locality* of the memory-trace," should read, once again, *"instead of* the memory-trace."]

[4] [It is still obtainable as such in England, where, however, it is also known as "Printator."]

ing." In the case of the Mystic Pad this scratching is not effected directly, but through the medium of the covering-sheet. At the points which the stilus touches, it presses the lower surface of the waxed paper on to the wax slab, and the grooves are visible as dark writing upon the otherwise smooth whitish-grey surface of the celluloid. If one wishes to destroy what has been written, all that is necessary is to raise the double covering-sheet from the wax slab by a light pull, starting from the free lower end. The close contact between the waxed paper and the wax slab at the places which have been scratched (upon which the visibility of the writing depended) is thus brought to an end and it does not recur when the two surfaces come together once more. The Mystic Pad is now clear of writing and ready to receive fresh notes.

The small imperfections of the contrivance have, of course, no importance for us, since we are only concerned with its approximation to the structure of the perceptive apparatus of the mind.

If, while the Mystic Pad has writing upon it, we cautiously raise the celluloid from the waxed paper, we can see the writing just as clearly on the surface of the latter, and the question may arise why there should be any necessity for the celluloid portion of the cover. Experiment will then show that the thin paper would be very easily crumpled or torn if one were to write directly upon it with the stilus. The layer of celluloid thus acts as a protective sheath for the waxed paper, to keep off injurious effects from without. The celluloid is a "protective shield against stimuli"; the layer which actually receives the stimuli is the paper. I may at this point recall that in *Beyond the Pleasure Principle* [trans., 1922, 22 ff.; new trans., 1950, 30 ff.]. I showed that the perceptive apparatus of our mind consists of two layers, of an external protective shield against stimuli whose task it is to diminish the strength of excitations coming in, and of a surface behind it which receives the stimuli, namely the system Pcpt.-Cs.

The analogy would not be of much value if it could not be pursued further than this. If we lift the entire covering-sheet —both the celluloid and the waxed paper—off the wax slab, the writing vanishes and, as I have already remarked, does not re-appear again. The surface of the Mystic Pad is clear of writing and once more capable of receiving impressions. But it is easy to discover that the permanent trace of what was written is retained upon the wax slab itself and is legible in suitable lights. Thus the Pad provides not only a receptive surface that can be used over and over again, like a slate, but also permanent traces of what has been written, like an ordinary paper pad: it solves the problem of combining the two functions *by dividing them between two separate but interrelated component parts or systems.* But this is precisely the way in which, according to the hypothesis which I mentioned just now, our mental apparatus performs its perceptual function. The layer which receives the stimuli—the system Pcpt.-Cs.—forms no permanent traces; the foundations of memory come about in other, adjoining, systems.

We need not be disturbed by the fact that in the Mystic Pad no use is made of the permanent traces of the notes that have been received; it is enough that they are present. There must come a point at which the analogy between an auxiliary apparatus of this kind and the organ which is its prototype will cease to apply. It is true, too, that, once the writing has been erased, the Mystic Pad cannot "reproduce" it from within; it would be a mystic pad indeed if, like our memory, it could accomplish that. None the less, I do not think it is too far-fetched to compare the celluloid and waxed paper cover with the system Pcpt.-Cs. and its protective shield, the wax slab with the unconscious behind them, and the appearance and disappearance of the writing with the flickering-up and passing-away of consciousness in the process of perception.

But I must admit that I am inclined to press the comparison still further. On the Mystic Pad the writing vanishes every time the close contact is broken between the paper which receives the stimulus and the wax slab which preserves the impression. This agrees with a notion which I have long had about the method in which the perceptual apparatus of our mind functions, but which I have hitherto kept to myself.[5] My theory was that cathectic innervations are sent out and with-

---

[5] [It is hinted at in *Beyond the Pleasure Principle* (English translation, 1922, 32; new translation, 1950, 33).]

drawn in rapid periodic impulses from within into the completely pervious system Pcpt.-Cs. So long as that system is cathected in this manner, it receives perceptions (which are accompanied by consciousness) and passes the excitation on to the unconscious mnemic systems; but as soon as the cathexis is withdrawn, consciousness is extinguished and the functioning of the system comes to a standstill. It is as though the unconscious stretches out feelers, through the medium of the system Pcpt.-Cs., towards the external world and hastily withdraws them as soon as they have sampled the excitations coming from it. Thus the interruptions, which in the case of the Mystic Pad have an external origin, were attributed by my hypothesis to the discontinuity in the current of innervation; and the actual breaking of contact which occurs in the Mystic Pad was replaced in my theory by the periodic non-excitability of the perceptual system. I further had a suspicion that this discontinuous method of functioning of the system Pcpt.-Cs. lies at the bottom of the origin of the concept of time.

If we imagine one hand writing upon the surface of the Mystic Writing-Pad while another periodically raises its covering sheet from the wax slab, we shall have a concrete representation of the way in which I tried to picture the functioning of the perceptual apparatus of our mind.

XIV

Negation[1] (1925)

THE MANNER IN WHICH our patients bring forward their associations during the work of analysis gives us an opportunity
for making some interesting observations. "Now you'll think
I mean to say something insulting, but really I've no such
intention." We see at once that this is a repudiation, by means
of projection, of an association that has just emerged. Or
again: "You ask who this person in the dream can have been.
It was *not* my mother." We emend this: so it *was* his mother.
In our interpretation we take the liberty of disregarding the
negation and of simply picking out the subject-matter of the
association. It is just as though the patient had said: "It is
true that I thought of my mother in connection with this person, but I don't feel at all inclined to allow the association to
count."

There is a most convenient method by which one can sometimes obtain a necessary light upon a piece of unconscious
and repressed material. "What," one asks, "would you consider was about the most unlikely thing in the world in that
situation? What do you think was furthest from your mind at
the time?" If the patient falls into the trap and names what he
thinks most incredible, he almost invariably in so doing makes
the correct admission. A nice counterpart of this experiment
is often met with in obsessional neurotics who have been
initiated into the meaning of their symptoms. "A new obsessive idea came over me; and it immediately occurred to me
that it might mean so and so. But of course that can't be true,
or it couldn't have occurred to me." The explanation of the
new obsessive idea, which he rejects in this way upon grounds
picked up from the treatment, is of course the right one.

Thus the subject-matter of a repressed image or thought

---

[1] ["Die Verneinung." First published *Imago*, 11 (1925), 217;
reprinted *Ges. Schr.*, 11, 3, and *Ges. W.*, 14, 11. Translation, reprinted from *Int. J. Psycho-Anal.*, 6 (1925), 367, by Joan Riviere.]

can make its way into consciousness on condition that it is *denied*. Negation is a way of taking account of what is repressed; indeed, it is actually a removal of the repression, though not, of course, an acceptance of what is repressed. It is to be seen how the intellectual function is here distinct from the affective process. Negation only assists in undoing *one* of the consequences of repression—namely, the fact that the subject-matter of the image in question is unable to enter consciousness. The result is a kind of intellectual acceptance of what is repressed, though in all essentials the repression persists.[2] In the course of analytic work we often bring about a further very important and somewhat bewildering modification of the same situation. We succeed in defeating the negation too and in establishing a complete intellectual acceptance of what is repressed—but the repression itself is still not removed.

Since it is the business of the function of intellectual judgement to affirm or deny the subject-matter of thoughts, we have been led by the foregoing remarks to the psychological origin of that function. To deny something in one's judgement is at bottom the same thing as to say: "That is something that I would rather repress." A negative judgement is the intellectual substitute for repression; the "No" in which it is expressed is the hall-mark of repression, a certificate of origin, as it were, like "Made in Germany." By the help of the symbol of negation, the thinking-process frees itself from the limitations of repression and enriches itself with the subject-matter without which it could not work efficiently.

The function of judgement is concerned ultimately with two sorts of decision. It may assert or deny that a thing has a particular property; or it may affirm or dispute that a particular image [*Vorstellung*] exists in reality. Originally the property to be decided about might be either "good" or "bad," "useful" or "harmful." Expressed in the language of the oldest, that is, of the oral, instinctual impulses, the alternative

[2] The same process is at the root of the familiar superstition that boasting is dangerous. "How lovely that I've not had one of my headaches for such a long time!" But this is in fact the first announcement of a new attack, of whose approach the patient is already aware, though he is as yet unwilling to believe it.

runs thus: "I should like to eat that, or I should like to spit it out"; or, carried a stage further: "I should like to take this into me and keep that out of me." That is to say: it is to be either *inside* me or *outside* me. As I have shown elsewhere, the original pleasure-ego tries to introject into itself everything that is good and to reject from itself everything that is bad. From its point of view what is bad, what is alien to the ego, and what is external are, to begin with, identical.[3]

The other sort of decision made by the function of judgement, namely, as to the real existence of something imagined, is a concern of the final reality-ego, which develops out of the previous pleasure-ego (a concern, that is, of the faculty that tests the reality of things). It is now no longer a question of whether something perceived (a thing) shall be taken into the ego or not, but of whether something which is present in the ego as an image can also be re-discovered in perception (that is, in reality). Once more, it will be seen, the question is one of *external* and *internal*. What is not real, what is merely imagined or subjective, is only *internal*; while on the other hand what is real is also present *externally*. When this stage is reached, the pleasure principle is no longer taken into account. Experience has taught that it is important not only whether a thing (an object from which satisfaction is sought) possesses the "good" property, that is, whether it deserves to be taken into the ego, but also whether it is there in the external world, ready to be seized when it is wanted. In order to understand this step forward, we must recollect that all images originate from perceptions and are repetitions of them. So that originally the mere existence of the image serves as a guarantee of the reality of what is imagined. The contrast between what is subjective and what is objective does not exist from the first. It only arises from the faculty which thought possesses for reviving a thing that has once been perceived, by reproducing it as an image, without its being necessary for the external object still to be present. Thus the first and immediate aim of the process of testing reality is not to discover an object in real perception corresponding to what is imagined, but to *re-discover* such an object, to convince oneself that it is

---

[3] Cf. "Instincts and their Vicissitudes," *supra*, p. 99.

still there. The differentiation between what is subjective and what is objective is further assisted by another faculty of the power of thought. The reproduction of a perception as an image is not always a faithful one; it can be modified by omissions or by the fusion of a number of elements. The process for testing the thing's reality must then investigate the extent of these distortions. But it is evident that an essential pre-condition for the institution of the function for testing reality is that objects shall have been lost which have formerly afforded real satisfaction.

Judging is the intellectual action which decides the choice of motor action, which puts an end to the procrastination of thinking, and which leads over from thinking to acting. This procrastinating character of thought, too, has been discussed by me elsewhere.[4] Thought is to be regarded as an experimental action, a kind of groping forward, involving only a small expenditure of energy in the way of discharge. Let us consider where the ego can have made a previous use of this kind of groping forward, where it can have learnt the technique which it now employs in intellective processes. It was at the sensory end of the mental apparatus, in connection with sense perceptions. For upon our hypothesis perception is not a merely passive process; we believe rather that the ego periodically sends out small amounts of cathectic energy into the perceptual system and by their means samples the external stimuli, and after each such groping advance draws back again.

The study of judgement affords us, perhaps for the first time, an insight into the derivation of an intellectual function from the interplay of the primary impulses. Judging has been systematically developed out of what was in the first instance introduction into the ego or expulsion from the ego carried out according to the pleasure principle. Its polarity appears to correspond to the opposition between two of the groups of instincts which we have assumed to exist. Affirmation, as being a substitute for union, belongs to Eros; while negation, the derivative of expulsion, belongs to the instinct of destruction.

[4] [Cf. *supra*, "Formulations Regarding the Two Principles in Mental Functioning," p. 21.]

The passion for universal negation, the "negativism" displayed by many psychotics, is probably to be regarded as a sign of the defusion of the instincts due to the withdrawal of the libidinal components. The achievement of the function of judgement only becomes feasible, however, after the creation of the symbol of negation has endowed thought with a first degree of independence from the results of repression and at the same time from the sway of the pleasure principle.

This view of negation harmonizes very well with the fact that in analysis we never discover a "No" in the unconscious, and that a recognition of the unconscious on the part of the ego is expressed in a negative formula. There is no stronger evidence that we have been successful in uncovering the unconscious than when the patient reacts with the words "I didn't think that" or "I never thought that."

XV

Some Elementary Lessons in Psychoanalysis[1] (1938)

AN AUTHOR WHO SETS out to introduce some branch of knowledge—or, to put it more modestly, some branch of research—to the lay public must clearly make his choice between two methods or techniques.

It is possible to start off from what everyone knows (or thinks he knows) and regards as self-evident, without in the first instance contradicting the learner. An opportunity will soon occur for drawing his attention to facts in the same field, which, though they are known to him, he has so far neglected or insufficiently appreciated. Beginning from these, one can introduce further facts to him of which he has *no* knowledge and so prepare him for the necessity of going beyond his earlier judgements, of seeking new points of view and of taking new hypotheses into consideration. In this way one can get him to take a part in building up a new theory about the subject and one can deal with his objections to it during the actual course of the work. A method of this kind might well be called *genetic*. It follows the path along which the investigator himself has already travelled. In spite of all its advantages, it has the defect of not making a sufficiently striking effect upon the learner. He will not be nearly so much impressed by something which he has watched coming into existence and passing through a slow and difficult period of growth as he would be by something that is presented to him ready-made as an apparently self-consistent whole.

[1] ["Some Elementary Lessons in Psycho-Analysis"—the original title is in English—was written in London during the second half of 1938 and left unfinished. It appears to be the beginning of a fresh version of the *Outline of Psycho-Analysis* (1938b). It was first published in *Schriften aus dem Nachlass* (London, 1941), p. 141; identical with *Ges. W.*, 17, 141. Some portions of it had previously been printed *Int. Z. Psychoanal., Imago*, 25 (1940), 21; translated *Int. J. Psycho-Anal.*, 21 (1940), 83. Translation by James Strachey.]

It is precisely this last effect which is produced by the alternative method of presentation. This other method, the *dogmatic* one, begins straight away by stating its conclusions. Its premises make demands upon the audience's attention and faith and very little is adduced in support of them. And there is then a danger that a critical hearer may shake his head and say: "All this sounds most peculiar: where does the fellow get it from?"

In what follows I shall not rely exclusively upon either of the two methods of presentation: I shall make use now of one and now of the other. I am under no delusion about the difficulty of my task. Psychoanalysis has little prospect of becoming popular. It is not merely that much of what it has to say offends people's feelings. Almost as much difficulty is created by the fact that our science involves a number of hypotheses —it is hard to say whether they should be regarded as postulates or as products of our researches—which are bound to seem very strange to ordinary modes of thought and which fundamentally contradict current views. But there is no help for it. We must begin our brief study with two of these hazardous hypotheses.

The Nature of the Mental

Psychoanalysis is a part of the mental science of psychology. It is also described as "depth psychology"—we shall later discover why. If someone asks what "the mental" really means, it is easy to reply by enumerating its constituents: our perceptions, ideas, memories, feelings and acts of volition—all these form part of what is mental. But if the questioner goes further and asks whether there is not some common quality possessed by all these processes which makes it possible to get nearer to the *nature*, or, as people sometimes say, the *essence* of the mental, then it is harder to give an answer.

If an analogous question had been put to a physicist (as to the nature of electricity, for instance), his reply, until quite recently, would have been: "For the purpose of explaining certain phenomena, we assume the existence of electrical forces which are present in things and which emanate from them. We study these phenomena, discover the laws that govern them and even put them to practical use. This satisfies us provisionally. We do not know the *nature* of electricity. Perhaps we may discover it later, as our work goes on. It must be admitted that what we are ignorant of is precisely the most important and interesting part of the whole business, but for the moment that does not worry us. It is simply how things happen in the natural sciences."

Psychology, too, is a natural science. What else can it be? But its case is different. Not everyone is bold enough to make judgements about physical matters; but everyone—the philosopher and the man in the street alike—has his opinion on psychological questions and behaves as if he were at least an *amateur* psychologist. And now comes the remarkable thing. Everyone—or almost everyone—was agreed that what is mental really *has* a common quality in which its essence is expressed: namely the quality of *being conscious*—unique, indescribable, but needing no description. All that is conscious, they said, is mental, and conversely all that is mental is conscious: that is self-evident and to contradict it is nonsense. It cannot be said that this decision threw much light upon the nature of the mental; for consciousness is one of the fundamental facts of our life and our researches come up against it like a blank wall and can find no path beyond it. Moreover the equation of what is mental with what is conscious had the unwelcome result of divorcing mental processes from the general context of events in the universe and of setting them in complete contrast to all others. But this would not do, since the fact could not long be overlooked that mental phenomena are to a large extent dependent upon somatic influences and on their side have the most powerful effects upon somatic processes. If ever human thought found itself in an *impasse* it was here. To find a way out, the philosophers at least were obliged to assume that there were organic processes parallel to the conscious mental ones, related to them in a manner that was hard to explain, which acted as intermediaries in the reciprocal relations between "body and mind," and which served to re-insert the mental into the texture of life. But this solution remained unsatisfactory.

Psychoanalysis escaped such difficulties as these by energetically denying the equation between what is mental and what is conscious. No; being conscious cannot be the essence of what is mental. It is only a *quality* of what is mental, and an unstable quality at that—one that is far oftener absent than present. The mental, whatever its nature may be, is in itself unconscious and probably similar in kind to all the other natural processes of which we have obtained knowledge.

Psychoanalysis bases this assertion on a number of facts, of which I shall now proceed to give a selection.

We know what is meant by ideas "occurring" to one—thoughts that suddenly come into consciousness without one's being aware of the steps that led up to them, though they, too, must have been mental acts. It can even happen that one arrives in this way at the solution of some difficult intellectual problem which has previously baffled one's efforts. All the complicated processes of selection, rejection and decision which occupied the interval were withdrawn from consciousness. We shall not be putting forward any new theory in saying that they were unconscious and perhaps remained so.

In the second place, I shall pick a single instance to represent an immensely large class of phenomena.[2] The President of a public body (the Lower House of the Austrian Parliament) on one occasion opened a sitting with the following words: "I take notice that a full quorum of members is present and herewith declare the sitting closed." It was a slip of the tongue—for there can be no doubt that what the President intended to say was "opened." Why, then, did he say the opposite? We shall expect to be told it was an accidental mistake, a failure in carrying out an intention such as may easily happen for various reasons: it had no meaning—and in any case contraries are particularly easily substituted for each other. If, however, we bear in mind the situation in which the slip of the tongue occurred, we shall be inclined to prefer another explanation. Many of the previous sittings of the House had been disagreeably stormy and had accomplished nothing, so that it would be only too natural for the President to think at the moment of making his opening statement: "If only the sitting that's just beginning were finished! I would much rather be closing than opening it!" When he began to

[2] Cf. *The Psychopathology of Everyday Life* (1904), Chap. V.

speak he was probably not aware of this wish—not conscious of it—but it was certainly present and it succeeded in making itself effective, against the speaker's will, in his apparent mistake. A single instance can scarcely enable us to decide between two such different explanations. But what if every other instance of a slip of the tongue could be explained in the same way, and similarly every slip of the pen, every case of mis-reading or mis-hearing, and every faulty action? What if in all those instances (one might actually say, without a single exception) it was possible to demonstrate the presence of a mental act—a thought, a wish or an intention—which would account for the apparent mistake and which was unconscious at the moment at which it became effective, even though it may have been conscious previously? If that were so, it would really no longer be possible to dispute the fact that mental acts which are unconscious do exist and that they are even sometimes active while they are unconscious and that they can even sometimes get the better of conscious intentions. The person concerned in a mistake of this kind can react to it in various ways. He may overlook it completely or he may notice it himself and become embarrassed and ashamed. He cannot as a rule find the explanation of it himself without outside help; and he often refuses to accept the solution when it is put before him—for a time, at all events.

In the third place, finally, it is possible in the case of persons in a state of hypnosis to prove experimentally that there are such things as unconscious mental acts and that consciousness is not an indispensable condition of [mental] activity. Anyone who has witnessed such an experiment will receive an unforgettable impression and a conviction that can never be shaken. Here is more or less what happens. The doctor enters the hospital ward, puts his umbrella in the corner, hypnotizes one of the patients and says to him: "I'm going out now. When I come in again, you will come to meet me with my umbrella open and hold it over my head." The doctor and his assistants then leave the ward. As soon as they come back, the patient, who is no longer under hypnosis, carries out exactly the instructions that were given him while he was hypnotized. The doctor questions him: "What's this you're doing? What's the meaning of all this?" The patient is clearly embarrassed. He makes some lame remark such as: "I only thought, doctor, as it's raining outside you'd open your umbrella in the room before you went out." The explanation is obviously quite inadequate and made up on the spur of the moment to offer some sort of motive for his senseless behaviour. It is clear to the spectators that he is in ignorance of his real motive. We, however, know what it is, for we were present when the suggestion was made to him which he is now carrying out, while he himself knows nothing of the fact that it is at work in him.[3]

The question of the relation of the conscious to the mental may now be regarded as settled: consciousness is only a *quality* or attribute of what is mental and moreover an unstable one. But there is one further objection with which we have to deal. We are told that, in spite of the facts that have been mentioned, there is no necessity to abandon the identity between what is conscious and what is mental: the so-called unconscious mental processes are the organic processes which have long been recognized as running parallel to the mental ones. This, of course, would reduce our problem to an apparently indifferent matter of definition. Our reply is that it would be unjustifiable and inexpedient to make a breach in the unity of mental life for the sake of propping up a definition, since it is clear in any case that consciousness can only offer us an incomplete and broken chain of phenomena. And it can scarcely be a matter of chance that it was not until the change had been made in the definition of the mental that it became possible to construct a comprehensive and coherent theory of mental life. . . .

Nor need it be supposed that this alternative view of the mental is an innovation due to psychoanalysis. A German philosopher, Theodor Lipps, asserted with the greatest explicitness that the mental is in itself unconscious and that the unconscious is the truly mental. The concept of the unconscious has long been knocking at the gates of psychology and asking to be let in. Philosophy and literature have often toyed

---

[3] I am describing experiments made by Bernheim at Nancy in 1889 at which I myself assisted. In these days there is no need for me to discuss any doubts as to the genuineness of hypnotic phenomena of this kind.

with it, but science could find no use for it. Psychoanalysis has seized upon the concept, has taken it seriously and has given it a fresh content. By its researches it has led to a knowledge of characteristics of the unconscious mental which have hitherto been unsuspected, and it has discovered some of the laws which govern it. But none of this implies that the quality of being conscious has lost its importance for us. It remains the one light which illuminates our path and leads us through the darkness of mental life. In consequence of the special character of our discoveries, our scientific work in psychology will consist in translating unconscious processes into conscious ones, and thus filling in the gaps in conscious perception. . . .